D1669969

# Poisonous Parenting

**The Family Therapy and Counseling Series**
Series Editor
Jon Carlson, PsyD, EdD

**Kit S. Ng**
*Global Perspectives in Family Therapy: Development, Practice, Trends*

**Phyllis Erdman and Tom Caffery**
*Attachment and Family Systems: Conceptual, Empirical, and Therapeutic Relatedness*

**Wes Crenshaw**
*Treating Families and Children in the Child Protective System*

**Len Sperry**
*Assessment of Couples and Families: Contemporary and Cutting-Edge Strategies*

**Robert L. Smith and R. Esteban Montilla**
*Counseling and Family Therapy With Latino Populations: Strategies That Work*

**Catherine Ford Sori**
*Engaging Children in Family Therapy: Creative Approaches to Integrating Theory and Research in Clinical Practice*

**Paul R. Peluso**
*Infidelity: A Practitioner's Guide to Working With Couples in Crisis*

**Jill D. Onedera**
*The Role of Religion in Marriage and Family Counseling*

**Christine Kerr, Janice Hoshino, Judith Sutherland, Sharyl Parashak, and Linda McCarley**
*Family Art Therapy*

**Debra D. Castaldo**
*Divorced Without Children: Solution Focused Therapy With Women at Midlife*

**Phyllis Erdman and Kok-Mun Ng**
*Attachment: Expanding the Cultural Connections*

**Jon Carlson and Len Sperry**
*Recovering Intimacy in Love Relationships: A Clinician's Guide*

**Adam Zagelbaum and Jon Carlson**
*Working With Immigrant Families: A Practical Guide for Counselors*

**David K. Carson and Montserrat Casado-Kehoe**
*Case Studies in Couples Therapy: Theory-Based Approaches*

**Shea M. Dunham, Shannon B. Dermer, and Jon Carlson**
*Poisonous Parenting: Toxic Relationships Between Parents and Their Adult Children*

# Poisonous Parenting

## TOXIC RELATIONSHIPS BETWEEN PARENTS AND THEIR ADULT CHILDREN

SHEA M. DUNHAM
SHANNON B. DERMER
JON CARLSON
EDITORS

Routledge
Taylor & Francis Group
711 Third Avenue
New York, NY 10017

Routledge
Taylor & Francis Group
27 Church Road
Hove, East Sussex BN3 2FA



Printed in the United States of America on acid-free paper
10 9 8 7 6 5 4 3 2

International Standard Book Number: 978-0-415-87908-8 (Hardback)



**Library of Congress Cataloging-in-Publication Data**

Poisonous parenting : toxic relationships between parents and their adult children / [edited by] Shea M. Dunham, Shannon B. Dermer, and Jon Carlson.
p. cm. -- (The family therapy and counseling series)
Includes bibliographical references and index.
ISBN 978-0-415-87908-8 (hbk. : alk. paper)
1. Parent and adult child. 2. Parenting. 3. Families--Psychological aspects. 4. Family counseling. I. Dunham, Shea M. II. Dermer, Shannon B. III. Carlson, Jon.

HQ755.86.P62 2011
155.9'24--dc22 2010052732

**Visit the Taylor & Francis Web site at**
**http://www.taylorandfrancis.com**

**and the Routledge Web site at**
**http://www.routledgementalhealth.com**

Dedicated to my grandfather, Don Scott, who believed you are never too old or too smart to learn something new.

**Shannon B. Dermer**

To every mentor and every critic, thanks for all your unknowing encouragement. I have learned the best lesson from all of you: *Nothing happens to you; it happens for you.*

**Shea M. Dunham**

# Contents

# Series Foreword

What a child doesn't receive he can seldom later give.

**P.D. James, *Time To Be Earnest***

Our relationship with parents impacts not only our entire lives but those of future generations. Understanding how the relationship with primary love objects impacts trans-generational patterns is beyond the scope of this foreword and this book. However, *Poisonous Parenting* clearly addresses how destructive relationships with parents will lead to unhealthy relationships throughout the lifespan unless they are effectively addressed.

The chapters of this important book allow the reader to not only understand how to use the material with clients but also how to better understand their own parental relationships, regardless of the depth or type of toxicity or health. As the editors state, "Whether overtly or covertly, children learn about who to love, how to love, how to be loved, and how (or even if) a child should love himself/herself." This experience provides the foundation for all future relationships.

The degree of bonding with parents falls along a continuum from secure and healthy to insecure and poisonous. This book is devoted to the poisonous, but I urge the reader to become familiar with the literature on healthy attachment in order to know not just what causes problems but to better understand what leads to healthy connections.

In my 60,000-plus hours of providing therapy, I have learned the importance of these early childhood relationships. People often joke that all problems lead back to Mom and Dad, but there seems to be more truth than humor to this statement. I seldom see clients who have healthy parental ties with clear boundaries and differentiation. It is more common to hear stories of one parent being a saint and the other a sinner, which leads to overinvolvement with one and under or no involvement with the other.

I urge you to carefully study these important words and apply the concepts not only to your clients but also to your own life patterns. Along with the editors and the chapter contributors, I wish that your attachments be secure and your relationships satisfying.

**Jon Carlson, PsyD, EdD**
*Lake Geneva, Wisconsin*

# About the Editors

**Jon Carlson, PsyD, EdD, ABPP,** is a distinguished professor of psychology and counseling at Governors State University and a psychologist at the Wellness Clinic in Lake Geneva, Wisconsin. Jon has served as an editor of several periodicals, including the *Journal of Individual Psychology* and *The Family Journal*. He holds diplomas in both family psychology and Adlerian psychology and has authored 150 journal articles and 55 books including *Time for a Better Marriage*, *Adlerian Therapy*, *Inclusive Cultural Empathy*, *The Mummy at the Dining Room Table*, and *Bad Therapy*. He has created over 250 professional trade video and DVDs with leading professional therapists and educators. In 2004, the American Counseling Association named him a "living legend," and in 2009 the Division of Psychotherapy of the American Psychological Association named him "distinguished psychologist" for his life contribution to psychotherapy. He has received similar awards from four other professional organizations. Most recently, he has a syndicated advice cartoon, "On the Edge," with cartoonist Joe Martin.

**Shannon B. Dermer, PhD,** is an associate professor and chair of the Division of Psychology and Counseling at Governors State University. She has a PhD in marriage and family therapy from Kansas State University and an MA in psychology from Illinois State University. She has published and presented work on the topics of training beginning counselors and therapists, working with African American couples, social justice, sexuality, solution-focused therapy, and more.

**Shea M. Dunham, PhD, MSW, MSEd,** is currently an assistant professor in the Division of Psychology and Counseling at Governors State University. She is a counselor, educator, and marriage and family therapist specializing in emotion-focused therapy, working with parents and their adult children, and with couples. She has recently published and presented on topics including African Americans and intimacy, emotional skillfulness in African American couples, training counselors and marriage and family therapists, and family social advocacy.

# About the Contributors

**Jennifer I. Durham, PsyD,** began her work in school and community psychology as an intern at The Consultation Center of Yale University Medical School. She left Yale in 1992 to do direct service work as a school psychologist for the Teaneck Board of Education. In 1999, Jennifer was hired as the executive director of Communities in Schools of Newark, Inc. Her work in the areas of social justice, culturally competent services, and racial disparities within health and educational settings has resulted in numerous awards, including the Donald Peterson Prize and the Baldwin Fellowship. Currently Jennifer is an assistant professor at the Derner Institute of Advanced Psychological Studies at Adelphi University in Garden City, New York.

**Matt Englar-Carlson, PhD,** is an associate professor of counseling at California State University–Fullerton. Matt coedited *In the Room With Men: A Casebook of Therapeutic Change* (APA) and *Counseling Troubled Boys: A Guidebook for Professionals* (Routledge), and was the featured professional in the APA DVD, "Engaging Men in Psychotherapy." With his father, Jon Carlson, he is the series editor of the Theories of Psychotherapy (APA) book series, and coauthor of the book *Adlerian Therapy*. In 2007, he was named the researcher of the year by the Society for the Psychological Study of Men and Masculinity. He is also a member of the APA Working Group to Develop Guidelines for Psychological Practice With Boys and Men. As a clinician, he has worked with children, adults, and families in school, community, and university mental health settings.

**Hannah R. Farber** is a student at Boston University. She is a candidate for a Bachelor of Arts degree in psychology. She hopes to further study parent–child attachment.

**Sondra Goldstein, PhD,** is a clinical psychologist in private practice in Encino, California. She is also a supervising psychologist in the UCLA Psychology Clinic, and a clinical associate professor in the Department of Psychology at UCLA. She has written and lectured locally and nationally on the neurobiology of attachment in relationships.

**Terry Hargrave, PhD,** is a professor of marriage and family therapy at Fuller Seminary in Pasadena, California, and is president of and in practice at the Amarillo Family Institute, Inc. He is nationally recognized for his pioneering work with intergenerational families. Terry has authored numerous professional articles and 10 books, including *Restoration Therapy: Guiding Healing in Marriage and Family Therapy.* His work has been featured in several national magazines and newspapers, as well as ABC News *20/20*, *Good Morning America*, and CBS *Early Morning*. He has been selected as a national conference plenary speaker and as a master's series therapist by the American Association for Marriage and Family Therapy.

**Judith V. Jordan, PhD,** is the director of the Jean Baker Miller Training Institute and founding scholar of the Stone Center at Wellesley College, where she and her colleagues have been developing Relational-Cultural Theory (RCT) since the late 1970s. She is an assistant professor of psychology at Harvard Medical School and served as the director of psychology training at McLean Hospital where she was the founding director of the Women's Treatment Program. Judith authored *Relational-Cultural Therapy*, co-authored *Women's Growth in Connection,* and edited *Women's Growth in Diversity, The Complexity of Connection,* and *The Power of Connection*. She is the recipient of the Massachusetts Psychology Association's Career Achievement Award for Outstanding Contributions to the Advancement of Psychology as a Science and a Profession.

**Melanie H. Mallers, PhD,** is an assistant professor at California State University, Fullerton, in the Department of Human Services. Her research areas include stress, health, and coping across adulthood, with emphasis on parent–child relationships. Currently she is exploring the link between disrupted parent–child attachments during childhood with daily stressor reactivity during middle adulthood. She also has an extensive background in family systems theory, social ecology, and biopsychosocial models of human development. In addition to her research, Melanie is highly involved in community work, including leading caregiving workshops for families struggling with dementia.

**Donald J. Olund, MA, LCPC,** is currently a marriage and family counselor and owner and executive director of Lifework Counseling Center, in Oak Brook, Illinois. Don is also a university lecturer at Governors State University where he received his BA in psychology and his MA in marriage and family counseling. He was nominated for and selected as a student speaker for commencement services at Governors State University and is a member of Chi Sigma Iota. Professional interests include marriage and family counseling and helping families adjust to lifecycle changes, particularly those with parent and adolescent transitions. In addition, Don specializes in play therapy and is a contributing author in two recent clinical books on the subject. Don is also interested in integrating spirituality and counseling.

**Patricia A. Robey, EdD, LPC, NCC, CTRTC,** is an assistant professor of counseling at Governors State University, University Park, Illinois. She is a licensed professional counselor and specializes in applying reality therapy and choice theory in her work with individuals, couples, families, and groups. Dr. Robey is a senior faculty member of the William Glasser Institute and has taught the concepts of choice theory and reality therapy in the United States and internationally.

**Daniel J. Siegel, MD,** earned his degree from Harvard University and did postgraduate training in pediatrics, child, adolescent, and adult psychiatry at UCLA. He has studied family interactions with an emphasis on how attachment experiences influence emotions, behavior, autobiographical memory, and narrative. He is currently a clinical professor of psychiatry at the UCLA School of Medicine where he is also on the faculty of the Center for Culture, Brain, and Development. Daniel is also codirector of the Mindful Awareness Research Center at UCLA and executive director of the Mindsight Institute. He has published extensively on parenting, therapy, and attunement from an interpersonal neurobiological perspective.

**Catherine Ford Sori, PhD, LMFT,** completed her doctorate at Purdue University, West Lafayette, Indiana, in child development and family studies with a specialization in marriage and family therapy. She is an associate professor at Governors State University, and is an associate faculty member at the Chicago Center for Family Health (an affiliate of the University of Chicago). She has authored/edited six books, including *The Therapist's Notebook for Children and Adolescents* and *Engaging Children in Family*

*Therapy.* She has written and presented on topics related to families coping with illness and bereavement, integrating play in family therapy, and training clinicians to work with children and families. A clinical member and an AAMFT-approved supervisor, Catherine is also a member of ACA and IPTA, and serves on the boards of several leading journals.

**Len Sperry, MD, PhD,** is professor of mental health counseling at Florida Atlantic University, and clinical professor of psychiatry and behavioral medicine at the Medical College of Wisconsin. He is a life fellow of the American Psychological Association, a life fellow of the American College of Preventive Medicine, a distinguished life fellow of the American Psychiatric Association, and is board-certified in psychiatry, preventive medicine, and clinical psychology. He has more than 600 publications, 60 of which are professional books, including *Recovery of Intimacy in Love Relationships.* He also is a member of 12 editorial boards, including the *American Journal of Family Therapy, The Family Journal,* and the *Journal of Marital and Family Therapy.*

**Susan Thau, PhD,** has a doctorate in clinical psychology. She is a member of the Institute of Contemporary Psychoanalysis in Los Angeles, where she is a supervising and training analyst. Her involvement in the study of attachment and affect regulation includes being a member of a study group with Allan Schore, PhD, as well as completing training and certification in Susan Johnson's emotionally focused therapy (EFT). She is in private practice in Santa Monica and Encino, California, where she treats adolescents, individuals, and couples from the perspective of attachment and neurobiology. Over the years, she and Sondra Goldstein, PhD, have lectured and written on the application of these principles to clinical work.

**Scott R. Woolley, PhD,** is a distinguished professor and systemwide director of the MFT masters and doctoral programs in the California School of Professional Psychology at Alliant International University. He is a founder and director of the San Diego Center for EFT at Alliant (TRI EFT Alliant). Scott has trained therapists in EFT in Asia, Europe, Central and South America, as well as throughout the United States.

# Introduction

SHANNON B. DERMER and SHEA M. DUNHAM

Do your adult clients sometimes feel like they can never please their parents no matter what they do? Do their parents ridicule them to their face or behind their back? Even though they are adults, do your clients create situations to draw themselves closer to their parents—catastrophizing and creating drama to test whether their parents will step up and save them even though they know they won't? Do your clients hate their parents and hate themselves when they interact with their parents, but are unable to do things differently and unable to rewrite their story? When they talk to their parents on the phone do they hang up and ask themselves, "Why did I call?" Yet does their insecurity drive them to seek the acceptance of their parents while cursing themselves for wanting their approval? If you answered "yes" to several of these questions, then your clients are more than likely suffering the toxic effects of a poisonous relationship with their parents.

Whether parents are "good" or "bad" caretakers does not determine whether children and adult children are attached to their parents. Humans are hard-wired to attach (form a strong emotional, cognitive, and physiological bond) to caregivers, whether those caregivers are responsive in a healthy way or not (Hazan, Gur-Yaish, & Campa, 2004). Attachment styles describe people's tendency to seek soothing and security from their attachment figure and the expectations that their attachment figure will meet their needs for security, attention, support, and warmth. Those who are securely attached have responsive caretakers who are effective at helping soothe children, especially in times of distress, and at encouraging exploratory behavior. Insecurely attached children are not confident in a caretaker's ability to provide warmth and security in a way that also supports exploratory behavior. "Again, insecure babies and children are differently, but no less, attached than their secure counterparts. So what do they have in common? It is that all of their attachment-defining behaviors are organized around a specific individual. This person may or may not be reliably responsive, may or may not be effective in alleviating distress, may or may not be approached for contact comfort in threatening situations. But she or he is nonetheless the selective target toward whom attachment behaviors are oriented" (Hazan et al., 2004, p. 64). Even when parents are a destructive force, their children and adult children still yearn for comfort and will orient their attachment behaviors toward a parent or another attachment figure (e.g., friend, mentor, therapist, romantic partner). In this book, readers are shown how to recognize poisonous parenting and how to recognize adult children who are suffering from poisonous parenting attitudes and behaviors. Different poisonous parenting styles are described in Chapter 1 by Shea Dunham and Shannon Dermer. Readers will learn when to try to save the relationship, when to proceed with caution, and when to disconnect to keep the poison from spreading. Many of the chapters in this book focus on the development of insecure styles of attachment in the infant–parent relationship and insecure strategies in the adult child–parent relationship. The effects of poisonous parenting are often seen in individuals' expectations and behaviors in other relationships.

## Overview

The roles of child, parent, and partner share the commonalities that they are likely to activate intense emotional reactions (both positive and negative) and fulfill the typical human interactions of dependency or caretaking. The child is dependent on the parent and evokes caretaking behaviors in others; parents are caretakers and tend to the dependency needs of children, not vice versa. Loving partners take turns evoking and fulfilling dependence and caretaking needs in each other. In adult romantic relationships, both sides of the "attachment coin" can be seen in each partner—the ability to be effectively dependent on someone and the ability to be effectively dependable. Although there are similarities in the attachment between parent and child and romantic partners, caretaking is supposed to be unilateral in parent–young child relationships, and couple relationships are supposed to be bilateral and reciprocal.

Attachment theory has been used as a framework to understand the emotional bond called love in both children and adults (Brumbaugh & Fraley, 2006; Mikulincer, 2006). Whether it is filial, platonic, or romantic love, the core process in creating a healthy attachment to another person is the repeated exposure to someone who is attuned to (accurately perceives nonverbal and verbal cues) and appropriately responds to the other's needs especially during times of distress. These processes can be understood from a relational perspective or a physiological one. In Chapter 2

Patricia Robey and Catherine Ford Sori review several major therapeutic models and how good parenting is understood within these paradigms. While Robey and Sori review parenting models from a systemic–relational perspective, in the two following chapters the focus is interpersonal neurobiology and the parent child and adult–child relationship. In Chapter 3 Hannah Farber and Daniel Siegel present the idea of "mindsight" and how one can create internal security through knowledge of how the brain, mind, and attachment are interrelated. In Chapter 4 Sondra Goldstein and Susan Thau also explore how interpersonal neurobiology can be used to understand relationships and focus on how to overcome early insecure attachments through earned security.

In childhood, parents are usually the most important attachment figures; in adulthood, romantic partners often become primary attachment figures (Mikulincer, 2006). For couples, a secure attachment predicts a happy, stable, committed relationship (Mikulincer). However, when one or both partners do not perceive the other as accessible and responsive, the relationship can be marked by anxiety, agitation, tension, and anger. Given enough threats to attachment over time, it ultimately can damage one's relationship and influence future relationships. For example, in Chapter 5 Shea Dunham and Scott Woolley discuss attachment injuries, their effect on the relationship, and how to repair them to strengthen couple relationships. In addition, in Chapter 6 Len Sperry discusses how to understand and assess relationship dynamics that have been influenced by poisonous parenting patterns and how, left unchecked, those dynamics may be passed to the next generation. As Sperry states, "The couple bridges at least two families of origin and their rules, relationships, and cultures. When the romantic relationship, whether it is brief or long-term, results in children, it is also one of the devices for passing relational patterns and quality of relationships to the next generation."

In addition to a future focus on how poisonous parenting can affect relationships, it is also helpful to look at the past. People who have destructive parenting styles often were the victims of malevolent parenting themselves. Parents may play out their own insecurities, deficiencies, and fears from childhood in their relationships with their own children. In some cases it's easy to see how poisonous parents are wounded, and in their pain they lash out and wound others or, conversely, hold children so close that they stifle their children's ability to grow. Particular types of attachment insecurity may manifest themselves in abusive relational patterns. When attachment anxieties are triggered by relational distance, conflict, fears of rejection, separation, or abandonment, parents may lash out with abusive behaviors to control children and to force emotional and physical proximity (Bartholomew & Allison, 2006). Others may manifest attachment as extreme avoidance—neglecting, abandoning, or cutting off emotionally from their children.

Clinicians can explore specific types of parent–child relationships or can widen their focus to include society. Melanie Horn Mallers, Matt Englar-Carlson, and Jon Carlson discuss the unique aspects of father–son relationships compared with other parent–child dyads in Chapter 7. In addition, a societal lens can be used to understand poisonous relationships. In Chapter 8 Judith Jordan uses relational-cultural therapy to question using *poison* as a metaphor for understanding relationships and instead explores how society can create extreme disconnection. Furthermore, in Chapter 9 Jennifer Durham explores the intersection between poisonous parenting and African American culture. It is important to acknowledge and understand how oppression can impact parenting. Although one can trace familial patterns of poisonous parenting throughout a family tree, focusing on only the family may be too narrow of a lens. Perhaps including a critique of society and its influence on families may be fruitful for some clinicians and families.

Besides using attachment theory to describe the affectional bonds between parents and children and between partners, some have hypothesized that the same styles can be used to understand people's relationships with a higher power. In addition, religion can be a source of great comfort or can be used as a way to impose guilt and control children and adults. In Chapter 10 Don Olund discusses how religion can be used as a weapon in the hands of a poisonous parent.

Overall, the various chapters in this book help the reader explore the effects of poisonous parenting on individuals, family relationships, romantic relationships, and friendships. The goal is to help clients and clinicians recognize and understand the toxicity associated with particular parenting styles and attachment injuries and how people carry contaminated views of themselves and their relationships into their adulthood. If one can identify poison and begin treatment to counteract the toxic effects of the poison as it infiltrates a system, then one may be able to recover and lead a healthy life. Terry Hargrave, in Chapter 11, discusses the healing power of forgiveness and how it can neutralize poisonous interactions. Nevertheless, forgiveness is not always possible. Like physicians, clinicians do not want to amputate but sometimes find it necessary to preserve the health of the larger system. Chapter 12, by Shannon Dermer and Shea Dunham, provides strategies for working with poisonous parents.

## Conclusion

The intergenerational pattern of destructive parenting, or what the others here have labeled poisonous parenting, can be understood from an attachment perspective. An attachment perspective is used by many of the authors in this book, although other perspectives are explored in several chapters. No matter what the theoretical perspective, all the authors share the view that poisonous parenting can have detrimental effects for parents, children, and the future platonic, filial, and romantic relationships of children of poisonous parents. Nevertheless, adult children of poisonous parents are not doomed. It is possible to gain earned security through healthy, secure relationships with friends, mentors, and partners. In addition, the goal of therapy with adult children is to find a way to intervene in the parent–adult child relationship in a way that either alters destructive interactional cycles that activate insecure attachment strategies or finds a way for adult children to gain empathy and forgiveness for the limitations of their parents. In the end, the goal is to create healthier relationships within generations and across generations.

We hope that this book will be a starting point for clinicians in exploring parent–adult child relationships and how unresolved attachment injuries with parents may have detrimental effects on adult children's current relationships. The book was written in an easy-to-read and informative style. Although it is meant for clinicians, assigning specific chapters to clients may prove useful in therapy. However this book is used, it was our goal, in creating it, that clinicians will better understand the impact of parent–child relationships on all people and to gain insight in how to work effectively in this area.

## References

Bartholomew, K., & Allison, C. J. (2006). An attachment perspective on abusive dynamics in intimate relationships. In M. Mikulincer & G. S. Goodman (Eds.), *Dynamics of romantic love: Attachment, caregiving, and sex* (pp. 102–127). New York: Guilford.

Brumbaugh, C. C., & Fraley, C. R. (2006). The evolution of attachment in romantic relationships. In M. Mikulincer & G. S. Goodman (Eds.), *Dynamics of romantic love: Attachment, caregiving, and sex* (pp. 71–101). New York: Guilford.

Hazan, C., Gur-Yaish, N., & Campa, M. (2004). What does it mean to be attached? In W. S. Rholes & J. A. Simpson (Eds.), *Adult attachment: Theory, research, and clinical implications*. New York: Guilford.

Mikulincer, M. (2006). Attachment, caregiving, and sex within romantic relationships: A behavioral systems perspective. In M. Mikulincer & G. S. Goodman (Eds.), *Dynamics of romantic love: Attachment, caregiving, and sex* (pp. 23–44). New York: Guilford.

CHAPTER 1
# Poisonous Parenting

SHEA M. DUNHAM and SHANNON B. DERMER

Parents are the ultimate teachers. They teach their children what to think about the world, what is important or unimportant, and about their own self-worth (Hughes, 2009). Whether overtly or covertly, children learn from their parents about who to love, how to love, how to be loved, and how (or even if) they should love themselves.

In the professional field of teaching, a person's view of how to teach is called pedagogy. Whether parents realize it, this applies to them as well—a systematic way of disciplining and shaping their children's lives. Practices deemed harmful to children and contrary to supporting healthy emotional development into adulthood have been referred to as *poisonous pedagogy* (translated from Rutschky's 1977 "black pedagogy"; as cited in Miller, 2002).

At first, *poisonous* may seem overly harsh in describing a parenting style. Yet, upon further reflection, poisonous parenting styles are analogous to poisonous substances. Poisonous substances are complex in that they are not always harmful and, given certain circumstances and uses, can even be helpful. Similarly, parenting behaviors can be innocuous or helpful in certain circumstances and doses, and those same behaviors can have long-lasting, detrimental effects when not administered properly. In chemistry, a poison is a substance that obstructs or inhibits a reaction; for purposes of this book, poison is a relational style that inhibits the formation of a secure attachment between two people. A poisonous parent is one whose ways of teaching children about life and styles of interaction damage children's abilities to form healthy connections with family members, friends, and eventually romantic partners and offspring. While every parent makes mistakes, it is the frequency and intensity of certain interactions that make them "poisonous."

The poisoning of a relationship can be chronic (happening over long-term, repeated exposure), or it can be acute (occurring immediately after exposure). For example, the poisonous effects of criticism may accumulate in the lifeblood of the relationship over years, or the effect of an action on the relationship could be immediate, as when a parent severely beats a child. Whether chronic or acute, poison sours a relationship that should be warm, supportive, and enjoyable.

## Definition of Poison

Paracelsus, a 16th-century physician who is considered the father of toxicology and who dedicated much energy to defining what is poisonous, once wrote, "While a thing may be a poison, it may not cause poisoning ... [and] every cathartic is a poison if not administered in the proper dose" (Deichmann, Henschler, Holmstedt, & Keil, 1986, pp. 210–211). In other words, the amount of a particular substance may make something harmless, curative, or poisonous depending on the dose and circumstance. The same can be said for parenting. Doses of a particular behavior may be healthy for a child at particular levels, stage of development, and context. For instance, showing affection to a child is a beneficial way to express caring, warmth, and love. Moderately excessive affection can feel intrusive and stifling to children, and extremely excessive affection can step into the realm of sexual abuse. However, the same kinds of behaviors (e.g., touching, stroking, kissing, intercourse) that would constitute sexual abuse (poisonous) in an inappropriate relationship may be perfectly healthy and healing (cathartic) in a romantic relationship. The toxicity (the level of harmfulness) varies based on many factors: level of exposure, recurrence of exposure, preparation, purpose, and the particular sensitivities of the person absorbing the substance. Parents and their systematic style of interacting with their young and adult children may be medicinal or poisonous to interpersonal relationships (Mikulincer, Shaver, Bar-On, & Ein-Dor, 2010). Particular behaviors such as competition, teasing, humor, control, and punishment can all have healthy or harmful effects depending on the intensity of expression, the number times they occur, the context in which they are expressed, and the psychological and interpersonal needs and sensitivities of the child.

## Definition of Poisonous Parenting

For purposes of this book, the authors of this chapter are defining poisonous parenting as chronic toxicity at a dose level that will eventually severely impair the parent–adult child relationship. Poisonous parents are those whose ways of teaching children about life and styles of interaction damage children's ability to form healthy connections with family members, friends, and eventually romantic partners and offspring. While every parent makes mistakes, it is the frequency and intensity of certain interactions that is damaging. In addition, not only does poisonous parenting have negative effects for the long-term relationship between parent and child; it also has implications for the self-worth, friendships, and romantic relationships of their adult children (Mikulincer et al., 2010). The parent–child relationship, whether healthy or unhealthy, serves as a template for all other relationships. Based on these interactions persons create an internal working model of what to expect from relationships.

## The Secure Bond: The Glue That Holds Relationships Together

Although necessary, meeting children's basic physical needs is not enough to sustain them and to foster healthy relationships. Certainly the groundbreaking studies of John Bowlby and Harry Harlow demonstrated the importance of a physical and emotional connection to a comforting figure who is a responsive caregiver. Bowlby demonstrated the deleterious effects on infants who did not have stable, caring, affectionate relationships. Harlow experimented with rhesus monkeys to show the detrimental effects of maternal deprivation and of not having a caregiver available to soothe the baby monkeys in anxiety-producing situations. Bowlby and Harlow looked to nature and instincts to learn about human emotional needs. So what does nature teach us about healing the human heart? We need only look, with an open mind, to the relationships between animals and humans and their offspring. The basic nature of healthy relationships is reflected in instinctual caretaking.

Over time, parents' level of attentiveness, ability to soothe children's anxieties and fears, tendency to enhance children's feelings of security, and willingness to accept their children's vulnerability helps determine a child's future relational patterns. The parent–child relationship is supposed to be one of security, soothing, love, and closeness. The focus of the parent–child relationship is on fulfilling the physical and emotional needs of the child to form a secure bond between child and caretakers. The secure attachment of the child to the parent means that the child trusts that the parent will be available and responsive to needs in a warm, caring manner and that the child feels valued (Greenberg, 2002). The securely attached relationship is one in which there is closeness and, as the child develops, freedom and space for the child to grow and explore the world without resentment from the parent. Although parents certainly gain things from the relationship, in healthy parent–child relationships the onus for fulfilling needs is on the parents, not on the child, to fulfill the needs and desires of the parents.

Parents who are physically near, emotionally responsive, and able to soothe with touch and vocalizations are likely to create a safe, comforting connection with an infant. Over time, these experiences accumulate to provide children "with a core sense of worth, of being loved, and of being able to love in turn" (Hughes, 2009, p. 8). Consequently, parents are seen as valuable and caring by the children. The developing children create internal working models of themselves, others, and relationships based on repeated interactions with caregivers (Mikulincer et al., 2010).

Sometimes children do not have caregivers attuned to their needs and form an insecure relationship with caregivers. Without an intervening secure relationship, whether it be a parent or another stable presence in the person's life, children insecurely attached to parental figures tend to develop into adults who construct insecure attachment strategies.

When children are trained, they learn how to train others in turn. "Children who are lectured to, learn how to lecture; if they are admonished, they learn how to admonish; if scolded, they learn how to scold; if ridiculed, they learn how to ridicule; if humiliated, they learn how to humiliate; if their psyche is killed, they will learn how to kill—the only question is who will be killed: oneself, others, or both" (Miller, 2002, p. 90).

The secure bond and attachment of the young child to a parent sets the stage for other relationships as the child matures into adulthood. People's attachment orientation, developed based on close relationships, creates relational expectations, emotions, and behaviors congruent with a person's unique attachment (Fraley & Shaver, 2000; Mikulincer et al., 2010). Children who trust a parent usually become adults who trust others. Appropriately compassionate and responsive parents cultivate adults who are trusting, comfortable with affection, have clear boundaries, are able to identify and express emotions, and maintain a sense of spontaneity and playfulness along with a responsible, caring nature. These are the types of adults who are good spouses or partners, parents, friends, and coworkers. Compassionate parents are like fertilizer—helping a seedling get the nutrients it needs to grow strong and healthy.

Conversely, when parents careen off the path of creating a secure bond and attachment they can be poison to their children and their children's future relationships. Rather than becoming securely attached to an unresponsive or unpredictably responsive parent, children may become avoidant or ambivalent about the affectional bond. Being insecurely attached to a parent creates a relational template wherein adult children are less likely to form secure, trusting, stable, affectionate relationships with others. Insecurely attached adults tend to show extreme patterns in their relationships (Mikulincer et al., 2010). They show disturbances in their abilities to trust or be trustworthy. A parent's lack of responsiveness, abandonment, betrayal of trust, or inability to comfort and soothe children in times of distress creates, over time, an attachment injury that is not easily healed (Johnson, Makinen, & Millikin, 2001). The injury, like scar tissue, may be minor and relatively unnoticeable or, with repeated trauma, may become large and interfere with functioning. Attachment injuries, when left unattended, can be gangrenous and create an impasse in current and future relationships that is not easily escaped (Johnson et al.).

## The Insecure Bond: The Foundation for a Poisonous Relationship

Typical parents may face the birth of a child with intermingled excitement, hope, fear, and anxiety; the helplessness of an infant can trigger both caretaking behaviors and resentment in parents. For many people the instinct to care for and emotionally bond with an infant is instinctual. On one hand, for typical parents, babies enhance adults' predisposition for nurturing through genetically programmed behaviors that have evolved to elicit responses from caretakers and enhance the emotional bond between parent and child (e.g., prolonged eye contact, smiling, crying, babbling, clinging). On the other hand, what evokes caring, attentive, affectionate responses from most parents may be experienced by poisonous parents as annoying, frustrating, selfish, and demanding (Laing in Firestone, 1990, p. ix). Alternatively, some poisonous parents have an insatiable craving for the attention and affection of their children to the point where the relationship becomes about meeting the parents' needs and desires for love and security rather than about the child's needs. Regardless of whether adults are abdicating the parental role, resenting it, or craving it, the needs of the child evoke the unmet needs within the parents (Firestone, 1990; Miller, 2002).

It is the pursuit of trying to heal or avoid one's own unmet needs that partly makes some parents destructive to the emerging psyche and relationships of their children. The term *attachment* describes children forming a bond with their parents or caretakers, not vice versa. Poisonous parents try to get their own needs met by attempting to repair their injuries through childbearing and child rearing. They see their children as a means to an end—helping them to feel loved, worthy, virile, important, or competent. They seek healing through a means that can never heal them. Parents have an affectional bond with a child, but they are not attached to the child (Hughes, 2009). Being securely attached to a parent, the child will turn to the parent for support and feelings of safety. It is not appropriate for the parent to turn to the child for those same things. Adults should seek feelings of support, warmth, and safety, from partners, friends, or their own parents but not from children.

Poisonous parents behave as they do for one or more of several reasons: as a means of expressing their anger and resentment toward their own parents, to restore their belief in love, or simply because they have never learned the skills for accurately perceiving others' needs or the ability to express loving behaviors in an attuned manner. They may display ambivalence toward their children—wanting to nurture their children but stunting their growth, stifling their joy, and altering their desires. Whether it is through emotionally or physically abusing, smothering, or deserting their children, poisonous parents repeatedly act in unloving and destructive ways. Regardless of how damaging these patterns may appear to others, poisonous parents may be oblivious to the effect they have on their children or adult children. One of the reasons it is difficult to intervene in these relationships is that parents may be blind to their malevolence or even perceive their actions as benevolent. For example, absent parents may believe their presence has no impact on a child's life or parents who are harsh and criticizing may believe they are preparing their children for a cruel world.

As children of poisonous parents develop and experience damage to their emotional connection to parents, a multigenerational legacy of poison is created. There are multiple people with attachment injuries trying to get their needs met. As children develop, the relationship between parents and adult children may become increasingly reactive, conflictual, and anxiety ridden. To change the legacy, adult children need to learn different ways of tilling the soil in which they intend to cultivate new relationships.

## Styles of Poisonous Parenting

Various styles of poisonous parenting are described in this section. For ease of comprehension, labels to describe typical patterns are used, and examples from books, movies, and clinical work are cited to help illustrate patterns. Although the styles are described separately, caretakers may be a combination of several types of change styles depending on the developmental stage of their offspring. The *pageant parent, dismissive parent,* and *contemptuous parent* describe the three main styles, and each style is broken down into subcategories.

### *The Pageant Parent*

Pageant parents try to create a child who is the mirror image of who they wish they were. This type of parent gains pseudo self-worth through the child's accomplishments—real or imagined. Children and adult children are pushed into taking on the parents' wishes and desires as their own. Subcategories of the pageant parent include the showbiz parent, fictitious parent, and the superstar parent.

*The Showbiz Parent* Showbiz parents may appear to love their children and want what is best for them, but they push their children in a driven, single-minded way to become the smartest, the most athletic, the most talented, or the most famous. These parents are sending the message, "Be what I was, or what I wanted to be, but even better." Pushing the child or adult child to be better stems from parents' needs rather than from a desire to do what's truly best for the child or adult child.

The quintessential example of a showbiz parent is the relationship between Gypsy and her mother, Rose. *Gypsy* is a Broadway musical (1959) based off the memoir of Gypsy Rose Lee, a vivacious burlesque dancer in the 1930s. The musical is a dramatization of Gypsy's life and fame but most notably of her relationship with her show business mother. Although Gypsy desired stardom, she desired her mother's support and acceptance more. Her mother constantly pushed Gypsy to be a star and to provide financial stability to the family through her stardom. When Gypsy was faced with love (a boyfriend wanted to get married and run away with her) and normalcy without her mother, Gypsy chose loneliness, chaos, and her show business mother. After Rose died, Gypsy was finally free to pursue some of her own life's interests and begin the healing process by writing her memoir.

*The Fictitious Parent* Fictitious parents glorify their children to the outside world, but in a fantasy way that demeans the reality of who the child actually is. They create a story with a grain of truth but exaggerate the child's accomplishments, goals, personality traits, or the quality of the parent–child relationship. In overexaggerating the child or adult child's life, these parents send a message that who the child or adult child actually is doesn't meet their expectations. For example, one client's mother had a chess set in the living room for decoration. One day a visitor asked the mother why she had the chess set since she didn't play chess. The mother replied, "Oh, my daughter loves to play chess. She plays all the time." The daughter looked at her mother incredulously because she had never played chess a day in her life. Another client reported that after going out on a date with a prominent politician's daughter once he overheard his father talking to someone about how his son was dating the mayor's daughter. His father stated this even though the son had told his father that he didn't like the woman and didn't want to ask her on another date. In both cases the message was that the child wasn't good enough.

A variation of the fictitious parent is where, instead of exaggerating the child's accomplishments to the outside world, parents exaggerate their relationship with the child. They may refer to their son or daughter as "my best friend." They may get jealous if someone gets too close to their child because the other person may usurp their position as the most important in their child's life. These types of parent may procreate to create someone who can love them unconditionally. They look to their children to fulfill their need for love, acceptance, and self-worth.

*The Superstar Parent* Superstar parents compete with their offspring. They remind their children that they will never be as good as they are. They get involved in things the child is interested in and do it better. They tend to minimize accomplishments and goals that the child has. Superstar parents might make comments such as, "That's great that you got all As and Bs, but I remember when I was in grade school I got all As and I had a full-time job." Or, as one client's mother stated when a friend commented on how beautiful her daughter was, "Of course she is beautiful; look at her mother."

Making a joke once in a while or an off-handed comment like these does not make someone a poisonous parent. It is the systematic, long-term "one-upping" of children along with occasional doses of criticism that undermine the security of children and adult children. In addition, the superstar parent often sends mixed messages. On one hand, these parents may push a child to be successful. On the other hand, they sabotage or criticize the child's accomplishments.

### *The Dismissive Parent*

Dismissive parents are not connected to the child in a meaningful way. Parents may be unavailable physically, emotionally, or financially. The dismissive parents may be home every day, but they are so involved in their own lives that they are not involved in the child's life. They may provide the basic necessities, and from their point of view that is parenting. However, what is missing is the secure bond—the emotional connection. These parents are not someone that the child can go to in times of distress and may be around but are not available emotionally. Secure, compassionate parents engage emotionally. Not engaging emotionally sends the message that the child doesn't matter and that there is little or no connection between the child and his or her parents. Any response, even anger, is better than no response. This may also hold true when the child becomes an adult—the parent is always too involved with work, too involved with dating, or too involved with friends to make time for adult children or their family. Dismissive parents go through the motions and follow a checklist, but the most important things are missing from that checklist. Dismissive parents may focus more on the quantity than the quality.

*The Stepford Parent* Stepford parents do what they think they are supposed to do because it is what is expected rather than because they are genuinely engaged with their children. These people may have children because they feel like they are supposed to rather than because they want to. From the outside it may appear that the children are taken care of. This makes it even more difficult for the children. The adult children may feel like they should be grateful for what they got but still feel empty and disconnected. Stepford parents are involved their children's lives, but they do not seem to be emotionally invested. In her memoir, *sTORI Telling*, Tori Spelling (2008) describes her childhood as filled with storybook experiences. Nevertheless, she felt disconnected from her "perfect" mother and felt more of an affinity to her nanny.

*The Prerogative Parent* Prerogative parents believe that parenting is a choice and that children should be grateful for being born and for whatever they get—if they get anything, big or small, something, or not at all. The choices the parents make aren't related to their duty to their child but are influenced instead by what pleases or works for them in the moment. These types of parents may be attentive to their children at times, but it's about meeting their own needs for attention, affection, or validation rather than a selfless act for their children's sake.

*The Acquaintance Parent* Some parents provide for the basic necessities of their children and are polite and kind to their children, but in a way one would reserve for acquaintances. An acquaintance relationship has no depth to it. It lacks intimacy. Gottman (1999), a renowned relationship expert, refers to the depth of information people have for their loved ones as a "cognitive love map." He also highlights the importance of accepting a bid for attention from loved ones and valuing one another by sharing dreams and admiring each other's venerable attributes. The more detailed the map, the more attention that is given to one another, and the more people admire one another, the more easily people navigate their relationship. Acquaintance parents' love map, ability to give meaningful attention, and ability to express admiration for the children and adult children are stunted. Their relationship with their children is more like ships passing in the night.

*The Donor Parent* Donor parents are truly absentee parents. They are basically egg or sperm donors—parents in name or biology only. Their offspring are latchkey children from birth—their parents are never home or have only barely been a part of their children's lives. Donor parents may resurface once in a while and appear to want a connection with their children, only to disappear again. Children cannot predict when their donor parents will appear and disappear. They may wrestle with yearning for a connection while knowing that their parents cannot be trusted to stay around.

*The Contemptuous Parent*

Contemptuous parents are the judge and jury regarding their children's behavior, needs, wants, and dreams. They tend to belittle, criticize, condemn, and emotionally blackmail their children. Contempt conveys disgust and is always poisonous to a relationship (Gottman & Silver, 1999). Sarcasm, cynicism, name calling, eye rolling, sneering, mockery, and hostile humor all convey contempt (Gottman & Silver).

Criticism, a close cousin to contempt, is also damaging to relationships and may be especially difficult for all parents to contain. Parents can complain about a child or adult child's behavior, but criticism is a global complaint that denigrates someone's character or personality (Gottman & Silver, 1999). Contemptuous parents will label children a "liar" when they accidentally provide misinformation, a "slob" when they don't clean up from dinner, and "lazy" when they do not immediately do what is asked. Although these are typical teenage behaviors, children will be maligned and their character assassinated for any transgressions. It's okay to be angry—that doesn't make one a contemptuous parent. If the anger is appropriate, genuine, and out of caring and concern and is directed at a particular behavior, then it can be helpful to a relationship. However, anger may turn into criticism and contempt when accompanied by demeaning comments that convey a sense of disgust with a child.

*The Zealot Parent* Zealot parents are fanatical about their point of view and will use their power and authority to dominate, control, or manipulate their children. The power may be based on money, religion, or affection. The control is often based on withholding or fear. These types of parents may threaten to cut their children off financially every time they do not fulfill their wishes, may threaten to damage and disparage a valued relationship to another person, may withhold affection from their children and exaggerate affection with other family members to make their children jealous and to live in fear of losing "love." Adult children may respond to these threats with submissiveness or rebelliousness.

Power and fear based on religion may be especially damaging because it includes a higher power than parents. Religious zealot parents shackle children and adult children to themselves out of fear of punishment from them and from God. One may be able to escape parents, but one can never escape God.

*The Seesaw Parent* Seesaw parents are sometimes up and sometimes down. Even when they are up they are still contemptuous, but the contempt is usually more indirect—expressed through snide comments and sarcasm. Seesaw parents are not easy to predict. There is always an underlying undercurrent of contempt, but when the seesaw is up the contempt is covert, and when the seesaw is down the contempt is overt. This type of style can be particularly confusing for children and adult children: When these parents are "up" there is a glimmer of hope that the relationship can be good, but their children and adult children are constantly snapped back to reality by their parents' ever-present harshness. For instance, this type of mother may rave about her adult child's engagement party, how beautiful her daughter was, and what a great time she had. Five minutes later, she may complain that the food wasn't that great and that her daughter's dress was inappropriate for the occasion. The "down" of the seesaw might be wildly obvious to everyone, or it may be just little swipes that would catch the attention and hurt the feelings only of the adult child. Whether the seesaw moving down is obvious or more subtle, when the seesaw falls, it falls fast and hard.

*The Mommy or Daddy Dearest Parent* Some parents are extremely physically and emotionally abusive. While the other types of contemptuous parents may hurt their offspring mostly with their words and threats, Mommy and Daddy Dearest literally pummel their children. These parents are the reason abuse hotlines were created. Their cruelty and viciousness is not subtle or hard to recognize. Punishments are swift and severe for seemingly minor transgressions. These types of poisonous parents take everything their children do outside of their wishes as a personal affront. They attribute adult motivations to childlike actions.

The term "Mommy Dearest" comes from the biography of Joan Crawford written by her daughter, Christina. One famous scene involves her mother hitting her with wire hangers after finding one among the cloth hangers in her closet; this vicious verbal and physical assault exemplifies the Mommy or Daddy Dearest parent.

Joan Crawford rants at her daughter:

> No … wire … hangers. What's wire hangers doing in this closet when I told you, "No wire hangers EVER!"? I work and work till I'm half-dead, and I hear people saying, "She's getting old." And what do I get? A daughter … who cares as much about the beautiful dresses I give her … as she cares about me. What's wire hangers doing in this closet? Answer me. I buy you beautiful dresses, and you treat them like they were some dishrag. You do. Three hundred dollar dress on a wire hanger. We'll see how many you've got if they're hidden

somewhere. We'll see … we'll see. Get out of that bed. All of this is coming out. Out. Out. Out. Out. Out. Out. You've got any more? We're gonna see how many wire hangers you've got in your closet. Wire hangers, why? Why?

## Case Example

Rita (mother) and Maya (adult daughter) sought counseling to better their relationship. Maya contacted the agency because she and her mother had always had a contentious relationship. When Maya was 3 years old she was sent to live with her grandmother. She returned to live with her mother when she was 7 years old. Both mother and daughter claimed that their relationship had been difficult ever since Maya came back to live with her mother. Rita stated during therapy that she was ready to cut her daughter off when she turned 18, but then Maya became pregnant and Rita wanted to be in her granddaughter's life. "I was looking forward to 18. I'm done. I'm free. Then she had the baby, and I wanted to make a difference in Keisha's life."

Both mother and daughter have a laundry list of complaints about one another, but there is fear and an underlying sadness beneath their words: fear that they will never truly have a secure mother–daughter relationship; fear that the pattern of distance between mothers and daughters will continue to be passed down through the generations. Maya sees her mother as hard and argumentative and thinks that she makes her love contingent upon Maya living her life exactly as Rita wants her to. Rita perceives her daughter as ungrateful, untrustworthy, and selfish. Throughout the session she calls her daughter a liar. "She lies. She's a pathological liar. She lies for the sake and joy of lying."

Maya has a fearful-avoidant attachment style with her mother, and, based on comments that Rita made about her own relationship with her mother, she most likely had an avoidant attachment style with her mother. The session starts with Maya stating that she wants to have a better relationship with her mother for her sake and her daughter's sake. Rita does not trust her daughter's motives. The mother consistently takes an attacking-protective stance with her daughter.

*Therapist:* Okay. So let's start off by saying, why did you make the phone call?

*Maya:* Well, I made the call because I'm 28, and for as long as I can remember my mother and I have had some type of rift. I now have my own daughter; she's 10. And this rift between my mother and me is starting to come out in me and my daughter.

*Therapist:* So you want to have a better relationship with your mother for your sake and your daughter's sake?

*Maya:* I want to have a much better relationship. Not just for me and my mother, but for my daughter as well. And I want a positive support system, but until we fix it or get help for whatever is the problem with us it's not going be right.

*Therapist:* Rita, how do you see it? Does that sum it up pretty good, or do you have something to add?

*Rita:* It sums it up. I don't think she and I can fix our "conflict" until we each individually fix what is causing us to act the way that we do. So, while this is good, I think it's jumping the gun.

*Therapist:* So you would prefer to see you do some individual work, she do some individual work, and then come back together?

*Rita:* Exactly. Because until we are honest with ourselves about ourselves, we're going to sit in here and lie. My plan is when the lying starts, I'm gone. And that's whether I'm telling it or it's being told. I agreed to do this as one last attempt to fix the problems, but I am tired.

*Therapist:* You're tired of conflict.

*Rita:* Mm-hmm.

*Therapist:* And how long has this conflict been going on?

*Rita:* Twenty-two years. Since she was 7. Since she came back from living with her grandmother. She's been lying since she was 7 years old, and it's never stopped.

*Maya:* She told my daughter I lie to people. So this is putting strain on where my daughter is like, "Should I believe Mama?" I'm Mama, so if I say the sky is purple, my daughter should say the sky is purple.

*Rita:* How should she deal with those lies she hears you tell? Because she comes to me and asks, "Why does my mother lie?"

*Maya:* That's not true. I do hope that we can bring my daughter in eventually. I have her in her own individual counseling in hopes that she and I can stay on track in my house, in our home.

*Rita:* You don't lie? So why don't I believe you then? Why have I learned not to trust anything you say?

*Therapist:* You know, Rita, that's a good question. Clue me in on that.

*Rita:* I want her to answer that though since I'm the bad guy.

*Maya:* I don't know. I'm asking you. I'd like to know. I'm not making you to be the bad guy. See, that's what I don't want, Mom. If I could afford it I would take a polygraph test and answer whatever questions she wants to prove I am not a liar.

*Rita:* [Rolls her eyes] She lies. She's a pathological liar. She lies for the sake and joy of lying. Every darn thing that I am able to believe is after proving it. I should not have to go that way with her, but I have learned over the years this is the only way; otherwise I play the fool. I learned years ago how to protect myself from being the fool. So, anything she tells me I have to dig into it. I have to ask questions. I have to dig and prove that she's telling the truth because she's lied so much for so long.

*Therapist:* So why do you think she's here now?

*Rita:* Because she needs a new audience. You're it. She doesn't need me. Truthfully, I won't be back because she wants to come in here and play a game. She has been in counseling for years. As long as I had "authority" over her, the school required that she get counseling. She's been to counseling, counseling, counseling, counseling. She played the same game with those people that she intends to play with you.

*Therapist:* But one thing I hear is that you both want to heal somehow this relationship.

*Rita:* I just want peace. She's grown. She cannot reinvent the wheel. Whatever kind of mother I was or wasn't, deal with it. Do what you need to do to fix you. I've been telling her this too. You can't change the past, but what I did I thought was the right thing to do.

*Therapist:* I understand that.

*Rita:* And I don't owe her anything. And I'm here to stop it. I can't do this anymore.

*Therapist:* I understand, Rita, that you're tired. I understand that.

*Rita:* I'm tired. Truly. I love her, but … I hope she gets the help that she needs.

*Maya:* I would like to have a mother and daughter relationship where we are not cussing at each other, arguing. I want something better than this; we have to have something better than this. And I don't know at what point it's going to stop with the "you're a liar." That's why I want the polygraph test, because the only thing she can say I lied about were normal kid things in my youth. "Did you have company in the house today?" "Well, no, Mom."

*Therapist:* Rita, what do you want? How do you want this to be better?

*Rita:* She has to start accepting responsibility for herself. She doesn't. She expects everything and everybody to go her way. And when it doesn't, you got a problem.

*Therapist:* What about the two of you, your relationship? What would you like to be better?

*Rita:* Well, if she stops trying to manipulate me and get angry with me when I don't follow her desires, we could have a better relationship. But she has to accept me as me and stop playing the game. Stop the lying, stop the manipulating, because I'm going to my grave calling her a liar because I haven't seen anything to prove different. That's why everything has to be proven because I learned not to trust anything she says.

*Therapist:* Are you open to her changing? If you say she's this big liar, and she said, "Okay, Mom. I'll do better," and the evidence proved that over time she's honest, are you open to giving her a chance?

*Rita:* If I thought it were possible, [but] I truly at this point do not even think it is possible. I don't think she knows how to be truthful anymore. She's learned how to manipulate, how to play a game. It automatically clicks.

*Therapist:* Has there been a moment when this has been good ever?

*Rita:* No. Never.

*Maya:* To me, there has.

*Rita:* Not in a long time.

*Maya:* To me there has, and more so in my adulthood.

*Therapist:* When it's good, do you feel connected to Rita?

*Maya:* Yes, but it's such a weird connection. I don't feel it's genuine. I can see the connection with some of my other friends and their parents and even with them and their siblings, and I want that so bad. But with my mother it's weird. [Daughter grabs a tissue and is wiping tears from her face.]

*Rita:* [Looks down and softens her face and demeanor.] The problems that I have … I have problems that have nothing to do with her.

*Maya:* Yes they do. They have been going from before I was even born. I found this out through my father. Mother, I am not here to upset you; I want to put it all out on the table so we can move on. She had a very abusive, terrible, terrible relationship with my father. I think because our problems stem from so young, she may just look at me and see him. He was terrible to her. I think I remind her of him, and it has always been too painful to look at me—to trust me.

*Therapist:* She trusted your father and then she felt like a fool?

*Rita:* No. [sigh] When I look at her, I see my face. I don't see him.… I can't act the way you want me to. I can't be the type of mother you have always wanted to me to be. But she is the good out of that relationship.

*Maya:* I couldn't be. Because at 7 this started.

*Therapist:* But your mom said something very important. She said you are the good out of that relationship.

*Maya:* She never treated me like that. I never thought that was true.

Both mother and daughter start to soften and become vulnerable with one another. Quickly, though, when faced with her daughter's feelings, Rita becomes defensive and distances herself again.

*Rita:* Because I didn't act the way she wanted me to, and if you don't act the way she wants you to it was wrong.

*Therapist:* Can we lay down the axe? Can we stop chipping away at each other?

*Maya:* Thank you. Thank you. Thank you. And that's why we're here.

*Rita:* I didn't particularly care for the way my mother raised me.

*Maya:* And you guys didn't get counseling; let's do something different.

*Therapist:* Is there love here?

*Maya:* I love my mother.

*Therapist:* Do you love her, Rita?

*Rita:* Mm-hmm.

*Maya:* I don't believe she does. I don't believe she does.

*Rita:* Because what would I need to do? Jump through that hoop and land on this left toe, and then [she shrugs her shoulders and sighs].... With my parents—my mother, I was angry with her, and I had to work through that. It's part of the process.

*Therapist:* Were you perfect with that anger? And didn't you sometimes hurt your mom and she sometimes hurt you?

*Rita:* Yes. But I didn't, as an adult; I did not go out of my way to hurt her or try to belittle her, to try to....

*Therapist:* Mom might say something different. If your mom was sitting right here, Mom would say, "Well, yeah, you did."

*Rita:* I didn't involve her in my hurt, in my pain. I didn't involve her in it. I limited my contact with her until I felt strong enough to deal with her. Okay?

*Therapist:* So cutting off doesn't hurt?

*Rita:* But I'm entitled to make those types of choices, as long as I don't blame her: "Oh it's your fault, it's your fault." It's not her fault. I'm an adult, doing what I want to do. Now some of the things I thought I was angry with her about, or maybe I was really angry with her about, I came to the realization that was okay, but I can't go back and reinvent the wheel. She couldn't change the parent that she was, and I accepted that.

The mother is demonstrating her avoidant style of dealing with unfulfilled attachment needs. Rather than being vulnerable and displaying her hurt, she distances and convinces herself that she does not need a close relationship with her mother. Over time she came to realize that she could not be vulnerable with her mother and that her mother could not soothe her in the ways that she needed. In some ways Rita may resent that her own daughter cannot do the same. Each time Maya reaches out to her mother it's like placing pressure on a sensitive wound. Rita either backs off or lashes out in anger.

*Therapist:* How did you come to that place, Rita? How did you do that?
*Rita:* It took some years, and...
*Therapist:* Did you talk to Mom?
*Rita:* I tried. But my mother is not one of those people. She will never see herself for the way we see her. There's four of us girls. She won't see it. She will refuse. So, we got that, have to deal with it ourselves. But we give her the respect of our mother. With just living life, I came to understand why she did or said a lot of the things because then I experienced life and then it's like, "Oh, now I get it." So that dissipated a lot of the anger.
*Therapist:* But would you have liked to have a conversation with her to lessen some of that pain you went through for a longer period of time?
*Rita:* I did that, a little here and there, to see what kind of response I was going to get. No, it's not going to happen, so I'm going to deal with the fact that it's not going to happen.
*Therapist:* And why wouldn't it happen with your mother? Why wouldn't it happen?
*Rita:* She was not that way.
*Therapist:* She was not open?
*Rita:* No. Never has been.
*Therapist:* So, it kind of seems like in some ways life is repeating itself. Here your daughter is, asking to work on things and to be more connected to you. If you won't do that then she's going to have to come to some kind of resolve on her own like you did with your mother.
*Rita:* She has to fix herself, and she refuses.
*Therapist:* Wouldn't it have been so helpful for you if you could've had that chance between you and your mother?
*Rita:* I accept what you're saying. Truthfully, though, my daughter and I have had some heart-to-heart conversations. She knows I love her. I love her dearly. And a lot of times, she throws out, "Oh you just want me to live my life because you didn't do this or you didn't do that." Well, isn't that what a parent wants? We want to see our children do better than we did. I want the world for her. She can have it, but she's afraid to reach for it. Okay? She's afraid to reach for it. So she stays in this rut. And if it's me that's holding her in this rut, then I want to step aside so she can climb out.

## Analysis of the Case Example

Rita and Maya had a conflictual-avoidant style that plagued their relationship for over two decades. Rita's poisonous parenting style was a combination of both a contemptuous (subtype zealot) and a dismissive (subtype prerogative) parent. Rita was a harsh judge of her daughter and peppered her conversation with criticism and contempt. She used hostile sarcasm, rolled her eyes, called her daughter a "pathological liar," and often threatened to disconnect from Maya emotionally and physically. Rita's character assassinations of her daughter were relentless. Even when Rita made herself temporarily vulnerable, she quickly reverted to degrading her daughter.

Per the usual style of a zealot parent, Rita used the threat of removing her affection and literally her presence in her daughter's life. In addition, Rita threatened to damage Maya's relationship with her daughter by letting her granddaughter know that Maya was untrustworthy. Rita exaggerated her affection for her son (who was accused of sexually molesting Maya), which only heightened Maya's feelings of being worthless and unlovable in her mother's eyes. Maya responded to her mother's parenting and affectional style by wavering between submissiveness and rebelliousness.

Besides being contemptuous, Rita also displayed dismissive strategies. Dismissive parents are not connected to children in a meaningful way. Maya commented that even when she got along with her mother there seemed to be a disconnection as if something was missing. Her bond with her mother did not seem comparable with connections that she saw among her friends and their parents.

Sometimes, out of financial necessity, Maya was separated from her mother for long periods of time. When Maya lived with her mother Rita was often out of the home working and too tired to accept her daughter's bids for attention when she was home (Gottman & DeClaire, 2001). As Maya became older their financial picture brightened when Rita married, but Rita became focused on her new husband. Again, Maya continued to feel invisible and unimportant.

Like a prerogative parent, Rita seemed to imply at times that her daughter should've been grateful for her mother working to provide a home for her and not complain and whine about the fact that she couldn't be around with milk and cookies whenever Maya came home. It wasn't that Maya had to stay with family for a couple of years when she was younger or that Rita was often gone working that made her a prerogative parent. These were necessities for survival. What made her a prerogative parent was the attitude that her daughter shouldn't want more than the basic necessities met and that Rita could choose when to emotionally connect with her child or not to connect with her. Rita seemed to find it insulting that her daughter wanted more than just the basic physical necessities. Children want a parent's presence, not their presents. Even when parents have little time and money, compassionate parents go out of their way to emotionally connect with a child to make them feel special and loved with the time they do have. Also, they are receptive when their children seek them out for connection. Although meeting the basic physical needs of a child is necessary, just as crucial, if not more crucial, is providing for their emotional needs and desire to be loved.

Overall, Maya felt that her mother put her needs and the needs of others (i.e., late husband and son) above Maya's emotional needs. Rita learned from her own poisonous parents that to trust others was to make oneself vulnerable to hurt and disappointment. Rita's attachment strategy of contempt and avoidance was created as a way to cope with her own unmet needs as a child and as an adult. She operated from an internal working model that made it dangerous to depend on others or to have them depend on her.

The struggle in working with poisonous parents is maintaining empathy for both the parents and children without making excuses for attachment injuries. Rita experienced her own hurt, her own poisonous parenting. Rita's and Maya's fathers were both donor parents—not part of the lives of the mothers of their children or part of their children's lives.

It was hard for Rita to see herself as a poisonous parent. She had already experienced not measuring up to her own mother's expectations, and she didn't measure up to her child's expectations either. Rita believed that her daughter should've been grateful to have a parent who worked hard to provide for the basic necessities of her children. Rita felt that what she gave wasn't good enough and never would be good enough for her daughter. When it came to Maya, "I gave a little, and she complained that wasn't enough; she wanted all of me." She felt her basic responsibility to her children was to provide for them financially; therefore, "Don't ask me for more." She never expressed her sorrow for not being there for her children. She ignored (especially Maya's) pleas to be acknowledged and sometimes degraded and berated her for wanting time and affection from her and from other people. Although Rita would not or could not meet Maya's attachment needs, she resented when Maya sought earned attachment from others.

Until Rita can recognize how her own unmet needs with her parents impacted her, she will probably not be able to accept and fulfill her daughter's attachment needs. Rita needs her yearning for emotional connection and pain associated with attachment injuries validated. Until she can grieve for her own lackluster attachment to her mother and father, Rita will have a hard time accepting and validating her daughter's needs. To repair her relationship with her daughter, Rita will need to reduce her defensiveness and accept responsibility. While it is true that Rita cannot change the past, she can change the present and the future.

## Poisonous Parent: Evil or Wounded?

Even in the previous short session excerpt, one can see a parent vacillating between contemptuous, cold, and sometimes cruel to hurt, sad, and suffering, with trouble connecting with her own mother. Rita resigned herself to the fact that she would never be able to have a fulfilling relationship with her mother and was trying to help her daughter come to the same resolution with her. For Rita it seemed easier to deal with the pain of cutting off rather than dealing with the pain of unfilled desires for closeness and acceptance.

Should clinicians view parents like Rita as evil or wounded? Whether one is a voluntarist (believes in the existence of evil) or an intellectualist (believes people are a product of their physiological, psychological, relational, and cultural contexts), it isn't particularly helpful to conceptualize parents as "evil" (Simon, 2002). Language is powerful, so is it fair to label relationships or people as poisonous?

Judith Jordan (Chapter 8) questions whether the term should be used. Does labeling a person or a relationship abdicate the responsibility of others or of a society that makes it more difficult for some parents to parent? Do such terms mask cultural and generational differences in parenting? Perhaps it is easy for a term such as *poisonous* to do all of these things, yet there is great danger for the individuals directly involved in poisonous relationships, collateral relationships, and future relationships. There may be dangers in labeling something poisonous, but it may also be necessary. For instance, some household products are poisonous, but it doesn't mean they aren't useful or should be eliminated. Nevertheless, attention must be called to their potential danger. While parents may not be 100% culpable for creating poisonous styles, it doesn't make the styles any less destructive.

The necessity of warning people of the dangers of poisonous styles mandates use of language that will get people's attention. Just like a skull and crossbones captures one's attention and warns of danger, the term *poisonous parenting* advises parents, partners, and children of the dangers of particular parenting methods. Even though poisonous styles are dangerous and produce emotional and relational damage, poisonous parents also hold the key to restoring a relational bond that is a source of strength, hope, and safety. Poisonous parents cannot alter the past, but they can amend the future. The antidote to the damage done in the past is compassionate parenting. Despite Rita bemoaning, "Whatever kind of mother I was or wasn't, deal with it.... You can't change the past," parents can make reparations for the past.

Rita has the opportunity to be the antidote to the poison that has been coursing through the familial veins for generations. She can help change the legacy that has been passed down from generation to generation. It may not be easy or quick; nevertheless, the journey is one that will be healing for parent and adult child. Healing of such relationships has effects far beyond the people immediately involved. Restoring security, warmth, and compassion into the parent–child relationship has the synergistic effect of revitalizing an entire system.

## The Effects of Poisonous Parenting

So are the children of poisonous parents doomed to unsatisfying relationships with family members, friends, and romantic partners? Well, the answer is that it depends. People with traumatic childhoods tend to report a relationship history of intense, ambivalent, and unstable relationships, report fears of being abandoned, and have less conviction about their own sense of self and what they want in life (Moran, Forbes, Evans, Tarabulsy, & Madigan, 2008). Additionally, people with unresolved trauma from childhood tend to have more challenges with emotional regulation, emotional awareness, emotional responsiveness, making accurate attributions about people's behaviors, and interpersonal connectedness (Moran et al.). Yet those who may not have continually secure relationships with parents can create "earned security" through a significant, emotional relationship with a friend, mentor, romantic partner, therapist, or someone else who provides a secure relationship over time (Roisman, Padrón, Sroufe, & Egeland, 2002; Siegel, 1999). Childhood is fertile ground for establishing the roots of our beliefs for relationships. This period is a time of expansive amounts of learning about the self, relationships, and the world. The brain changes in response to relational, cognitive, and environmental experiences (Cozolino, 2006; Goldstein & Thau, 2004; Schore, 2001; Siegel & Hartzell, 2003). The relationships people have do not just teach children through modeling and reinforcement; relational experiences actually influence brain development.

During infancy, the brain is a hotbed of activity and growth. Internal working models (Bowlby, 1982) about the security of relationships are formed based on the relationship between caregiver and child and are used to predict future interactions with the caregiver and other relationships. The behaviors and experiences that create the internal working model also correspond to actual structural changes in the brain itself (Hughes, 2009; Goldstein & Thau, 2004). Emotion and its expression have an impact on both brain growth and cognitive mastery of experience (Trevarthen, as cited in Hughes, 2009). Parent–infant interactions affect brain development and set the stage for emotional intelligence, self-esteem, cognitive skills, and social skills (Siegel & Hartzell, 2003). A secure attachment helps ensure optimal brain development. "We are entering a new era regarding our understanding of how the human brain is designed to work in good relationships, and how such relationships are central to the cognitive, emotional, social, behavioral, and even biological development of the person" (Hughes, 2009, p. 5).

While it may be true that early childhood is a time of unparalleled learning and neural growth in the brain (times of neural growth are called sensitive periods), humans maintain the capacity to learn and influence their brain structure across a lifetime (Cozolino, 2006). Through intervention, in the form of secure relationships with other intimate relationships (e.g., relatives, friends, romantic partners) or through treatment relationships, individuals can alter their brain structure and corresponding emotions and internal working models of relationships. "We can't change what happened to us as children but we can change the way we think about those events.... By freeing ourselves from the constraints of our past, we can offer our children the spontaneous and connecting relationships that enable them to thrive" (Siegel & Hartzell, 2003, pp. 3–4). Interventions for poisonous parents should free them to become more attuned to comprehending the intentions, thoughts, feelings, beliefs, goals, and motivations of self and others. It is never too late to help the Christina Crawfords of the world help themselves. This book was written to aid clinicians in assisting children of poisonous parents to stop suffering from the poisonous effects of their childhood and from spreading the venom of their childhood to other relationships in their lives.

In the late 1980s, attachment researchers began to expand the application of attachment theory from infants' love and attachment for their parents to adult romantic relationships (Mikulincer, 2006). From an adult perspective, love involves both partners' needs and abilities for attachment, caregiving, and sex, and relational distress is caused by dysfunction in one or more of these systems, leading to relational stress, conflicts, dissatisfaction, and sometimes results in relationship dissolution (Mikulincer). A romantic partner may become an attachment figure depending on the extent to which the partner acts as "(1) a target for proximity seeking; (2) a source of protection, comfort, support, and relief in times of need (*safe haven*); and (3) a *secure base*, encouraging the individual to pursue his or her goals in a safe relational context" (Mikulincer, p. 26, italics in original).

Adults who have a poisonous parent tend to have conflicting feelings toward their parents. They love their parents and want their parents to love them differently than they have their entire lives. They want a loving relationship with the parent but also hate the parent for never being able to live up to the idealized version of parenting they yearn for. Adult children of poisonous parents starve for a place to call home and true feelings of love and acceptance; they feel guilt and struggle with a sense of loneliness and a feeling that they are not worthy of love. Sometimes these adult children are like addicts, self-medicating through outside validation (e.g., sex, substance abuse, multiple relationships, material possessions) and struggling with being overly reactive (bully their way through life) or underreactive (sleep their way through life). They want their parents to be their biggest fans, but as they accomplish the things they think their parents want the list gets longer; the ladder gets higher. Adult children of poisonous parents will never be able to fulfill their parents' expectations. The adult children of poisonous parents, barring intervention, may become poisonous partners and parents themselves.

## References

Bowlby, J. (1982). *Attachment and loss: Vol. 1. Attachment* (2nd ed.). New York: Basic Books.

Cozolino, L. (2006). *The neuroscience of human relationships: Attachment and the developing social brain.* New York: W. W. Norton.

Deichmann, W. B., Henschler, D., Holmstedt, B., & Keil, G. (1986). What is there that is not poison? A study of the *Third Defense* by Paracelsus. *Archives of Toxicology, 58*(4), 207–213. doi: 10.1007/BF00297107.

Firestone, R. W. (1990). *Compassionate child-rearing: An in-depth approach to optimal parenting.* New York: Glendon Association.

Fraley, R., & Shaver, P. (2000). Adult romantic attachment: Theoretical developments, emerging controversies, and unanswered questions. *Review of General Psychology, 4*(2), 132–154. doi:10.1037/1089-2680.4.2.132.

Goldstein, S., & Thau, S. (2004). Integrating attachment theory and neuroscience in couple therapy. *International Journal of Applied Psychoanalytic Studies, 1*(3), 214–223. doi:10.1002/aps.73.

Gottman, J. M. (1999). *The marriage clinic: A scientifically based marital therapy.* New York: W. W. Norton.

Gottman, J. M., & DeClaire, J. (2001). *The relationship cure: A 5 step guide for building better connections with family, friends, and lovers.* New York: Crown Publishers.

Gottman, J. M., & Silver, N. (1999). *The seven principles for making marriage work.* New York: Three Rivers Press.

Greenberg, L. S. (2002). *Emotion-focused therapy: Coaching clients to work through their feelings.* Washington, DC: American Psychological Association.

Hughes, D. A. (2009). *Attachment-focused parenting: Effective strategies to care for children.* New York: W. W. Norton.

Johnson, S., Makinen, J., & Millikin, J. (2001). Attachment injuries in couple relationships: A new perspective on impasses in couples therapy. *Journal of Marital and Family Therapy, 27*(2), 145–155. doi:10.1111/j.1752-0606.2001.tb01152.x.

Mikulincer, M., Shaver, P., Bar-On, N., & Ein-Dor, T. (2010). The pushes and pulls of close relationships: Attachment insecurities and relational ambivalence. *Journal of Personality and Social Psychology, 98*(3), 450–468. doi:10.1037/a0017366.

Mikulincer, M. (2006). Attachment, caregiving, and sex within romantic relationships: A behavioral systems perspective. In M. Mikulincer & G. S. Goodman (Eds.), *Dynamics of romantic love* (pp. 23–46). New York: Guilford Press.

Miller, A. (2002). *For your own good: Hidden cruelty in child-rearing and the roots of violence.* New York: Farrar, Straus, & Giroux.

Moran, G., Forbes, L., Evans, E., Tarabulsy, G., & Madigan, S. (2008). Both maternal sensitivity and atypical maternal behavior independently predict attachment security and disorganization in adolescent mother–infant relationships. *Infant Behavior and Development, 31*(2), 321–325.

Roisman, G., Padrón, E., Sroufe, L., & Egeland, B. (2002). Earned-secure attachment status in retrospect and prospect. *Child Development, 73*(4), 1204–1219. doi:10.1111/1467-8624.00467.

Schore, A. (2001). Effects of a secure attachment relationship on right brain development, affect regulation, and infant mental health. *Infant Mental Health Journal, 22*(1–2), 7–66. doi:10.1002/1097-0355(200101/04)22:1<7::AID-IMHJ2>3.0.CO;2-N.

Siegel, D. J. (1999). *The developing mind: Toward a neurobiology of interpersonal experience.* New York: Guilford.

Siegel, D. J., & Hartzell, M. (2003). *Parenting from the inside out: How a deeper self-understanding can help you raise children who thrive.* New York: Penguin Putnam.

Simon, G. (2002). *Beyond technique in family therapy: Finding your therapeutic voice.* Boston: Allyn & Bacon.

Spelling, T. (2008). *sTori Telling.* New York: Simon Spotlight Entertainment.

CHAPTER 2

# Compassionate Parenting

## *The Antidote to Poisonous Parenting*

**PATRICIA A. ROBEY and CATHERINE FORD SORI**

> The only people who think parenting and teaching are easy are those who have never done either one.
>
> **Thomas W. Phelan, PhD (2003, p. 2)**

Compassionate parents, as opposed to poisonous parents, allow children to explore, learn, and grow in an environment of love, safety, and protection. This does not mean that children should be overindulged, given inappropriate freedom, or allowed to rule the household. Instead, parents must learn to provide the proper balance between freedom and control. Except for issues related to immediate concerns about safety, parents must take the long view of their roles. The ultimate goal of parenting is to enable children to become independent, competent, and loving citizens of the world and compassionate parents to their own children (Buck, 2000; Stosny, 1998).

Unfortunately, children do not come into the world with a set of directions that parents can follow. Unless parents make an effort to get parent education, much of what parents do is by instinct rather than purpose. Many parents adopt the parenting styles of their own parents; others, who did not appreciate the efforts of their parents, will go to great lengths to avoid becoming like their own parents (Buck, 2000, 2009; Good, 1992). A compassionate approach to parenting is based on an understanding that children need parents who will provide a balance between allowing children to have fun, be creative, and experience freedom while maintaining parental control by setting limits through appropriate structure and discipline (Glasser, 1998; Minuchin, 1974).

It is a fallacy to suggest that parental behavior influences a child's development in a linear fashion. Using the principle of reciprocity, a child's behavior and characteristics also affect parents, which, in turn, influence the parents' behavior toward the child. There are also many other influences on children, including the extended family, school, and peers. Everyone knows of good parents whose children go "wrong." Some parents err on the side of overinvolvement with their children, which can lead to enmeshment (Minuchin, 1974) or fusion (Nelson, 2003), whereas others are too distant or disengaged. In addition, it is very likely that the use of destructive and coercive poisonous parenting behaviors like criticizing, blaming, complaining, controlling, manipulating, demanding, and attacking will result in a breakdown of the parent–child relationship (Glasser, 1998; Stosny, 1998).

In this chapter the authors describe effective and ineffective parenting behaviors through the lens of three different approaches: structural family therapy, Bowen's intergenerational family systems approach, and choice theory/reality therapy. Each theory will be explored based on how healthy and unhealthy patterns of behavior in parent–child relationships are understood, and case examples will be used to illustrate how clinicians can work with families using these different approaches.

## Structural Family Therapy Approach to Compassionate Parenting

### *Theoretical Background*

Minuchin's structural therapy has been a beacon over the last 40 years to family therapists. This influential leader, perhaps, would not label parents "poisonous" but may label certain familial structures poisonous. Minuchin does not take a pathological view of families; rather, he sees them as becoming stuck in an organizational *structure* that no longer works, either due to developmental issues (e.g., an adolescent leaving home) or from external factors (e.g., an illness, loss of a job). Colapinto (1991) believes that "a healthy family is in a continuous process of structural growth (p. 425). Families need to be able to adapt their structures to developmental changes or adversity (Minuchin, 1974), and having a healthy family structure promotes resiliency in children (Klimes-Dougan & Kendziora, 2000). However, when a change in organization is called for, some families "dig in" and stubbornly stick to a system of roles and rules that are no longer functional (Minuchin & Fishman, 1981). For example, parents may try to apply the same rules to an adolescent that they did when the teen was in grade school.

An important aspect of family structure is the idea of *subsystems*, such as the parental, sibling, and spousal subsystems. Membership in subsystems is determined by factors such as roles, gender, and generation, and members of different subsystems serve various functions. There are boundaries both around individuals and subsystems that determine the type and amount of contact family members have with one another as well as who participates and how they interact (Minuchin, 1974).

One of the most important subsystems is that of the parental unit, since families function best when there is a strong parental *hierarchy* (Minuchin, Lee, & Simon, 1996). In fact, good parental hierarchy fosters security in children and helps meet children's developmental and nurturing needs (Faber, 2002; Fish, 2000). Conversely, a poor parental hierarchy is associated with conduct problems in children (Shaw, Criss, Schonberg, & Beck, 2004). Good hierarchy occurs when the boundaries between parents and children are permeable and allow for open communication between the generations but do not permit children to invade the generational boundary and become part of the parental subsystem. An example of this might occur in single-parent families, where an older child becomes *parentified*, assuming the role of parent to younger siblings. This may help a struggling single parent, but when this role becomes rigid it is developmentally unhealthy and inappropriate for the child, siblings, and parent.

*Boundaries* are invisible barriers that surround individual family members and subsystems and determine the amount of contact that ensues (Minuchin & Fishman, 1981). If boundaries are too inadequate or *diffuse*, the hierarchy is weak and children are not clear about the rules, consequences, and predictability of life. When this occurs families may be chaotic and *enmeshed*; children often become involved in an unhealthy manner in the parental subsystem, or a parent can become overfocused on a child at the cost of having a distant relationship with the spouse. Enmeshment impairs interpersonal growth and development, and children are not allowed to develop autonomy by learning from their own mistakes. In contract, when the boundaries between the parents and children are too *rigid*, communication between the generations is not sufficient for parents to be appropriately informed and involved in their children's lives. Children in these *disengaged* families may be emotionally isolated and learn to be independent, but at a cost of an emotional connection to the family. Interpersonal boundaries in a family can be likened to an artist's palette. A healthy family is like a palette with separate, vibrant colors representing individual family members; each color is distinct from the others. In enmeshed families, the colors on the palette have been blended together so much that the individual paints are blurred and no longer recognizable as distinct colors. Disengaged families could be represented on the artist's palette with colors that are so isolated that it would be difficult to mix any of the colors to create a pleasing hue.

### *Healthy Behaviors and Relationship Patterns*

Using the lens of structural family therapy theory, a healthy family is one that is organized in a way that facilitates the growth and development of individuals as well as the family as a whole. While there is no one "ideal" type of family structure, families that have *permeable boundaries* (neither diffuse nor rigid) around individuals, have subsystems (especially the parental system), and are able to adapt their structure when needed are likely to function well. These families are neither enmeshed nor disengaged but can strike a balance between togetherness and individuality by shifting their hierarchical structure over time as the needs of family members change. For example, parents of young children must be very involved in taking care of infants and toddlers, but the same degree of focus on adolescents would restrict the individual development of teens (see Faber, 2002; Fish, 2000).

Having a good executive subsystem is important at all ages and stages of child and family life cycle development, but the hierarchical structure needs to change over time (Colapinto, 1991). Fish (2000) discusses Wynne's epigenetic model of family development and believes that hierarchical relationships promote social, emotional, and cognitive development. Hierarchical relationships are synonymous with complementary (one is up, the other is down) relationships (Faber, 2002). It is only through a child's struggle to form more egalitarian (or symmetrical) relationships with parents that a change in the hierarchical relationships can occur (Faber; Fish).

### *Unhealthy Behaviors and Relationship Patterns*

What may appear as poisonous parenting, from a structural perspective, is a poisonous structure in which the boundaries between parent and child do not allow for appropriate amounts of communication, affection, guidance, and feelings of safety. Boundaries are either too diffuse and parents are intrusive in their children's lives or too rigid and parents are not accessible and responsive. Conversely, families who are not able to adapt their style of organization over time are likely to see problems develop in a child, spouse, or subsystem. For example, if a parent or child develops a serious illness such as cancer, the family must be able to adapt quickly and reorganize to meet the immediate and long-term needs of the ill person, well children, and adults (Rolland, 1994). Furthermore, if a child becomes critically ill one parent may need to quit work to oversee the child's health, research treatment options, and manage doctors' appointments, medications, meals, and therapy. Due to financial strain, the other parent may need to work longer hours or take a second job, resulting in less time with the family. This can lead to distance in the marital relationship, as parental roles become skewed and couples lack time for each other. Well siblings may have to assume extra responsibilities, help more with chores or care for younger children, or be forced to drop extracurricular activities. They often experience resentment (and subsequent guilt) toward the ill sibling who seems to be draining the family resources (Sori & Biank, 2006). Families need to be flexible and accept outside help to manage day-to-day living and to avoid caregiver burnout. However, some families hang on to old structures that are no longer functional or develop new rigid patterns that leave family members feeling isolated, unsupported, and emotionally distant (Rolland; Sori & Biank).

Children in families that are enmeshed do not develop autonomy and may never achieve the sense of individuality and self-esteem needed to be successful in life. Likewise, those from disengaged families may become independent thinkers but may struggle with close relationships. The first may occur in ill children whose parents continue to hover too closely, not allowing them to assume age-appropriate responsibility for their own health. The second may be seen in well siblings who often do not give voice to their own needs and concerns because they do not want to burden their already overstressed parents (Sori & Biank, 2006).

Often one parent may become overfocused on a child at the expense of other relationships in the family, and a *cross-generational coalition* can develop (Colapinto, 1991). This occurs when a child has an especially close relationship with one parent but is distant from the other parent and siblings. Other times parents may join in making one child a scapegoat, seeing that child as the source of all the family's problems. Instead of dealing with issues the couple may have, they submerge their own interpersonal issues and *detour their conflict* onto the child. Two parents may also attempt to enlist the loyalty of a child against the other parent, leaving the child in a no-win situation, where choosing one parent means sacrificing a close relationship to the other parent (Minuchin, 1974). Children need to have easy access to both parents, which means that triangles are not rigid but are able to shift and adapt according to the child's developmental needs.

### *Therapeutic Approach to Working With Parents*

Structural family therapy is a therapy of action (Colapinto, 1991), in which the therapist is very involved with the family and often assumes the role of conductor or director. Several key skills will be briefly introduced, and readers are referred to Minuchin (1974), Minuchin and Fishman (1981), and Kindsvatter, Duba, and Dean (2008) for more detailed descriptions.

First, it is essential that clinicians *join* with each family member to understand the family's world view and become part of the family (Figley

& Nelson, 1990) and then to *accommodate* to their ways (Minuchin, 1974; Minuchin & Fishman, 1981). This is necessary before any attempts are initiated to alter interactional patterns or change the family structure. The therapist develops an initial systemic structural *hypothesis* that guides the interactions with the family. It is not important whether the initial hypothesis is correct, as it can be altered based on observations of subsequent family interactions. Like many forms of family therapy, the structuralist privileges family process (*how* people talk) above content (*what* they talk about), especially since the process illuminates the structure of the family. However, often the content of the presenting problem is used to change interactions and restructure the family.

Structural family therapists believe it is not sufficient just to *listen* to families talk about their relationships; rather, it is essential to *observe* the family interacting. Minuchin is known for his directiveness, and one of the hallmarks of the structural approach is the use of *enactments* (Figley & Nelson, 1990; Minuchin, 1974; Minuchin & Fishman, 1981). Enactments might occur spontaneously when family members naturally begin talking to one another or can be orchestrated by the therapist. For example, Minuchin might ask a wife to turn to her husband and convince him that she is overworked and needs his help with the kids. The therapist may sit back and observe how long the couple can maintain a dialogue before it breaks down, may push it beyond their tolerance level, or may use the exchange to alter typical patterns of interaction and begin the process of restructuring. From this assessment, the therapist develops a *structural map* of the family that illustrates the hypothesis and informs the therapeutic process.

Restructuring is facilitated by interventions such as the following (Figley & Nelson, 1990; see Minuchin & Fishman, 1981):

- Blocking someone who attempts to speak for another while challenging people to speak for themselves
- Raising the intensity of interactions beyond the family's comfort level, pushing family members into a new way of interacting and altering their structure
- Reframing a presenting problem from being an individual concern to spreading the symptom to other family members
- Helping families find new ways of viewing things and discovering untapped resources they do not realize they have to solve their own problems in the future

Often these latent abilities have been lying dormant and unrecognized by the family. Once this restructuring occurs families are able to solve their own problems more freely, and individuals and the family as a whole can get back on track developmentally.

Attachment theory has increasingly been incorporated in family therapy (e.g., Giblin, 1994) and is the basis of Susan Johnson and Les Greenberg's research and development of emotionally focused couples therapy. Promoting good attachment between parents and children is a concept that also bridges the concepts of structural tenets (e.g., permeable boundaries and parental hierarchy), which promote healthy development in children and adults. The following case illustrates methods to integrate attachment-based family interventions with structural family therapy.

*Case Example of Structural Approach to Compassionate Parenting*

The Williams family was a three-generational African American family consisting of the mother, Sabrina, a newly practicing pathologist; her 13-year-old daughter, Sarah; and Sabrina's mother, Susannah. Sabrina initiated counseling because of the disrespect Sarah showed to her and Sarah's grandmother. Sabrina had been divorced for approximately 5 years from her husband, Tom, who saw Sarah every other weekend and on Wednesday evenings. Since recently starting at a new school, Sarah had developed severe stomach pains that had led to many invasive tests and hospitalizations. However, the diagnosis was inconclusive.

After joining with the family and hearing everyone's view of the problem, the therapist began to assess the family interactions and relationships. She learned that Mom was rather emotionally disengaged from her daughter. She did not know Sarah's best friends, favorite subjects, or which television programs she liked best. While Mom often worked long hours, Sarah would sometimes talk back or ignore Susannah, who already was not taking a very active coparenting role. By the time Sabrina got home from work and learned about Sarah's problem behaviors that day, she was usually too tired to deal with Sarah, and would retire to her room to read. Susannah would spend her evenings in her own bedroom watching television, leaving Sarah to talk on the phone, surf the Internet, or do whatever she pleased. The therapist hypothesized that the family was rather disengaged; neither the mother nor the grandmother was actively involved in each other's or in Sarah's life. That began to change when Sarah got sick.

As Sarah's symptoms had worsened over several weeks, Sarah's father began to be more involved in her life, often calling and asking to come by the house to see her. He and Sabrina spoke more about Sarah's behavior, and Mom spent more time with Sarah when she felt ill. However, Mom felt overwhelmed trying to manage Sarah's illness while supporting the family.

In an individual session, Mom shared that she wanted her mother to be more involved in helping to take care of Sarah. In exploring what Sabrina's relationship with her mother had been like when Sabrina was Sarah's age, Sabrina explained that her mother was often sick and depressed. At times she had barricaded herself in her bedroom, leaving Sabrina and her sisters to fend for themselves in their single-parent household.

The therapist held a conjoint session with Grandmother and Mom, where through an enactment they discussed Sabrina's feelings about her mother when she was Sarah's age, as well as her desire to have Susannah assume more parenting responsibilities with Sarah. Surprisingly, Susannah said she never knew that Sabrina felt somewhat abandoned as a child, nor did she realize that Sabrina really wanted or needed her help now. She told her daughter, "You always seemed so independent and self-assured, and I never wanted to butt in. Sometimes I've just been biting my tongue when Sarah mouths off, but I didn't want to interfere. But I'm happy to help you out." Next the therapist helped the two adults work out the terms of their "coparenting" arrangement and decide how to inform Sarah what the new rules were and how Grandmother was Mom's surrogate when she wasn't home, and would act on Mom's behalf.

In an individual session Sarah said she liked school, was doing well academically, and had many friends from her previous school. (All of this confirmed what the therapist had heard from the parents and the school.) However, Sarah confessed that she had been thinking she might like to live with her father, since he didn't have "all those stupid rules" and was more fun.

In thinking about the possible function of Sarah's mysterious stomach symptoms and that recently Dad had drawn closer to Sarah and Mom, the therapist hypothesized that there might be a cross-generational coalition developing between Dad and Sarah. She spent some time helping the parents talk together to develop a strategy on how to handle Sarah's medical problems as well as how to sidestep the "divide-and-conquer game." The therapist emphasized that, because of her health concerns and developmental stage, Sarah needed to have appropriate rules and consequences that were similar in both homes. Both parents were concerned for their daughter and were committed to doing what was best for her. With some help they developed a plan that would work in both houses, as well as strategies for handling problems as they arose.

Next the therapist spent time strengthening the relationship between Mom and Grandmother. First each one planned special activities to do with Sarah when she was feeling well. Then Mom and Grandmother began to talk more openly about their feelings and how they could support one another in day-to-day life. For example, when Grandmother's arthritis got bad and she was unable to cook, they agreed she would call Sabrina to get take-out on the way home. Mom also offered to hire a part-time housekeeper so Grandmother could spend more time interacting with her granddaughter and resting and less time cleaning house and doing laundry. Grandmother, a retired accountant, agreed to manage all of Sarah's medical files and bills. They also decided on some basic house rules and consequences that both would enforce, and together they presented the information to Sarah, emphasizing Grandmother's new role as coparent when Mom wasn't around.

To promote attachment among the family members, the therapist integrated methods from family play therapy (Dermer, Olund, & Sori, 2006; Gil, 1994; Gil & Sobol, 2000; Sori, 2006), including structural art activities (Sori, 1995). Through these playful activities the family learned a lot about one another and began to laugh more and enjoy having fun together. Theraplay activities, which are based on attachment theory (Jernberg & Booth, 1999; Munns, 2000), such as lotioning one another's hurts and writing messages on each others' backs, increased touch and fostered better attachment across the generations. They began to practice theraplay activities at home and to have weekly "family nights," where they played games, did crafts together, or worked on puzzles.

Over time not only did the family grow closer and Sarah's behaviors improve at home, but also her physical symptoms decreased in intensity and frequency. The therapist suggested that Mom encourage Sarah to invite friends over more as well as to attend more school functions. Mom also invited Dad to initiate extra visits when Sarah felt well so that he wasn't just seeing her more often when she was symptomatic. This freed up more opportunities for Mom to date or see friends and for Grandmother to play bingo and spend time with her friends from church.

At termination the family was happy with their progress. Mom and Grandmother were functioning pretty well individually and as a team, Sarah was more respectful, and her stomach symptoms had greatly improved. Mom and Dad were communicating well, and Sarah had more open access to her father. Sarah told the therapist that even though at first she thought all the rules and consequences were "a bunch of crap," now she realized that she actually felt more secure and liked to be with her family a lot more now. She thought it was cool that her parents got along so well, when many of her friends' divorced parents didn't. She was closer to her grandmother and happy to have so many people who loved her in her life.

The family presented the therapist with a parting gift, a cross-stitch that read, "The greatest of these is love." In explaining why this scripture was chosen, Mom turned the cross-stitch over so it showed a tangle of threads that had no apparent meaning. She said, "This is how our family was when we first came here; all loose ends and knots that didn't seem to fit too well together." Then turning it to the right side Mom continued, "But now we are like this verse—structured and stitched together in love and harmony—brightly colored, and our happiness shows."

### *Summary of the Structural Approach to Compassionate Parenting*

The structural approach to compassionate parenting really encompasses what Keim (2000) calls both the "softer and harder side of hierarchy." Evidence of the softer side of hierarchy includes parents who do the soothing, who provide fun times, reassurance, affection, nurturing, and empathy for their children. At the same time they are able to develop rules, set limits, apply consequences, create safety, and provide for their children—all evidence of the "harder" side of hierarchy. These two sides of hierarchy provide children with an optimal environment for healthy development. Parents and children have good attachment, and they enjoy and respect one another. Even though problems inevitably will arise, these parents are able to adapt and generate workable solutions to their problems.

## Bowen's Intergenerational Family Systems Approach to Compassionate Parenting

Murray Bowen began to develop his comprehensive and very eloquent intergenerational theory in his early work with schizophrenics but discovered that many of the same characteristics of psychotic families were present in families with less severe problems (Nichols & Schwarz, 2008). According to Bowen, individuals are in a constant struggle between two polarized forces: the desire for individuality and the desire to be connected to others. *Fusion* occurs when individuals' psychological boundaries are blurred and they experience too much closeness and not enough individuation. On the opposite side of the continuum is too much separateness, where individuals distance themselves and even *cut themselves off* from family members. Fusion and emotional cutoffs can be seen as two sides of the same coin, both illustrating lower levels of differentiation. People who are successful in balancing these two extremes are considered to have achieved *differentiation*—that is, the ability to balance thinking and feeling, the ability to choose to respond to pressures with self-restraint, and the ability to address anxiety without reacting emotionally to internal or external pressure (Kerr & Bowen, 1988).

From Bowen's psychodynamic perspective, the challenge for children and adults is to differentiate from their families of origin. This process is influenced by the level of differentiation experienced by one's parents. Parents who are emotionally cut off from or fused with their own parents and siblings experience emotional reactivity. This reactivity is projected onto relationships with spouses and children. Children of undifferentiated parents often become involved in *triangulation*, as the tension between parents is shifted onto the child, often resulting in anxious attachment. This focus may relieve tension in the couple but leaves the child vulnerable to developing emotional dysfunction. The child most involved in the family problems will achieve the lowest level of differentiation, whereas siblings outside of intense triangles will be more differentiated. A *multigenerational transmission process* occurs when this anxiety and lower level of differentiation is passed from generation to generation. The child who is the focus of a great deal of parental anxiety will be less likely to grow into an emotionally healthy and happy adult (Nichols, 2008; Schwartz, Thigpen, & Montgomery, 2006). Since people are likely to marry someone at a similar level of differentiation, succeeding generations will achieve lower levels of differentiation.

### *Healthy Behaviors and Relationship Patterns*

According to Bowen, adults with higher levels of differentiation in their family of origin can handle stress in relationships and avoid entanglement in rigid triangles. They are able to balance closeness and autonomy and can take an "I" position and are able to hold their stance while remaining calm and avoiding emotional reactivity.

Healthy children are those who are able to separate their identities from their parents while still being able to remain connected to them. According to Schwartz et al. (2006), the way that parents deal with their children's emotions plays a significant role in the ability of children to achieve individuation from their parents. Gottman and DeClaire (1997) suggest that supportive parents are *emotional coaches*. They are aware of their child's emotions, accept their child's feelings, and use displays of emotion as opportunities to label them, problem solve, and learn from them. This fosters healthy attachment.

### *Unhealthy Behaviors and Relationship Patterns*

In contrast, those who have lower levels of differentiation often are quick to react emotionally or give advice, preferencing their emotional system over their thinking system. When stress arises between two people, a third person is often triangulated in to relieve the stress between the original two. Bowen believed a triangle was the smallest stable unit. However, while a triangle may temporarily reduce tension between two people, problems tend not to be resolved.

Undifferentiated parents tend to poison their relationships with their children and create a pattern that is likely to be passed down across generations. When parents are fused with their own family of origin, this pattern often is reflected in current and future family relationships. Fusion between a parent and a child can affect many areas of development. Both parent and child may lack autonomy, or role-reversal may occur. In either case, the child's sense of identity and social-emotional development can be greatly impaired. Cutoffs also tend to reoccur across generations. When parents are cut off from their own families of origin, the child loses the opportunity to develop relationships with extended family. Children then cannot incorporate aspects of extended family members into their developing identity.

While Bowen believed the differentiated person would use the thinking system instead of the emotional (reactive) system, this does not mean that he was suggesting emotions should be eschewed. Parents should be encouraged to support their child's emotional development and not dismiss the child's emotions as trivial, unimportant, or even harmful. However, some parents are uncomfortable with displays of emotion and want to fix the problem as soon as possible rather than try to understand it. Gottman and DeClaire (1997) described three parenting behaviors as being especially harmful to children: *dismissing*, *disapproving*, and *laissez-faire*. In each of these situations children learn that their emotions are inappropriate instead of how to regulate or use emotions effectively for their own development or in relationship with others. These unhealthy approaches to emotions can interfere with the child's development of self and increase the likelihood of fusion or emotional cutoffs, resulting in lower levels of differentiation.

### *Therapeutic Approach to Working With Parents*

When parents bring their children to therapy there is usually a great deal of anxiety in the family system. This anxiety may be related not only to the problem but also to the parents' sense of themselves as being competent or incompetent in their roles as parents. Feelings of failure, anxiety, and questioning one's parenting ability are compounded for grandparents who must step into the role of parent because their adult child is not able to function in that capacity (Lever & Wilson, 2005). Parental anxiety exacerbates the family's problem, as parents often respond to a child's behavior by becoming more rigid and uncompromising in their attempts to control their child (Kerr & Bowen, 1988). Often parents bring children to counseling, hoping that the counselor will be able to "fix" the child (Bailey & Sori, 2000; Sori, Dermer, & Wesolowski, 2006). The identification of the child as the source of the problem relieves some of the parents' anxiety, as the focus of anxiety shifts from themselves to the child (Montgomery, DeBell, & Wilkins, 1998). The Bowenian therapist works to spread the symptom beyond the child and parents by examining related patterns that have occurred across generations.

Family therapists resist the idea of treating children separately from their parents or siblings. The belief is that family systems work is the most beneficial approach to working with family problems (Becvar & Becvar, 1996). However, seeing the family members together may heighten the family's anxiety in initial sessions, resulting in resistance, blaming, and locking in to familiar patterns of family behavior. When this occurs, family therapy may be counterproductive at that time, especially for the child who is often the target of blame (Wilson & Gottman, 1995). Therefore, the therapist must evaluate whether family, couple, individual, or some combination will be most effective for each particular family at different stages of treatment (Bailey & Sori, 2000; Montgomery et al., 1998; Sori et al., 2006).

Bowen's goal was always to promote differentiation by lowering the anxiety in systems, and he often accomplished this by working with couples or individuals, trusting that changes in even an individual will lead to reciprocal changes in the family system (see Bowen, 1978; McGoldrick & Carter, 2001). Clients are often coached on how to repair cutoffs by starting to build one-on-one relationships with distant family members, how to identify one's own role in a triangle, and how to begin the process of detriangulation (Bowen, 1978). Optimal development occurs in families who are fairly well differentiated, where anxiety is low, and when parents are in emotional contact with their families of origin (Schwartz, 2008).

In working with children and families from a transgenerational perspective, Montgomery et al. (1998) suggested that assessment of the system addresses several levels. Assessment of the child indicates whether the child is on target for emotional, physical, cognitive, and motor development. Assessing these areas helps the therapist begin to develop an appropriate therapeutic plan for the child and the family. Parents are assessed to gauge their understanding of developmental stages. Perhaps they have unreasonable expectations for their child, given the child's development. The relationship between parents is also assessed. Often problems in the parental relationship mirror the problems with the child. Finally, parents are assessed to determine the stories they hold regarding parenting and how these stories impact the level of anxiety they feel about parenting. Therapy can focus on addressing issues but can also provide an opportunity to educate parents so that they can be proactive in their responses to their own relationship issues as well as in their responses to their child's behavior.

Bowen's intergenerational family systems approach is psychoeducational in nature. Teaching parents how to respond to children's emotions may be an integral part of the therapeutic process. Parents can learn to use emotions as they occur as opportunities for learning and connecting (Gottman & DeClaire, 1997; Schwartz et al., 2006).

Genograms are also an important part of Bowen's therapy. Genograms help the therapist and clients see patterns of parenting styles, family roles, interactional patterns, triangles (and interlocking triangles), illness, abuse, and dysfunction that have occurred over generations (McGoldrick, Gerson, & Petry, 2008). A more playful approach to gathering transgenerational information at a more subconscious level is the family play genogram. In a play genogram, which was developed by Eliana Gil, family members select miniatures to represent their thoughts and feelings about each family member (Gil, 2003, 2008; Gil & Sobol, 2000). Play is the way that young children communicate and can help parents and children connect on a deeper level. Play genograms often provide rich insight to clients' emotional reactions to family members and can be a powerful motivation for change. Insight and recognizing patterns are first steps toward learning new ways to interact with one's children and one's own family of origin.

### *The Case of a Couple With a "Smother Mother"*

John and Judy were a young couple in their late 20s who had been married 5 years and had a 2-year-old daughter, Camellia. They initiated therapy due to conflict over problems with John's mother, whom John dubbed "Smother Mother." Every time she visited, problems arose between John's mother and wife, centering on issues related to Camellia's grandmother not respecting their approach to parenting. For example, if Judy asked her mother-in-law, Candace, not to give Camellia juice, as soon as Judy left the room she would hear Candace give the child juice, telling her how sad it is that Mommy didn't want her to have this good juice. Judy would fume, approach John, and demand that he go "set her straight" by telling his mother she needed to respect their rules. A dismayed John would freeze up emotionally, unable to discuss the problem with either Judy or Candace. Over time Judy's resentment had snowballed to the point that she refused to speak to Candace when she called on the telephone. John was clearly caught in a rigid triangle between his wife and mother, feeling loyalty to each but unable to take any action. The pressure from Judy to come up with a plan was intensifying, since Candace was due to visit soon. John and Judy both agreed to a goal of working together as a team, and John wanted to be able to set appropriate boundaries with his mother before her next visit.

The therapist began to take a detailed genogram of both John and Judy's families. John was an only child whose parents divorced when he was 12, the summer before he started middle school. Both parents told John that he could decide whom he wanted to live with; he could stay with his mother or move out of state with his father. John had always been very close to his mother, and he saw this as an opportunity to get to know his father better, who was rather distant. However, when John told his mother of his decision to move with his father, Candace was devastated. She took to her bed crying and depressed, asking what she would do without her "Little Johnny." John felt so guilty for causing his mother so much pain that he changed his mind. He stayed with his mother. His father moved away and became more distant than ever.

John talked about what a loss this was for him. Not only did he miss becoming closer to his father, but he also became responsible for his mother's emotions. It became his job to try to soothe her when she was upset and to cheer her up when she felt down. John expressed how difficult it had always been to disagree with his mother because of how upset she would get and then how guilty he would feel. When he said he still felt this way, Judy's eyes filled with tears. She never knew how the divorce had affected him and how responsible he still felt for his mother's feelings. Now she understood why it was so difficult for him to set boundaries related to her visits. Empathy soon replaced the frustration and anger Judy had previously felt toward John.

In a subsequent session, the therapist took Judy's family genogram. Judy had not said much about her family, so it was interesting to learn that she was very distant—almost cut off—from her parents and family of origin. With anger and profound sadness she told of how her parents never even came to her college graduation, even though they lived only 90 minutes from campus. She was very hurt by this as well as by their lack of interest in her wedding. After Camellia was born she came up with excuses to avoid visits. As she gradually revealed the sense of loss and abandonment underneath her anger, John shared how surprised he was to realize the depth of her sorrow and pain. He mirrored the understanding and empathy Judy had shown him.

A deeper level of insight occurred when they did family play genograms (Gil, 2003, 2008; Gil & Sobol, 2000). For example, John chose an eagle on wing to represent his father and a stone well for his mother, while Judy selected a stone wall to represent her relationship with her mother. They all explored how one might get close to a flying eagle and how one might scale a stone wall to discover what is on the other side. John said the well was like his mother because there was a danger of falling in and drowning. The therapist asked how someone could learn to drink from the well without drowning, and this metaphor was explored in subsequent sessions.

The genograms helped solidify the couple's desire to function as a "unified front" in dealing with Candace. Together John and Judy brainstormed possible scenarios that might occur before and during Candace's visit, and the therapist coached them on ways to respond in a manner that set appropriate boundaries around John and Judy and Camellia as a family yet allowed them all to be connected to Candace. These sessions were characterized by a good deal of humor and enjoyment.

The visit with Candace was a success overall. Although at first it was difficult for John to approach his mom to set some ground rules, with Judy's love and support (instead of her angry insistence) he was able to do it, and Candace responded appropriately. Judy was thrilled and much less anxious during the visit, which contributed to a good time for all.

In a follow-up session, Judy expressed a desire to reconnect with her distant family and discussed ways to begin to approach family members one at a time to develop one-on-one relationships. She called her mother and was happily surprised that her mother expressed such a desire to see her and her granddaughter. John continued to work on his plan to approach the flying eagle. Since eagles like to catch fish and his father used to take him fishing as a child, he decided to invite his father on a fishing trip. They enjoyed talking and making plans for the trip.

At the beginning of therapy, John and Judy reflected the two counter-balancing forces in Bowen's theory: John was fused with his mother, and Judy was too distant from her family. With determination, tenacity, and hard work, both achieved their individual goals and their levels of differentiation. They reported more intimacy in their marriage and were much more of a team in parenting Camellia. At termination, they shared the exciting news that they were expecting a second child and thanked the therapist profusely for helping them achieve more balance and harmony in their relationships.

*Summary of the Bowen's Approach to Compassionate Parenting*

Bowen strongly believed that to do multigenerational therapy trainees and clinicians first must begin by working on their own genograms and family-of-origin issues. This process has been shown to be transformative (Lim, 2008). As we recognize triangles, levels of differentiation, cutoffs, and fusion in our own families of origin and begin the long process of working on these issues, we are much more effective in helping our clients and their families.

## The Choice Theory and Reality Therapy Approach to Compassionate Parenting

Choice theory explains that the reason for much of the misery in the world is that we are trying to get our own needs met through the use of controlling behaviors that impose on the needs and wishes of others (Glasser, 1998). Although many poisonous parents would argue that the use of force, punishment, rewards, bossing, and other coercive behaviors seem to help maintain discipline or control in the short run, in the long run they create more resistance and destroy relationships. The *Journal of the American Medical Association* (JAMA) published a summary of a longitudinal research project whose objective was to identify risk and protective factors that impact on adolescent health. A significant finding was that "parent–family connectedness and perceived school connectedness were protective against every health risk behavior measure except history of pregnancy" (Resnick et al., 1997, p. 823). It is critical that we help parents develop new behaviors that will improve connectedness and eliminate coercion.

Both poisonous and nonpoisonous parents may believe that it is their duty to teach, convince, and control their children so that they will learn to behave as parents think they should. Parents use external rewards in hopes that children will find enough pleasure from the reward so that the desired behavior becomes the norm. Or parents may choose another approach—using punishment with the hope that children will not repeat the behavior to avoid pain. The use of punishments and rewards may have short-term effects but in the long term are ineffective and damage relationships (Kohn, 1999).

According to Glasser (1998), we are born with basic needs for love and belonging, power, freedom, fun, and survival. These needs provide the genetic instructions for how we live our lives, and our behavior is motivated toward getting our needs met. Understanding that we, and our children, have these needs can help us to create our own instruction manuals for more effective parenting. Instead of attempting to control children's attempts in getting their needs met, we can work *with them* to ensure safety while encouraging exploration (Buck, 2000).

### *Healthy Behaviors and Relationship Patterns*

Lipton (2005) explained that people respond to stimulus at a cellular level, with either a position of protection or of growth. Children cannot grow and learn if they are afraid, anxious, or worried. They can grow only when they feel safe and free to explore without negative consequences (Buck, 2009). So if parents can't use the "tried-and-true" methods of parenting, what is left? First, parents need to have an understanding of what motivates their children's behavior. According to Glasser (1998), all behavior is learned and has the purpose of helping us get what we want. Our wants include specific people, places, and things that satisfy one or more of our basic needs. Consider the 2-year-old child who balks when mother tries to put her in the car for preschool. Mother, who is trying to get her own needs satisfied (the need for power and control by being an effective mother), sees her daughter's behavior as frustrating and resistant. Mother takes it personally: "Why is she doing this? She knows better." In fact, Daughter was not resisting Mother. Instead, the child had noticed that her friend was outside and she wanted to go play (the need for belonging and fun). Although Mother still needed to get to work on time, the time and energy she put out to control her daughter could have been spent by letting her daughter say hello briefly before putting her into the car. The goal is to assess the situation, consider what needs the child is trying to meet, and to create a win–win situation for both if possible.

Once parents accept the fact that children's behavior is purposeful, they can stop asking why children do the things they do. The answer is that everyone's behavior is their best attempt to get what they want in the moment. A better question to ask is, "What does my child want that she is behaving so inappropriately to get?" The answer to this question will help parents understand what it is their children want. The follow-up then is to teach children more effective and responsible ways to get what they want (Buck, 2009).

Glasser (1998) identified seven caring habits that should be used in all relationships: supporting, encouraging, listening, accepting, trusting, respecting, and negotiating differences. Imagine this scenario. Josh, a 14-year-old high school freshman, has just announced that he wants to try out for the football team. His parents know that Josh has never been very successful in athletics. They are afraid he will be embarrassed or, even worse, will get hurt. Their initial response was to respond, "No way, Josh." Using the caring habits instead, Josh's parents were able to respond with "Yes, if…." Together with Josh they were able to negotiate a way for Josh to approach his goal with safety and responsibility. Josh's parents were able to address their want to have Josh be safe and happy, whereas Josh was able to make a plan to get his want of being on the football team: win–win.

### *Unhealthy Behaviors and Relationship Patterns*

In contrast to the seven caring habits are the seven habits that Glasser (1998) refers to as "deadly": criticizing, blaming, complaining, nagging, threatening, punishing, and bribing or rewarding to control. Imagine again the scenario with Josh. This time his parents use the deadly habits: "No way, Josh." Josh is angry and demands to know why he can't join the team. His parents respond, "You know you have never been good at sports (criticizing). The last time you did this we spent a lot of money and you quit (blaming). You always want to do things like this and then you neglect your chores (complaining). Let's forget about football, Josh. Hey, why don't we go take a look at that guitar you wanted (bribing or rewarding to control)?" Josh's parents are not bad parents. They are trying to protect him from being embarrassed and are concerned for his safety. If they can keep Josh off the team, they will feel better about their roles of parents. After all, they have kept Josh safe, haven't they? But in using the deadly habits to keep Josh safe, they have denied Josh's want to join the team. Josh goes away angry: win–lose.

### *Therapeutic Approach to Working With Parents From This Perspective*

The reality therapy approach to counseling was developed by William Glasser in 1965. Reality therapy is based on choice theory; understanding choice theory helps therapists use reality therapy more effectively. Since the source of almost all human problems is based on relationship problems, the goal of reality therapy is in helping people reconnect. Therapist behaviors include focusing on the present; avoiding discussion of problems and complaints; promoting change in actions and thinking (what clients can more effectively control); teaching clients to use caring habits and avoid deadly habits; encouraging self-evaluation of behavior; discouraging excuses; and helping clients make specific, workable, plans that will help lead them toward happier, healthier lives. Wubbolding (1989, 1991) created the acronym of WDEP to help therapists organize their thinking in this process. Therapists ask clients:

What do you WANT?
What are you DOING to get what you want?
Is it working (EVALUATION)?
What is your PLAN?

*The Case of Dave and Riley*

Dave called requesting counseling for his daughter Riley, 16. Dave's wife, Nancy, died from breast cancer when Riley was 12 years old. Dave, a computer technician, was required to travel often on business. He and Riley moved in with Dave's mother and father so that Riley could have consistent supervision and support while Dave was traveling.

Dave reported that Riley, an honor student, had changed dramatically in recent months. According to Dave, Riley had been going out with a bad crowd. Her grades had slipped, and she was spending most of her time at home in her room and avoiding her grandparents and her father. Recently, Riley had snuck out of the house and was gone all night. Riley was grounded until further notice and had lost her privileges at home.

In the initial sessions, Riley was angry and sullen, clearly resistant to being in therapy. Riley argued that she wasn't doing anything wrong. She was bored with school and tired of being stuck at home while all her friends were out having fun. Riley wanted to get her driver's license and get a job. Dave insisted that Riley improve her grades before he would even consider allowing her to drive. "You still think I'm a baby. You just don't trust me," she screamed at her father. "Why should I?" Dave responded. "You aren't worthy of trust."

When working with more than one person, the reality therapist will begin by establishing a relationship with each person and listening to each side of the story. The therapist will move as quickly as possible from the problem (the *don't want*) to the desired outcome (the *do want*). Ideally, the therapist will find an area of overlapping of wants, which helps to collapse the conflict and sets the stage for collaboration and negotiation. For example, after listening to the complaints from Dave and Riley, the therapist asked, "Would you like to figure out a way to make your relationship with each other better?" This question was simple and likely to elicit a positive response. Dave and Riley said yes. If the response to this question had been no, the therapist would have had to avoid a relationship question and might try a different question, such as, "Would you both agree that you would like to be happier?"

Once Dave and Riley agreed that they wanted a better relationship with one another, the focus shifted from the problem to how they could make that happen. The therapist asked them to explain what they had been doing so far to make the relationship better. Both agreed that there was a lot of yelling, door slamming, punishing, and lying. When asked if their behavior was helping or hurting their relationship and their ability to get their personal goals met, each said it was not.

After an evaluation has been made that the current behavior is not working, the clients are ready to move toward creating a plan for more effective behavior. The therapist helped Dave and Riley explain their own points of view and began to negotiate their differences. Dave explained that he was really worried when Riley was out late. Riley said she felt stifled at home and just wanted to be able to go to the mall and hang out with her friends. The therapist asked, "How can you work together to be sure that Riley gets some freedom while Dave feels confident that she is OK?" Dave promised to buy Riley a cell phone and to take her to the mall occasionally. Riley promised to check in regularly and to get her homework done so that her grades would improve. As sessions continued, the therapist worked with Dave and Riley on other challenges facing them. Before termination, the therapist taught them about the caring and deadly habits and told them to evaluate what behaviors they were using when they found they were in conflict.

### *Summary of the Choice Theory and Reality Therapy Approach to Compassionate Parenting*

Choice theory provides parents with a framework for understanding their children and themselves. In times of conflict, it is useful to ask oneself, "Is what I'm about to do or say going to bring us closer together or push us further apart?" It is not enough for parents to understand their children's needs, wants, and purpose of behavior. Parents must know that their own behavior is motivated by their own needs and wants. Buck (2009) referred to this as *conscious* parenting. To choose a different path, parents have to understand the path they have been on in the past. Buck noted that parents often respond in predictable ways based on unspoken, unrecognized rules they learned in their own past experience. When parents find themselves responding to parenting challenges in ways they don't like, Buck suggested that parents ask themselves the following questions (p. 34):

- What automatic behavior did I use to handle the frustration?
- Was I conscious of what I was doing at the time?
- Do I want to behave differently next time?
- If yes, what are the many different alternative choices available to me?
- Of all these choices, which option will I choose next time?

Finally, parents should avoid using the deadly habits on themselves. Most parents are doing the best that they can, given what they know about effective parenting. Understanding their children and themselves through the lens of choice theory and applying caring habits to all their relationships can help parents have healthier, happier, more connected relationships with their children.

## Summary

Just as there are many ways to describe poisonous parents, there are many approaches to compassionate parenting. The family systems concept of equifinality holds that there are many ways to reach a goal. Whether the approach examines the family structure and interactions among the immediate family members, traces patterns of parenting, anxiety, differentiation, and triangles across generations, or encourages people to examine goals, bad and healthy habits, and to think about the choices people make, with effort parents can improve their relationships with their children and with their own parents.

All of the approaches discussed in this chapter fit well with attachment theory as well as Gottman and DeClaire's (1997) concepts of emotionally intelligent parenting. As we have learned more about the impact of the family environment on the developing brain of a child, we now recognize the very detrimental effects a hostile home life has not only on children's brains but also on their hormonal system and their social and emotional development. How many children diagnosed with attention deficit hyperactivity disorder (ADHD), emotional or behavior problems, or poor school performance are really reflecting the anxiety or chaos they experience at home, and what is the cumulative effect on our culture when so many children struggle in life because of poor parenting or a hostile home environment? As a society and as a field, we must respond to this crisis and promote more compassionate parenting wherever we can.

## References

Bailey, C. E., & Sori, C. F. (2000). Involving parents in children's therapy. In C. E. Bailey (Ed.), *Children in therapy: Using the family as a resource* (pp. 475–501). New York: Norton.

Becvar, D. S., & Becvar, R. J. (1996). *Family therapy: A systemic integration* (3rd ed.). Boston: Allyn & Bacon.

Bowen. (1978). *Family therapy in clinical practice*. Northvale, NJ: Jason Aronson.

Buck, N. S. (2000). *Peaceful parenting*. San Diego, CA: Black Forest Press.

Buck, N. S. (2009). *Why do kids act that way? The instruction manual parents need to understand children at every age.* Charlestown, RI: Peaceful Parenting, Inc.

Colapinto, J. (1991). Structural family therapy. In A. S. Gurman & D. P. Kniskern (Eds.), *Handbook of family therapy* (Vol. 1) (pp. 417–443). New York: Brunner/Mazel.

Dermer, S., Olund, D., & Sori, C. F. (2006). Integrating play in family therapy theories. In C. F. Sori (Ed.), *Engaging children in family therapy: Creative approaches to integrating theory and research in clinical practice* (pp. 37–68). New York: Routledge.

Faber, A. J. (2002). The role of hierarchy in parental nurturance. *American Journal of Family Therapy, 30*, 73–82.

Figley, C. R., & Nelson, T. S. (1990). Basic family therapy skills, II: Structural family therapy. *Journal of Marital and Family Therapy, 16*(3), 225–239.

Fish, L. S. (2000). Hierarchical relationship development: Parents and children. *Journal of Marital and Family Therapy, 26*(4), 501–510.

Giblin, P. (1994). Attachment: A concept that connects. *Family Journal, 2*(4), 349–353.

Gil, E. (1994). *Play in family therapy.* New York: Guilford.

Gil, E. (2003). Play genograms. In C. F. Sori, L. L. Hecker, & Associates (Eds.), *The therapist's notebook for children and adolescents: Homework, handouts, and activities for use in psychotherapy* (pp. 49–56). Binghamton, NY: Haworth.

Gil, E. (2008). Family play genograms. In M. McGoldrick, R. Gerson, & S. Petry (Eds.), *Genograms: Assessment and intervention* (3rd ed.) (pp. 257–274). New York: Norton.

Gil, E., & Sobol, B. (2000). Engaging families in therapeutic play. In C. E. Bailey (Ed.), *Children in therapy: Using the family as a resource* (pp. 341–382). New York: Norton.

Glasser, W. (1965). *Reality therapy.* New York: HarperCollins.

Glasser, W. (1998). *Choice theory: A new psychology of personal freedom.* New York, NY: HarperCollins.

Good, E. P. (1992). *Helping kids help themselves.* Chapel Hill, NC: New View Publications.

Gottman, J., & DeClaire, J. (1997). *The heart of parenting: How to raise an emotionally intelligent child.* New York: Simon & Schuster.

Jernberg, A. M., & Booth, P. B. (1999). *Theraplay: Helping parents and children build better relationships through attachment-based play.* San Francisco: Jossey-Bass.

Keim, J. P. (2000). Oppositional behavior in children. In C. E. Bailey (Ed.), *Children in therapy: Using the family as a resource* (pp. 278–307). New York: Norton.

Kerr, M., & Bowen, M. (1988). *Family evaluation.* New York: Norton.

Kindsvatter, A., Duba, J. D., & Dean, E. P. (2008). Structural techniques for engaging reluctant parents in counseling. *Family Journal, 16*(3), 204–211.

Klimes-Dougan, B., & Kendziora, K. T. (2000). Resilience in children. In C. E. Bailey (Ed.), *Children in therapy: Using the family as a resource* (pp. 407–427). New York: Norton.

Kohn, A. (1999). *Punished by rewards: The trouble with gold stars, incentive plans, A's, praise, and other bribes.* Boston, MA: Houghton Mifflin.

Lever, K., & Wilson, J. J. (2005). Encore parenting: When grandparents fill the role of primary caregiver. *Family Journal, 13*(2), 161–171.

Lim, S. (2008). Transformative aspects of genogram work: Perceptions and experiences of graduate students in a counseling training program. *Family Journal, 16*(1), 35–42.
Lipton, B. (2005). *The biology of belief: Unleashing the power of consciousness, matter and miracles.* Santa Rosa, CA: Mountain of Love/Elite Books.
McGoldrick, M., & Carter, B. (2001). Advances in coaching: Family therapy with one person. *Journal of Marital and Family Therapy, 27*(3), 281–300.
McGoldrick, M., Gerson, R., & Petry, S. (2008). *Genograms: Assessment and intervention* (3rd ed.). New York: W. W. Norton.
Minuchin, S. (1974). *Families and family therapy.* Boston, MA: Harvard University Press.
Minuchin, S., & Fishman, H. C. (1981). *Family therapy techniques.* Boston, MA: Harvard University Press.
Minuchin, S., Lee, W., & Simon, G. M. (1996). *Mastering family therapy.* New York: John Wiley & Sons, Inc.
Montgomery, M. J., DeBell, C., & Wilkins, J. (1998). Calming anxiety: Developmental interventions for multigenerational parent–child therapy. *Family Journal, 6,* 87–93. doi: 10.1177/1066480798062003.
Munns, E. (2000). *Theraplay: Innovations in attachment-enhancing play therapy.* New York: Aronson.
Nelson, T. (2003). Transgenerational family therapies. In L. L. Hecker & J. L. Wetchler (Eds.), *An introduction to marriage and family therapy* (pp. 255–293). Binghamton, NY: Haworth.
Nichols, M. P. (2008). *Family therapy: Concepts and methods.* Boston, MA: Pearson Education.
Nichols, M. P., & Schwartz, R. C. (2008). *Family therapy: Concepts and methods* (8th ed.). Boston: Allyn & Bacon.
Phelan, T. W. (2003). *1-2-3 Magic: Effective discipline for children 2–12* (3rd ed.). Glen Ellyn, IL: ParentMagic, Inc.
Resnick, M. D., Bearman, P. S., Blum, R. W., Bauman, K. E., Harris, K. M., Jones, J., et al. (1997). Protecting adolescents from harm: Findings from the national longitudinal study on adolescent health. *Journal of the American Medical Association, 278*(10), 823–832.
Rolland, J. S. (1994). *Families, illness, & disability: An integrative treatment model.* New York: Basic Books.
Schwartz, J. P., Thigpen, S. E., & Montgomery, J. K. (2006). Examination of parenting styles of processing emotions and differentiation of self. *Family Journal, 14,* 41–48.
Shaw, D. S., Criss, M. M., Schonberg, M. A., & Beck, J. E. (2004). The development of family hierarchies and their relation to children's conduct problems. *Development and Psychopathology, 16,* 483–500.
Sori, C. E. F. (1995). The 'art' of restructuring. *Journal of Family Psychotherapy,* 6(2), 13–31.
Sori, C. F. (Ed.). (2006). *Engaging children in family therapy: Creative approaches to integrating theory and research in clinical practice.* New York: Routledge.

Sori, C. F., & Biank, N. (2006). Counseling children and families experiencing serious illness. In C. F. Sori (Ed.), *Engaging children in family therapy: Creative approaches to integrating theory and research in clinical practice* (pp. 223–244). New York: Routledge.

Sori, C. F., Dermer, S., & Wesolowski, G. (2006). Involving children in family counseling and involving parents in children's counseling: Theoretical and practical guidelines. In C. F. Sori (Ed.) *Engaging children in family therapy: Creative approaches to integrating theory and research in clinical practice* (pp. 139–158). New York: Routledge.

Stosny, S. (1998). *Compassionate parenting.* Washington, DC: CompassionPower.

VanFleet, R. (2003). Strengthening parent–child attachment with play: Filial play therapy. In C. F. Sori & L. L. Hecker & Associates (Eds.), *The therapist's notebook for children and adolescents: Homework, handouts, & activities for use in psychotherapy* (pp. 57–63). Binghamton, NY: Haworth.

Wilson, B. J., & Gottman, J. M. (1995). Marital interaction and parenting. In M. H. Bornstein (Ed.), *Handbook of parenting, Vol. 4: Applied and practical parenting* (pp. 33–55). Mahwah, NJ: Lawrence Erlbaum.

Wubbolding, R. E. (1989). Radio station WDEP and other metaphors used in teaching reality therapy. *Journal of Reality Therapy, 8*(2), 74–79.

Wubbolding, R. E. (1991). *Understanding reality therapy.* New York: HarperCollins.

CHAPTER 3

# Parental Presence

## *An Interpersonal Neurobiology Approach to Healthy Relationships Between Adults and Their Parents*

HANNAH R. FARBER and DANIEL J. SIEGEL

What makes for a healthy relationship between adult children and their parents? How can a clinician assess this important lifelong relationship and create a treatment strategy of intervention to help troubled families move toward health? This chapter addresses these questions by offering an outline of how difficulties develop within a relationship from the point of view of the interdisciplinary field of interpersonal neurobiology (IPNB).

The field of IPNB draws on a wide range of research disciplines to offer a fundamental definition of the human mind and mental health. From this perspective, the mind is seen as emerging from the interplay of relationships and the physical nervous system. As an embodied and relational process that regulates the flow of energy and information, the mind that gives rise to our sense of self is embedded within the emergent properties of the brain and our most intimate relationships (Siegel, 1999).

Adult children with a history of significant difficulty in their relationships with their parents do not have an integrated sense of self because there has been a breach in the interpersonal relationship patterns within which the brain developed. This compromised neural setup lays the foundation for even more challenges as the now-grown children reenter the family system that, if unchanged, continues to evoke the same unhealthy patterns of relating. A clinician empowered with the IPNB perspective is in a position to offer a holistic approach to assessment and treatment planning to optimize the results of therapeutic interventions.

## What Is Parental Presence?

*Parental presence* is the term we are proposing to identify the healthy functioning of parents in their relationships with their children. To be present as a parent, individuals must be open, receptive, and accepting of who their child is and what their child does. There must be a direct view of the child that is not excessively distorted by prior expectations, experiences, or judgments. Often, parental presence is accompanied by a curiosity, openness, acceptance, and love—a "COAL" state of mind—that is at the heart of being mindful (Siegel, 2007).

Mindfulness entails three different interpretations, each relevant to parental presence. "Being mindful" signifies being conscientious, caring, and intentional in what one does. "Mindful learning" involves the avoidance of premature closure of categories so that one remains open to new experiences and a variety of interpretations of incoming data (Langer, 1989). "Mindful awareness" entails openness to present-moment experience as it is happening, without being swept up by judgments (Kabat-Zinn, 2005).

Mindfulness and parental presence may go hand in hand. In fact, a recent study suggests that security of attachment in adults and mindful traits are correlated features of an individual (DiNoble, 2009). But what is attachment?

## The Science of Attachment

Attachment is an important process in the development of the individual. All mammals need the caring attention of their caregivers during infancy to survive. Our complex human development reveals that these important parent–child relationships early in life directly impact the development of a range of processes including self-regulation, self-understanding, empathy, and social skill acquisition. A parent–child relationship is about more than just survival; it is about developing these necessary foundational skills that enable a child to thrive.

Attachment research reveals that the patterns of communication between a parent and child that shape these regulatory functions fall into one of several groupings. For a "secure attachment," a child has to have consistently attuned communication in which her internal states of needs and feelings have been accurately perceived and responded to by the parent. In these securely attached relationships, when ruptures to such connecting communication have occurred, effective repair has generally taken place. What does that mean? Repair involves the identification of a rupture of various sorts and intensities and the initiation of a reconnection so that a sense of "being seen" is reestablished. Securely attached children grow up to become "securely attached" as adults. These are individuals who meet their intellectual potential, have rewarding relationships, and have emotional well-being in their lives.

Another type of parent–child attachment is termed an "avoidant attachment." Avoidantly attached children have had minimal close, emotionally expressive communication with their caregiver. As they grow up, these children tend to be controlling of others, distant from their own emotional lives, and, as adults, have what is called a "dismissing attachment" (Sroufe et al., 2005). The need for others is minimized as an adaptation to the emotionally barren family world in which they have grown. The healthy need for interrelatedness gets "pushed to the side" to enable children to do the best they can under difficult circumstances.

For a relationship that is inconsistently attuned and at times intrusive, these children develop an "ambivalent attachment" in which the need for others is actually amplified. In this subsection of the population, we see that the intermittent reinforcement has created an internal sense of uncertainty so that children are excessively dependent upon parental input for a sense of security even into the adult years. Such "preoccupied" states of attachment are filled with a deep sense of mistrust throughout adult relationships.

Overlapping with these prior three categories of organized attachment—one secure and two insecure—we have a fourth category called "disorganized." Disorganizedly attached children have had experiences with caregivers that are frightening or terrifying. The internal state of such a developmental path is thought to be fragmenting, and these individuals reveal the clinical condition of dissociation. One possible outcome of such experiences for the adult child is the state of "unresolved trauma or loss," which leads to a sense of disorientation and difficulty regulating emotions and having relationships with others. Fear is a common manifestation of the disorganized attachment relationship.

Families tend to maintain their patterns of communication over time. Since grown children's sense of self has been shaped by these patterns, returning to such a family environment will reactivate and reinforce these adaptive strategies. Even in the face of personal growth, "returning home" can be quite a challenge. To understand this process, it is helpful to recognize how experience shapes the structure of the brain.

## Neuroplasticity in a Nutshell

Communication in families involves the sharing of energy and information. This flow stimulates various regions of the brain to become active—and it is this activity that can change the structural connections within the brain itself. Neuroplasticity is the property of the nervous system in which neural firing patterns enable connections to be made or strengthened among the neurons firing at that time. In this way, the experiences that parents provide will directly shape brain structure so that lasting effects will be made on growing children.

From an IPNB perspective, the key to secure attachment and brain development can be seen in this way: when patterns of communication are "integrative," then the growth of the brain is "integrative." Integration is the connecting of differentiated elements of a system to one another. For a parent–child relationship, integrative communication involves the honoring of differences between parent and child and then the cultivation of compassionate and empathic communication between them.

In the brain, neural integration involves the linkage of widely separated areas to each other. The brain has many layers and parts. The region just behind the forehead, the prefrontal cortex, carries out important integration of input from the body proper, the lower brainstem and limbic regions, and the cortex at the top of the brain itself. This prefrontal region also makes maps of others' minds, taking in the signals from other brains so that it also links the input from the social world. Social, somatic, brain stem, limbic, and cortical input are all connected into one functional whole by the prefrontal cortex.

The functions of the middle aspect of this prefrontal region comprise the following list of nine important processes: (1) body regulation; (2) attuned communication; (3) emotional balance; (4) flexibility in response; (5) fear modulation; (6) insight; (7) empathy; (8) morality; and (9) intuition. The first eight of these functions are proven outcomes of secure parent–child relationships. All nine are outcomes of mindful awareness practices. How many of these nine functions do you feel describe the condition of mental health? At their heart, the connection among health, secure attachment, and mindfulness may rest in the common feature of integration (Siegel, 2010a, 2010b).

When a family is filled with individuals with internal neural integration, interpersonal integration naturally follows. These are the families we generally do not see in clinical practice. When adults have a history of insecure attachment, impediments to neural integration have been established in their development and are the source for continuing difficulties. When these adults return home, this vulnerable state of impaired integration makes them at risk of falling into the family system's impaired integrative relating. This setup perpetuates and deepens the impediments to health that so often fill clinical offices with suffering and a sense of despair. Change is possible but requires a careful assessment to illuminate the neural and interpersonal origins of impaired integration.

## Assessment

Anyone can have difficulties after leaving home when returning to visit family, but only certain situations may benefit from clinical intervention. To proceed with treatment planning, a clinician must understand patients' present situation and developmental past. In the present situation, current difficulties may be revealed as chaos or rigidity. Chaotic reactions can include anger, panic, fear, and rebellion. Similarly, rigid reactions can include detachment, stubbornness, depression, and a loss of identity within the family environment. This can result in resentment or hostility on the part of adult children. These situations can be helped by a careful understanding of the development of "the self."

## The Self as Verb

Though people often think of "the self" as a noun, the core aspect of our being that creates a sense of continuity may perhaps be better described as an active emergent process. The self continually emerges from the interplay between our interpersonal relationships and physiological synaptic connections. If relationship patterns remain toxic within a family, they will constantly reinforce toxicity within the self. The synaptic shadows of an insecure past will create internal traits that directly impact the capacity for flexible self-regulation. With security, as described already, individuals are given the prefrontal capacity to regulate the body, to balance emotions, to pause before responding, and to have insight and empathy. These integrative functions are the internal contributions to healthy interpersonal interactions.

Insecure attachment manifests itself in adulthood as impediments to self-regulation. For those with an avoidant history, a dismissing state of mind is present and reveals itself as a disregard for the internal experience of others or even of the self. This stance can induce others to also interact on a similar superficial level of communication. In other circumstances, a dismissing stance can activate a reactive attempt in others to elicit emotions from the individual. In these ways, the internal trait of a dismissing attachment state of mind can move a family toward rigidity or chaos. For those with an ambivalent attachment history, the preoccupied adult state of mind can amplify the perception of slights and misunderstandings into explosive reactivity. Ambivalence leads people to become inconsistent or unpredictable in their reactions to others; this is how we develop a tendency to make "mountains out of molehills." Disorganized attachment and unresolved trauma or loss predispose individuals to internal fragmentation that compromises interpersonal relationships. This dissociation may also make individuals more vulnerable to going down the "low road" during moments of challenging interactions. Such a time of "flying off the handle" or "flipping your lid" can be seen as a disengagement of the integrative functioning of the prefrontal cortex where any of its functions may be temporarily disabled.

Each of us is born with a fundamental need to be safe, seen, and secure. Our attachment category describes the way we have adapted these needs in response to the family environment in which we are born. Whatever the age of the person, these needs are still present. Because of the nature of neuroplasticity, our self-regulatory circuits have been shaped both by direct experience and by how we have adapted to those experiences. Attachment categories reveal how we have adapted the best we can to what we were given. For adults returning home, identifying with these self-regulatory patterns as "who they are" solidifies a sense of identity in these various forms of insecurity. In contrast, secure attachment yields a fluid and flexible self that is continually emerging. Part of the challenge for the clinician is to offer a sanctuary in which individuals can feel safe, seen, and secure so that they do not continue to seek fulfillment of those needs in unfulfilling environments. Without such clinical intervention, people continue to get lost in familiar places. Seeing the self as a verb is a reminder that we are forever emerging in our lives. When repeated patterns of chaos or rigidity imprison individuals, clinical intervention at the level of the family and self systems may be necessary.

## Systems Thinking

It is often more common to think in linear terms, where one thing leads directly to another. In contrast, in systems thinking, we envision the interaction of many elements having multidirectional influence on each other. Systems science involves the mathematical analysis of clusters of entities as they move and interact across time. One example would be a cloud: water molecules gather and "self-organize" across time in the sky. When a system is open to forces and elements outside of itself and is capable of chaotic behavior, we call it a complex system. Such systems are nonlinear, in that small inputs to the system lead to large and unpredictable outcomes. Sounds like a family, doesn't it?

Complex systems, including the mind and families, emerge across time through a self-organizing process that pushes the system to differentiate its elements and to link them to each other. This integrative process makes the natural movement of a complex system create flexibility and harmony. With impediments to self-organization, the system moves, instead, to chaos or rigidity.

Thinking in systems terms, then, we examine the external and internal constraints on a family. External factors include employment, neighborhood environment, religious affiliation, and cultural setting. Each of these can have a direct influence on how a family functions. Internal factors include established patterns of communication, individual temperament and attachment history, as well as psychiatric and medical conditions. When these constraints impede the capacity of the family to promote both differentiation and linkage, then dysfunction occurs.

Healthy functioning within the family system involves the cultivation of individual differences. With this differentiation, the family can then promote linkage in the form of compassionate and empathic communication. Dependable acceptance within a family system is the key to nurturing an independent, resilient sense of self. This is how individuals can be both a "me" and a part of a "we" with fluidity and freedom. With the linkage of differentiated individuals, integration results and harmony ensues.

Impaired differentiation occurs when parents in a family feel threatened by the independence and success of their offspring. A parent's own insecure attachment or narcissism may create such reactions to a child's healthy growth. Here, children are not allowed to be a separate "me" and instead must be solely defined by the "we."

Impaired linkage involves impediments to the sharing of energy and information flow between members of a family. Without the sharing of compassionate communication, the connections among family members will be limited. Not having family meals together, not sharing interests or activities, and dismissing emotional bids for connection are each examples of impaired linkage.

With both impaired differentiation and impaired linkage, members of a family may be prone to entering a "reactive state of mind." Reactive states involve the initiation of a fight-flight-or-freeze response. Such a state closes individuals down to sending or receiving subtle emotional communication. When integration is present, in contrast, individuals will likely be in a "receptive state of mind" in which they are open to receiving signals from the internal world of other people. Family systems that rapidly and frequently move from receptive to reactive states are dysfunctional. Assessing the internal and external constraints that shape such impairments to self-organization is important before designing a treatment strategy.

## Assessing Attachment

One way of evaluating adults' attachment "state of mind" is the Adult Attachment Interview (AAI; Hesse, 1999). This semistructured assessment involves an interviewer asking a series of questions about individuals' recollections of their childhood experiences (Siegel, 2010a, 2010b). Space in this chapter does not permit a comprehensive review of the AAI or its evaluation, but here we offer a brief overview of the essential findings that should be distinguished from the work in adult romantic attachment from the field of social psychology (Roisman et al., 2007).

The AAI includes questions about where persons grew up, who was in the family, and which parent they were closest to and why. A set of inquiries then explores how individuals remember their relationship as young children with each parent or other caregivers. The next set of questions investigates times when persons were separated from their parents, were distressed (medically, physically, or emotionally), were terrified by their parents, or were experiencing loss. The final questions explore how individuals' relationships with their parents changed over time, how it is presently, and how they feel it has affected their development as an adult. If individuals are parents, an additional segment of the interview queries about how individuals hope their own parenting will benefit their children.

Individuals are classified as secure, dismissing, or preoccupied depending on certain themes revealed in their narrative. A secure adult attachment is revealed in responses to these questions that show flexibility and self-reflection. Even individuals with AAIs that suggest a challenging past but that are filled with examples of how they have "made sense" of how these events have shaped their lives are said to have "earned security." A dismissing state of mind is revealed in an AAI in which individuals repeatedly insist that they do not recall their past and that relationships have had little, if any, impact on their development. Details are often idealized, and the interview demonstrates a paucity of self-reflective comments. A preoccupied state of mind yields an AAI in which the narrative frequently diverges from the asked question into often unrelated details and topics. This interview has the quality that individuals confuse past and present. With unresolved trauma or grief, an AAI has moments during the questions about being terrified or having experienced loss in which individuals become disoriented. Such fragmentation in linguistic output during the interview is thought to reflect impairments to resolution of significant trauma or loss.

Adults' attachment status will significantly influence how a family functions as a system. Each member of the family still has beneath these attachment adaptations the universal needs to be safe, seen, and secure. As individuals within a family carry out the intricate, automatic dance of advance and retreat, patterns of insecure attachment can be continuously reinstated and reinforced. If the parents in this adult family system are themselves filled with such insecure attachment adaptations, their ability to provide parental presence will be significantly compromised, causing the cycle of insecurity to continue. Intervention, taking all of these factors into account, can focus a spotlight on the system's constraints that create impediments to integration.

## Intervention

"Emotional communication" is often the focus of intervention in a family system. But what is "emotion?" Communication is the sharing of signals from one person to another through energy flow that often has symbolic meaning, but what does it mean to communicate emotionally? An IPNB perspective suggests that emotion is a "shift in integration" so that when we feel emotionally close to someone, our two minds are integrated. This positive relational state occurs when we cultivate our differences and promote our linkages. When a family is emotionally distressed, integration is diminished. Such impediments to well-being occur when differentiation or linkage is blocked and chaos and rigidity ensue.

How can a clinician promote integration and "emotional health" in a family? Parental presence is a key internal constraint to the family system that can open the gateways toward essential and lasting change. If the parents of the system cannot change in this way, the adult children can be helped by understanding the science of relationships and the brain that support a healthy mind. The first place to begin is in seeing the mind, brain, and relationships in a clear manner so that integration can be promoted. This ability is called "mindsight."

## Mindsight Skill Training

Mindsight is the skill that enables an individual to sense energy and information flow as it is shared in relationships, passes through the physical mechanism of the embodied brain, and is regulated by the mind. To stabilize the mindsight lens, people can learn to develop a "tripod" that consists of openness, objectivity, and observation. Imagine the recording of a video camera operated by a shaky hand; the result would be blurry, and the details would be difficult to perceive. With a tripod, the camera would now be stabilized, and the recording would have highly focused depth, detail, and richness.

"Openness" is the mind's capacity to receive things as they are and accept them without judgment and distortion. "Objectivity" is the way we perceive our own mental life without using it as our identity. "Observation" is that quality of awareness that enables us to reflect on our own participation in experience. A set of reflective exercises is available to develop the tripod of the mind (Siegel, 2010a, 2010b). (Audio exercise available at http://www.drdansiegel.com.)

One example of such a mindsight skill-building practice is the wheel of awareness exercise. The metaphor of the mind having a wheel in which the central hub represents awareness and the rim contains anything one can be aware of is a useful map. On the rim are four sections: the first includes the senses of sight, hearing, smell, taste, and touch that bring in information from the outside world; the second includes the sense of the interior of the body from the input from muscles and bones to the viscera of the torso, such as the heart and intestines; the third involves mental activities, which range from thoughts, feelings, images, and memories to intentions, beliefs, desires, and attitudes; and the fourth section has the sense of our relational connection to other people and entities in the world.

A wheel of awareness practice invites the individual to perform a rim review covering the entire circumference of the rim systematically. This exercise leads to "integration of consciousness"—the first of eight domains of integration that are a part of the IPNB approach to psychotherapy. By differentiating the hub's awareness from the rim's objects of attention, integration is created. Furthermore, by distinguishing the different rim elements from one another, integration is enhanced.

A clinical example of the use of the wheel is teaching an adult child this practice and then encouraging her to "remain in the hub" as she returned for a family reunion. After the event, the patient stated, "I can't believe how I was able to disengage from my sister's mean comments that in the past would have sent me into orbit. I focused on my breath, imagined the wheel and the tranquil hub, and could just accept that this was her rivalry that I could just sense was a point on the rim."

This woman's experience revealed that staying out of reactivity can alter the otherwise automatic patterns of family dysfunction. Having an inner compass that holds your course steady in the face of stormy family weather can be the difference that makes *all* the difference.

## Finding (and Maintaining) an Inner Compass in the Face of the Storm

Maintaining a flexible perspective while interacting in a family is the way your inner compass guides you to a new way of functioning. A reflective exercise, like the wheel of awareness, creates a state of mind with clarity, stability, and equilibrium within the hub of the mind. With repeated practice in the privacy of one's own inner world, this state can become a trait. This trait is a strengthened hub. This is how neural firing that is intentionally created with practice induces structural changes that establish new traits of flexibility and resilience in a person's life.

Whatever patterns of family communication exist, it is possible in an ideal world to observe these interactions with *c*uriosity, *o*penness, *a*cceptance, and *l*ove. This COAL state of mind reveals how we can be mindfully present in connecting with others. In the real world, this is sometimes more easily stated than achieved. When we are present in this open way, our own brain is integrated and the nine middle prefrontal functions are flexibly at work. But challenging family dynamics can push even seasoned therapists and mindfulness practitioners beyond the boundaries of a "window of tolerance." Within the window, an integrated state enables us to function well. Outside of the window, we break into states of rigidity or chaos that reflect a nonintegrated state. Unfulfilled emotional needs or unresolved trauma or loss can make anyone vulnerable to breaking through the window with explosive rage or emotional withdrawal. Such reactive states do not facilitate healthy communication, happiness, or change in a family. In fact, such reactivity usually reinforces the historical patterns of toxicity.

A clinician helping adult children can build on the mindsight skills described earlier to create an inner compass in the strengthened hub of the mind so that "reentry" into the family system may lead to change. By just observing one's own emerging reactivity but not becoming swept up by it, one can flexibly evaluate and choose a new way of responding. This is how we put a mental pause between impulse and action. When adult children are armed with these tools, they are then able to cope with the family in a way that is conducive to their health. Furthermore, they may use these tools to alter the family structure and behavior that may induce helpful changes in the family patterns of interacting.

## Know When to Hold 'Em, Know When to Fold 'Em

It is said that if individuals do not acknowledge the madness of their own environment, then they may go mad themselves. Likewise, if people place in the front of their mind that their environment is crazy, then they can maintain their own sanity in the face of the madness. Being aware of the truth can be painful, but it is a guiding principle that leads to health in the development of both individuals and a family. Sometimes a world is so disturbed that no amount of change is possible. At a minimum in this situation, acknowledging that this is not a "problem" that can be solved but rather a "situation" that needs to be dealt with across time can greatly help maintain the sanity, and the well-being, of individuals in a crazy environment.

We all need the basic elements of relationships: respect, trust, safety, and security. When these needs are not met, we adapt in ways that often shut down our awareness of these essentials of human connection. For adult children to be helped successfully, it is often useful to guide them toward recognizing and accepting that these needs are normal. Without the spaciousness of the hub, these unfulfilled needs are overwhelming and are therefore blocked from daily life. The key to change is having the open presence of a strengthened hub so that disappointments, sadness, longing, loneliness, frustration, and rage become tolerable. This is how the window of tolerance becomes widened for basic attachment needs.

Sometimes a solution cannot be found for adults whose relationships with their parents continue to be particularly tumultuous. Engrained patterns of insecure attachment can be passed through the generations of a family. These patterns of reactive communication and restrictive adaptations may be directly acquired through experience and shape the tension and dysfunction in a family. Sometimes even the best of efforts do not yield lasting, effective change. In such situations, patients may be helped by learning to keep a certain amount of distance between themselves and their parents. In other situations, one member can initiate significant change by starting "from the inside out" with a deeper self-understanding and widened windows of tolerance. This is the way individuals can inspire their family to change in a positive way.

All people need respect, trust, safety, and security. If individuals can be supported to have the courage to accept these as normal parts of human relationships—and to respond in their family with a receptive state rather than the reactivity of fight-flight-or-freeze—then change may be more likely in the family system as a whole. A strengthened hub allows individuals to express their sadness about their family's lack of respect or acceptance rather than becoming enraged.

The often quoted Serenity Prayer inspires us to have the serenity to accept the things we cannot change, the courage to change the things we can, and the wisdom to know the difference. Though the brain continues to change across the lifespan, not all social systems support this capacity. Nevertheless, individuals are empowered to see deeply into the nature of both the brain and relationships with the development of mindsight. These essential skills offer not only the pathway toward social and emotional intelligence but also an effective means with which persons can develop the wisdom to approach a dysfunctional family unit. As with poker, sometimes one simply needs to know when to hold 'em and when to fold 'em.

## (L)earning Security

Ultimately, whether individuals stay actively involved with their family, create emotional and physical distance, or separate entirely if the family remains hopelessly poisonous, the key to well-being rests in developing an internal state of security. Research suggests that no matter what our experiences in our family of origin have been, if we make sense of those experiences and how they have impacted our development, we can "earn" our security as adults (Siegel & Hartzell, 2003). The creation of security that enables adults to have successful relationships may be facilitated by mindsight skill training and relationally based therapies.

Healthy relationships—whether within the family of origin or a newly created social system—are essential for well-being. As a clinician, your task is to help the individuals and, if possible, the family as a whole develop toward integration. For the individual, integration means making sense of their life, being in touch with their emotional and bodily experience, and embracing the essential components of healthy relationships. For a family, integration involves the honoring of differences and the cultivation of compassionate connections. Whatever the limitations of your patients' poisonous parents, it is your privilege to help guide them toward liberating states of integration in their lives. Unyielding parents do not make therapy a failure. Instead, the journey toward the development of well-being is an empowering companionship between the two of you that allows for openness and freedom. Within this therapeutic relationship, adult children can successfully cultivate the integrative mindsight tools to create resilience and self-understanding for a lifetime of well-being.

## References


DiNoble, A. (2009). *Examining the relationship between adult attachment style and mindfulness traits.* Dissertation presented to the faculty of the California Graduate Institute of the Chicago School of Professional Psychology, January.

Hesse, E. (1999). The adult attachment interview: Historical and current perspectives. In J. Cassidy & J. C. Shaver (Eds.), *Handbook of attachment: Theory, research and clinical applications.* New York: Guilford Press.

Kabat-Zinn, J. (2005). *Coming to our senses: Healing ourselves and the world through mindfulness.* New York: Hyperion.

Langer, E. (1989). *Mindfulness.* Cambridge, MA: Perseus Books.

Roisman, G. I., Holland, A., Fortuna, K., Fraley, R. C., Clausell, E., & Clarke, A. (2007). The adult attachment interview and self-reports of attachment style: An empirical rapproachment. *Journal of Personality and Social Psychology,* 92(4), 678–697.

Siegel, D. J. (1999, 2011). *The developing mind,* 1st/2nd edition. New York: Guilford Press.

Siegel, D. J. (2007). *The mindful brain: Reflection and attunement in the cultivation of well-being.* New York: W.W. Norton.

Siegel, D. J. (2010a). *Mindsight.* New York: Oneworld Publications.

Siegel, D. J. (2010b). *The mindful therapist.* New York: W.W. Norton.

Siegel, D. J., & Hartzell, M. (2003). *Parenting from the inside out: How a deeper self-understanding can help you raise children who thrive.* New York: J.P. Tarcher/Penguin.

Sroufe, L. A., Egeland, B. E., Carlson, E., & Collins, W. A. (2005). Placing early attachment experiences in developmental context: The Minnesota longitudinal study. In K. E. Grossman, K. Grossman, & K. G. Waters (Eds.), *Attachment from infancy to adulthood* (pp. 48–70). New York: Guilford Press.

CHAPTER 4

# A Brain-Based Understanding From the Cradle to the Grave

SONDRA GOLDSTEIN and SUSAN THAU

Since the beginning of human existence, long before there was any record, people have been forming bonds with their primary mates and living in social groups. There is an important reason for this: We need each other to exist, to be safe, and for companionship. The threats to the caveman and his family were primarily animal and environmental forces that lurked outside their dwelling. The threats of modern life are of a very different kind. Modern life, with its myriad complexities, requires much more consciousness just to survive. Our lives are rarely tranquil. Living in the 21st century means we are being bombarded by the forces of nature with an ever-increasing intensity as the result of modern technology. To face the complexities of life, humans, from the past into modern times, have formed partnerships with family and friends. Our connections to intimate others, and how we relate to them, determine a great deal about the quality of our lives.

We know that just having another person by our side is not enough. It is how that relationship develops and endures that counts. Until recently the matter of how we engage in our most intimate relationships seemed pretty much a matter of chance or good luck. Now, with advances in our understanding of intimate relationships and the workings of the brain, partners can learn about the actual dynamics of their relationship and the transactional patterns of communications, both verbal and nonverbal, that occur. This look into each person's window of tolerance (Schore,

2003) has much to do with how conflict is handled or avoided—how the emotional state of both partners creates a thriving relationship or one that is primarily dysfunctional. The concept of having a window of tolerance refers to the emotional range of flexibility that individuals exhibit in their interpersonal relationships.

This change in our ability to understand the workings of relationship has come about because of the developments in the emerging field of neuropsychobiology. To understand what this is about, it is necessary to go back to the beginning of human development to when babies are conceived. We now know that experiences in the uterine world are far from passive (Raphael-Leff, 1991). The parents' DNA is joined at the moment of conception; shortly afterward developing fetuses are affected by the mother's body, and they pick up on the transmissions from the world around them. The mother's moods and arousal level are transferred directly into fetuses' developing nervous system—allowing ambient trauma to affect neonates. Once babies are born there is even more direct opportunity for transmission of parental anxiety to occur.

While infants come into the world with a specific wiring pattern, the nervous system is shaped and formed in the ordinary and repetitive interactions between the mother and her infant. The awesome result of the interaction of these powerful forces determines the beginning capacity to form the attachments that are so significant from cradle to grave (Bowlby, 1982). Warm, appropriate responsiveness by parents is essential for infants' capacity to experience caring, to learn to regulate themselves, and to be able to venture out in the world. This means feeling safe enough in their own world to develop a growing interest in what lies beyond. But how does this all begin? What are the actual mechanisms that create this regulatory process? Again, what has been learned about relationships and the developing brain provides a way of conceptualizing this intense experience.

The focus of this chapter is interpersonal neurobiology, which examines the way our bodies and minds together create either harmony and consonance or discord and dissonance. Without question, those who are fortunate enough to have been born into health-promoting experiences will experience pathways in life with others that are easier and probably more satisfying. We consider why this is so and what can be done when these earliest experiences do not foster comfortable attachments. We suggest ways that security can be earned throughout the life cycle through experiences and relationships that both supplement and override the previously detrimentally destructive relationships. This perspective comes directly out of the perspective of neuropsychobiology—that our brain and body have an innate resiliency and capacity to repair.

### Attachment and Affect Regulation

John Bowlby's name is immediately mentioned whenever attachment is discussed. Bowlby's lifetime work began when he became interested in imprinting in animals. As a follower of Konrad Lorenz and Charles Darwin, he concluded that certain behaviors in animals and birds could develop only during a particular time period and under certain conditions (Karen, 1994). He saw unmistakably that if birds were not exposed to one of their own species during the crucial time period, certain aspects of development did not occur (Bowlby, 1958). From these interesting studies, he began to generalize to human infants as well. His conclusions came from working with orphaned infants and children during the traumas of World War II. From observing these children, he came to wonder what would happen if caretakers were either completely absent or were inconsistent in their availability. Would infants behave and relate differently if they had parents present and regularly responsive? What happened to children who had to endure permanent separations from their caregivers?

The emerging theory that Bowlby proposed was based on the assumption that the relationship between a mother and infant has a profound and lasting influence upon the developing child's capacity to function and persevere (Bowlby, 1958). Attachment theory is a theory of emotional regulation (Schore, 1994). Bowlby proposed that infants respond and need the physical proximity of a caring and attuned parent to develop a sense of security and safety. The combination of physical proximity and emotional attunement act as a buffer protecting the developing child from feeling alone and unwanted in the vast and uncertain world.

Mary Ainsworth and Mary Main, followers of Bowlby, created a series of experiments to determine how small children would respond to their primary caregiver departing suddenly and then reappearing. This famous experiment, known as the Strange Situation (Ainsworth, Blehar, Waters, & Wall, 1978), focused on the emotional disruption caused by this act of separation. These results continue to be replicated across cultures and in different experimental conditions, and the outcomes continue to verify the significance of the attachment bond as a stabilizing force in the emotional life of a growing child. This bond provides a way of understanding the role of emotions in our interpersonal relationships. From the moment of birth, the caregiver's emotional state is being transmitted on a moment-to-moment basis from right brain to right brain (Schore, 2003).

This transmission, which goes on dyadically, is the most basic way human infants learn about the world. It begins at birth long before conscious and intentional thought is possible. The human brain is uniquely constructed to make this incredible learning possible. The complexity of the human brain means that its midstructures, specifically the limbic system, are in place at birth. This part of the brain acts as a receptor for the signals of transmission both internally and externally and is involved in learning, memory, motivation, and emotion (Cozolino, 2002). The amygdala, the part of the limbic system that is receiving these signals, comes online shortly after birth. The amygdala's job, as the internal red alert system, is to determine whether the conditions in the surroundings are safe, and thus the amygdala directly affects how this regulation system develops.

The transmissions affecting this alert system are ongoing with automatic and rapid processing occurring instantaneously. That is how our autonomic nervous system develops its responsiveness. When the response to infants is primarily consistent and caring, it is more likely that infants' nervous systems will be in a nondistressed state. In effect, the caretaker is transmitting through her emotional right brain, which is picked up in the infant's right brain, so they continue to transfer their emotional states back and forth, creating a sense of mutuality. In other words, there is minimal autonomic arousal or triggering, and infants remain calm. In contrast, if the mother is in a more agitated, dysregulated state, her transmissions will contain unmetabolized affect. Young children cannot defend against the bombardment of any intense emotionality and in effect will be overwhelmed by the conditions from which they cannot escape. If this inescapable dysregulation occurs with some regularity, young children's ability to maintain their own homeostasis will be compromised. The overwhelming inescapable state of being trapped, which is the fate of highly dependent infants, is the pathway, the genesis, of the undoing of children's regulatory capacity.

Intense emotionality triggers the limbic system (specifically the amygdala) to be alert and to signal the sympathetic nervous system's response of flight or fight; either response creates arousal, and this arousal has the potential to permanently alter the developing child's delicate nervous system. Fight and flight both affect the HPA axis, the neuroendocrine system responsible for excretion of the neurochemical cortisol. This substance is known for its adverse effects on our body and health, including its association with autoimmune disorders, diabetes, and chronic heart disease (Kiecolt-Glaser & Newton, 2001; Schmidt, Nachtigall, Wuethrich-Martone, & Strauss, 2002).

We humans are born with our own unique wiring pattern, which is the result of each individual's genetic background. Along the continuum of emotional regulation, some generalizations can be made. This capacity is what we commonly call our nature. It can be conceptualized in a number of ways including flexibility versus rigidity, calm veresus distressed, or tense versus relaxed. This innate capacity to regulate is affected directly by the regulatory capacity of the primary caregivers. In addition, primary caregivers' capacity to maintain homeostatic balance is either enhanced or interfered with by their own support system. Caregivers who have a good enough relationship with others will more likely be able to feel secure in the complicated task of bonding with their child (Lieberman, Padron, Van Horn, & Harris, 2005).

Caregivers' ability to tolerate and inhibit their own arousal system creates the building blocks that will eventually be the foundation and scaffolding of the developing child. While some caregivers, through reflection and self-awareness, are aware of this awesome responsibility, others function in a highly self-focused state, which in effect acts as a barrier in terms of forming a real attachment to their children. The developing children respond and thrive when there is a real feeling of mattering to another, a sense of being held in their caregiver's mind (Siegel, 1999). This is the pathway that occurs on an ongoing basis between caregivers and their children.

The result of this regular interaction involving emotional transmission is the laying down of the tracks that form part of the foundation of children's regulatory capacity. This capacity is thought of as the ability to self-regulate, or to calm down when in a state of arousal. Physiologically it is often referred to as having good vagal tone (Schore, 2003). To function adequately, it is also necessary to be able to seek comfort, to use the regulatory capacity of another, and to seek mutual regulation. One of the hallmarks of good affect regulation is that individuals have developed the ability to shift back and forth between both modes of emotional functioning—to use both self- and mutual regulation. Neuropsychobiologically, this means that even when experiencing arousal others are felt to be safe enough and consistent enough that their presence is desired and is both comforting and soothing. This is the definition of a secure attachment.

Again, our brain's multiplicity of functions gives us the capacity to be in the presence of others and to read and take in their emotional cues, the external indication of emotional states. Human communication is exceedingly complex because of the intricate system of facial muscles that enable the transmission of emotional states. This rapid sequence of changing facial expressions reveals quickly these internally experienced, body-based emotions. This capacity to read the emotional states of others begins shortly after birth, involving rapid processing right brain to right brain between the infant and its caretaker. This processing goes on as a means of survival long before any of the higher cortical functions come on line. As we develop the capacity for language, we are able to name these emotional states that are both transitory and highly significant in terms of being able to feel safe enough to be with other people. The states euphemistically referred to as *feelings* are generally defined as states of being that are processed internally, automatically, and without any language or conscious thought. Feelings are implicit or interoceptive (Schore, 2003) and are experienced as sensations emanating from the body in transient ways.

### Affect Regulation and Internal Working Models

Until recently the matter of how we engage in our most intimate relationships was considered an innate or intuitive function. However, many people are emotionally ignorant both of their own cues as well as those of others. Conceptually these individuals tend to be primarily oriented to their left brain—to language and linear thinking. They have limited awareness of their body arousal and feeling states. In contrast, others may be primarily right-brain dominant with a great sensitivity to their own emotional processes as well as those of people around them. These individuals are more likely to have a strong sense of their internal experience and are highly attuned to the emotional states and cues of others. Part of the dyadic process of relating from a neuropsychobiological perspective has to do with how well this process of transmission goes between the partners, which includes all forms of dyads, caregiver and child, husband and wife, siblings or close friends.

In all these relationships, there is both the capacity for regulation based on attunement as well as failures because one or both individuals are unable to read these emotionally transmitted cues. This emotional blindness, or inability to read and be sensitive to the cues of others, may cause very difficult dyadic interactions. Nevertheless, this is where it all starts. These ordinary, regular, moment-to-moment transmissions, though not consciously learned, form the basis of how young children experience themselves in the world. This is called implicit relational learning, and it occurs without any conscious awareness, emerging as a result of the actual lived experience. The result of these ordinary, repetitive interactions can be gleaned from the perspective and expectations that individuals reveal as they live and interact with the others with whom they have a relationship. Bowlby (1982) referred to these inner interpretations of relationships and the world as our internal working models. These internalized schemas or templates in effect determine the expectations, hopes, and fears that form the foundation of what individuals will come to expect from others during the rest of their lifetime. In this way, this implicit knowledge, while not consciously held, determines whether other people or situations are experienced as safe or unsafe. It also relates to the important ability to experience hope and positive perspectives and a state of basic trust in others. This attitude is carried forward from early childhood, often without interpretation or cognitive processing, and is just part of a person's sensibility because of the nature and quality of these earliest attachment experiences.

The types of behaviors that bond children to a caretaker are not just creating expectations; they are also the basis of actual structural changes in the brain itself. This is because emotions are not just feelings; they correspond to actual structures and activity. Attachment experiences directly affect the wiring of the brain (Goldstein &Thau, 2004). The pathway of transmission of the signals from the top down (i.e., limbic system to the gut, or the enteretic nervous system) and from the top up (i.e., limbic system to the cerebral cortex) is rapid, continuous, and automatic. But it is how these pathways are layered that essentially determines that flexibility or rigidity of developing children's emotional and attachment schemas.

## Secure and Insecure Attachment Models

To gain a perspective on the development of these cortical and subcortical structures in the early maturing brain, it is helpful to examine the differences in the way these early interactions occur. There is no such thing as perfect attunement, but when there is a good enough responsiveness, there is usually a balance in terms of quietness and arousal. These emotional signals are transmitted automatically from the right brain of the caregiver into the developing right brain of the infant where they have to be metabolized and integrated into the emergent nervous system, neuron to neuron. The consistency of the caregiver provides an expectation that is translated into children's response systems in terms of flexibility, fluidity, and resiliency. Gradually, this will likely develop into what we call security in terms of having a sense of basic trust in oneself as well as in others.

We know that secure individuals are able to interact in a variety of situations and move through these with an ease that differentiates them from individuals who cannot do this. This means that difficult situations are managed by people's internal capacity to experience the emotion, manage their state, whatever it is, and still maintain their sense of self both cognitively and emotionally. This congruence forms the scaffolding that allows the cohesiveness of individuals to be maintained even when challenges to their nervous systems are experienced as difficult to manage. Secure attachment bonds allow a safe exploration of the world, flexibility in dealing with change and stress, trust with intimate others, free expression of emotions, and a positive outlook with self and others. Secure attachment bonds between caregiver and child foster an ongoing sense of possibility and hope and a generally optimistic outlook.

The good enough bond between parent and child that fosters secure attachment relationships does not always occur in early development. If the key ingredients of affect regulation, reliable emotional and physical availability, and emotional attunement are not provided consistently by the primary caregiver, children are unable to develop effective affect regulation skills and ability to trust in a developmental progression. Rather than developing a secure attachment bond, children tend to develop an insecure attachment bond. The children's internal working models, predictors of interpersonal experiences, lead them to expect negative or untrustworthy behavior from other people. The nature of the children's insecure attachment bond may vary depending on their experiences with the primary caregiver. If the caregiver is emotionally distant, unavailable, or rejecting, the children may develop an avoidant attachment style (George & Solomon, 1999). Fear of emotional closeness with an expectation of unavailability and rejection are the defining characteristics of the insecure avoidant attachment style. In answering the attachment question, "Can I count on other people to be there for me?", insecure avoidant children will answer no.

Insecure ambivalent attachment styles emerge from infant–caregiver interactions characterized by unpredictable caregiver vacillation which includes rejection and intrusive, often emotionally unpredictable behavior. Intrusive parents believe that their "helpless" children must be protected against experiences of failure and unfairness in life. Hovering over the children, they gain a sense of parental efficacy and security by controlling their every action. In this age of technology, intrusive parents may "check on" children by e-mail, cell phone, text messages, and global positioning systems (GPSs), which track children who drive. They may require that their children call them several times daily and report on their every move. These children feel under scrutiny by their parent. Insecure ambivalent children behave in highly anxious, vigilant ways, preparing for their caregiver's erratic behavior (Sable, 2000). These children tend to be fearful and uncertain about the trustworthiness of relationships and fear engulfment and control (rather than true closeness). Their answer to the attachment question, "Can I count on others to be there for me?" is maybe.

A third insecure attachment category is the insecure disorganized attachment style. This style emerges from caregiver–infant interaction characterized by affect dysregulation, emotional or physical abuse, and volatility with threatened and actual abandonment. The source of potential security, the caregiver, becomes instead the source of danger for these children. The dilemma facing the children is very real in that they are drawn to the caregiver for comfort yet feel that the caregiver may be dangerous and frightening. The children develop an insecure disorganized attachment style characterized by erratic and contradictory behavior. For instance, they may display hopeful-seeking behavior followed by avoidance, freezing, or dazed behavior. Crying for the caregiver after separation may be followed by rage upon reunion. Children with insecure disorganized attachment style are unable to use consistent strategies when alarmed. They cannot seek support and comfort from the caregiver (secure attachment), shift attention away from the caregiver (avoidant attachment), or oscillate between seeking and resisting comfort (anxious-ambivalent attachment). Insecure disorganized children's answer to the attachment question, "Can

I count on others to be there for me?" is a confused I don't know and I don't know what to do (Sable, 2000).

## Insecure Attachment and Stress

Although different in manifestation and prediction about the dependability of others, the three insecure attachment styles have common characteristics. Poor stress management is found in all of these insecure attachment working models. Securely attached children have a history of an attuned caregiver who can correctly assess and respond to their positive and negative affect. If there is misattunement on the caregiver's part, the caregiver guides an interactive repair, which allows the child to safely recover from the misattunement. The child–caregiver dyad transitions smoothly between positive to negative and back to positive affect. The fluidity of affect change in secure attachment creates greater resilience in dealing with stress.

In the environment of the insecure caregiver–child dyad, there are frequent and enduring high levels of negative affect and low levels of positive affect. Because the caregiver cannot participate in affect-regulating dyadic interactions, the child shows a greater tendency for negative emotional states to endure beyond the initial stressful event. Insecurely attached individuals have poor adaptability to environmental change, negative mood when stressed, and intensity of negative reactions over time and different situations.

As a result of repeated episodes of unrepaired misattunement and dysregulation between caregiver and child, these children come to expect that they will not benefit from the caregiver's attempts to manage their emotional state or reaction to stress. This is a significant feature of all insecurely attached individuals. These representations are then stored outside conscious awareness as prototypes of interactions with others (internal working models of insecure attachment). Dysfunction of affect regulation in insecurely attached individuals is most obvious under stressful conditions that call for flexibility and effective affect regulation (Schore, 2003).

The ability to reach out to other people for problem-solving help, support, and comfort is invaluable in dealing with stressful life situations. A disadvantage shared by individuals with insecure attachment styles is their lack of trust in family and friends. Children's experience with caregivers' intrusiveness, unavailability, rejection, abandonment, and failure to promote and facilitate affect regulation results in their belief that it is futile to reach out to other people for assistance and support. They cannot count on others to be there in times of need. To reach out to others in managing stress, expression of emotion is essential. Often communication skill in expressing emotion is underdeveloped in insecurely attached individuals. Insecure attachment styles usually involve "hiding" emotional needs because of negative experience with inconsistent caregiver availability and caregiver failure to encourage children's communication skills for affect regulation. The ability to ask others for help and express emotional needs is less available to insecurely attached individuals, creating a handicap in their management of stress (Kobak, 1999).

Good dyadic affect regulation between caregiver and child builds confidence in children about their ability to transition from positive to negative and back to positive states. This smooth dyadic regulation of affect creates a positive outlook regarding self and others. Insecurely attached children do not experience these successful emotional transitions and develop a more negative view of self and others. The fluidity and flexibility of emotional transactions are not experienced in insecure attachments. A rigid style of problem solving may allow insecurely attached persons to feel some security and direction in facing challenges. However, this rigid style of thinking and navigating life challenges does not allow the flexibility required to effectively think creatively and successfully face the unexpected "curve balls" in life. Adults assessed as having an insecure attachment have greater difficulty in managing the vicissitudes of life generally, and interpersonal relationships specifically, than those assessed as securely attached (Shaver & Mikulincer, 2007).

Stressful life situations may trigger a dangerous psychobiological "cycle of fear." When danger is sensed in relationships or life crises, the amygdala and autonomic nervous system (ANS) are triggered within milliseconds to go into "fight-or-flight" mode. Management of triggered reactions by securely attached individuals is very different from the insecurely attached. When faced with a difficult life challenge, securely attached people react with initial fear, but the high levels of anxiety begin to subside as they successfully regulate and modulate the negative emotions. This ability to regulate emotion has evolved from a regulating and safe relationship between caregiver and infant (George & Solomon, 1999). The caregiver has provided much of the modulation of states and has facilitated the infant or child to transition from a positive state to a negative state and back to a positive state. These early experiences with disruption and repair form children's abilities to withstand negative states and transition back to a positive state.

Neural connections are firmly developed between the amygdala and orbitofrontal cortex, the area of the cerebral cortex involved in social and emotional behaviors, regulation of body and emotional states, and critically involved in the attachment process. These neural connections occur as a result of the caregiver providing secure dyadic experiences of affect regulation, which are internalized as internal working models of attachment. Thompson (1999) wrote that emotion is initially regulated by others, but over the course of development it becomes increasingly self-regulated as a result of neurophysiological development. People with secure attachment styles can self-regulate and address initial fear and anxiety created by a stressor with a positive outlook. Their internal working model of a helpful other will allow them to turn to other people for help if needed. The ability to think flexibly increases the possibility of problem solving in dealing with the stressor.

A different caregiver relationship may be found in insecurely attached persons' developmental history. As a result of episodes of caregiver–infant dysregulation or misattunement, infants learn to expect that they cannot benefit from the caregiver's participation in management of their affect arousal (Beebe & Lachmann, 1988). Their internal working models may contain prototypes of the caregiver as rejecting or unavailable but also one of themselves as unworthy of help and comfort (Bretherton & Munholland, 1999). This internal working model of insecure attachment will preclude turning to interactive regulation and support during times of emotional crisis. Schore (2003) notes that the dysfunction of psychobiological systems is most obvious under stressful and challenging conditions that call for behavioral flexibility and affect regulation. Insecurely attached individuals may face a crisis or stressor by fight-or-flight responses such as volatility, conflict, fear, or dismissive avoidance. None of these responses is flexible and problem solving. Frustration and difficulty in facing life's challenges and interpersonal problems may create an ongoing stress response. Physiological stress responses may be acute or chronic. When homeostasis is disrupted, allostasis, an essential psychobiological coping process, engages to meet biological needs of the moment. Allostasis is the process of achieving stability through physiological or behavioral change and involves the autonomic nervous sytem, the HPA axis, and the cardiovascular, metabolic, and immune systems, which act to protect the body. It is an additional process of reestablishing homeostasis but one that responds to challenge instead of subtle ebb and flow. Allostasis is a process of maintaining physiological stability through change. Paradoxically, this process can protect and restore as well as damage the body. Allostatic load refers to the cumulative cost to the body of allostasis, with allostatic load being a state in which serious pathophysiology can occur (McEwen & Wingfield, 2003).

Two types of allostatic load have been identified. Type 1 is acute and occurs during unpredictable natural disasters, which may stimulate survival reactions. These physiological stress responses are temporary and are related to dealing with the immediate crisis. Type 2 allostatic load and overload are physiological responses to social conflict that may persist over time. In Type 2 allostatic overload, increased energy expenditure fails to be effective in reducing the stressors during life and work (McEwen & Wingfield, 2003). Chronic fear of pending interpersonal danger maintains excessive stimulation in the stress response and amygdalar systems, heightening cortisol, the "stress hormone." Excessive stimulation of cortisol is associated with Type 2 overload and creates wear and tear on the body. Heightened cortisol is associated with many medical conditions such as obesity, diabetes, hypertension, cardiovascular risks, and high cholesterol.

The element of danger in interpersonal relationships is heightened for insecurely attached individuals. The related possibility of Type 2 allostatic overload with its health risks is important to consider as a reaction to chronic stress of "danger" in relationships. In addition, insecurely attached persons do not trust others to be helpful; their answer to the attachment question, "Can I count on you to be there for me?" is no, maybe, or I don't know. The lack of trust may lead to social isolation and poor social support systems. In general, adults assessed as having an insecure attachment have greater difficulty in managing the vicissitudes of life generally, and interpersonal relationships specifically, than those assessed as securely attached (Shaver & Mikulincer, 2007).

Sroufe (1988) conducted longitudinal research indicating that attachment styles tend to be intergenerational with a high correlation between the caregiver's attachment status and the attachment status of the infant with that particular caregiver. Bowlby (1973) wrote that "the inheritance of mental health and mental ill health through the medium of family microculture … may well be far more important than is their inheritance through the medium of genes" (pp. 322–323). Belsky (2005) also concluded that the process of intergenerational transmission of attachment status is experiential in nature. He found that the quality of parenting and interactive regulation experienced by children is a strong predictor of attachment style. He also noted that attachment style experienced in adulthood shapes subsequent parenting behavior and facilitates either security or insecurity in offspring.

## Earned Secure Attachment

Fortunately, insecure attachment status is not necessarily permanent in parent or child. Bowlby (1969) wrote that people could accommodate new information that allows their internal working models to be updated. Thus, people possess the capacity for change in patterns of attachment security over time. Additional research has found that change in attachment status can occur throughout the lifespan. The term *earned secure* attachment has been used to describe individuals who experience malevolent or dysregulated parenting from which an insecure attachment status would be likely to evolve yet instead develop a secure attachment. Although individuals who are securely attached have continuous attachment from early childhood, "earned secure" individuals have risen above difficult early childhood experiences and are later assessed in adulthood as securely attached (Pearson, Cohn, Cowan, & Cowan, 1994).

How does earned secure attachment occur? Although the primary caregiver is most influential in shaping attaching status, most children have more than one caregiver. These caregivers (e.g., grandparents, uncles, aunts, siblings, teachers, mentors) play important roles in shaping children's internal working models predicting security versus insecurity in interpersonal relationships. Earned secures have found meaning in their difficult childhoods, may have found ways to forgive their parents, or could have otherwise defused the emotional impact of the adverse parenting they received (Simpson, Rholes, & Winterheld, 2010). Forming a secure relationship with an additional caregiver may be one way of defusing their negative past.

The nature of the relationship needed to develop earned secure status is characterized by repetitive, secure interactions with a significant other (e.g., spouse, family member, teacher, mentor, therapist). Examples of repetitive secure interactions that enhance and create security are (1) attunement and conscious reciprocity, (2) self-reflection and recognition of one's own behavior, (3) attention to nonverbal cues of the other, and (4) recognition of the need to repair disjunctions when they occur. Many others forms of repetitive secure interactions foster the recognition of emotional needs of the other, including touching, speaking, eye contact, and remembering. As these repetitive secure interactions occur, they alter brain circuitry.

Psychotherapy and other secure experiences may accomplish alterations in brain functioning because the orbital frontal cortex retains a capacity for plasticity throughout life (Schore, 2003). The flexible right frontal regulatory system within the secure, affect-regulating environment of therapy (or other important secure relationships) may become more flexible and efficient. This neurobiological change may mediate an expansion of individuals' right hemispheres (allowing affect regulation) and the transformation of an insecure into an earned secure attachment (Phelps, Belsky, & Crnic, 1998).

There are naturally occurring protective factors promoting resilience and development of earned secure attachment. Children live multifaceted lives within multiple contexts (e.g., school peer groups, sports teams, religious organizations). Teachers, mentors, and adult models are available. Each context is a potential source of protective factors that allow and promote earned secure attachment status. Secure mentor relationships may promote more security and foster resilience, creating hope for the child (Egeland, Carlson, & Sroufe, 1993). When a greater sense of security occurs, children may have greater physical and mental flexibility. When children or adults feel more secure, this state is characterized by increased release of the hormone oxytocin, which is an antidote to stress. Oxytocin is a hormone related to good health and a sense of well-being.

## Clinical Examples of Earned Secure Attachment

A clinical example of earned secure attachment is Sam, whose primary caregiver was an alcoholic mother. His father was often absent because of his business travel. Whenever he left, Sam felt unprotected from his mother's irrational and unpredictable rage states when she drank heavily. Sam was verbally abused by his mother with name calling, harsh criticism, and verbal attacks in which his mother would accuse him of "bad" behavior. At times he was physically abused when his mother would beat him with a belt or large metal cooking spoon. He reports being fearful and distrustful of relationships during his childhood. When Sam was 11 years old, his parents divorced, and primary custody was awarded to his father on the basis of his mother's alcoholism and abusive behavior. Initially Sam had supervised visits with his mother once a week until his mother proved to the court that she was sober and attending regular Alcoholics Anonymous (AA) meetings. Sam then saw his mother occasionally and only when he chose to see her. His father traveled less and was more physically and emotionally available to Sam. The father's girlfriend, who lived with Sam and his father (and later became Sam's stepmother), was very caring and accepting of Sam and became a secure caregiver. Through the repetitive secure interactions with his father and stepmother from ages 11–18 (when he went away to college), Sam became more trusting and earned secure in his attachments to these primary caregivers. He became more forgiving and understanding of his mother, whose childhood had been marred by her own parents' alcoholism. When Sam attended college he developed mentor relationships with two professors who supported and guided his intellectual growth and success. These were additional secure relationships allowing secure repetitive interactions that also contributed to his sense of earned security. After college he married a woman who served as a secure base and safe haven; together they have created a secure and enduring attachment bond. Currently, Sam is working successfully as a corporate executive. However, he chose not to have children out of a fear that he might not be a "good" parent due to childhood experiences with his abusive and emotionally unavailable mother. We will never know whether his earned secure status could have resulted in his being a secure and loving parent, ending the intergenerational cycle of insecure caregiver transactions.

Janice is another clinical example of earned secure attachment. Earning security has not come easily for Janice. How could it? What looked like a perfectly fine family was part of the problem. On the outside, her family life was quite upper-middle class. Her mother, an artist, was home with the children, and her father had a good job in law. But that is where any semblance of normality stopped. Janice's mother had never resolved her own feelings of hatred for her mother and in turn began to turn away from

Janice almost at birth. Janice, a middle child, lived with daily neglect bordering on actual abuse. In addition, she was left in the care of relatives who furthered this frightful cycle. Because of the profound scorn that Janice's mother had for her father, he was not available to her to offset this cycle of profound neglect. How is it possible then for someone who had such minimal experience with good attachments to survive and grow in a healthy way? But much like a cactus flower in a barren desert, Janice somehow had the implicit instinct to find what she has needed. While she was in college, suffering from extreme addiction, she began therapy with a skilled and sensitive therapist. Even though she did not acknowledge the will to live, she continued to go to therapy, stating unequivocally that she had no idea why she was there. This was the important beginning of building a real relationship with someone who actually listened to her experiences and validated the horror of what she had to live through, allowing repetitive secure transactions over a continuous time span.

Time has passed, and Janice's behavior has shown a new kind of spirit such as her courage to move across the country to make a new life for herself. Gradually, she brought into her life new and meaningful connections including a significant boyfriend, several girlfriends, and a new therapist. She has forged the attachments to these new relationships, and each in its own way has contributed to her building a secure foundation that in the past was illusive at best.

The remnants of Janice's past are most evident in her profound resignation that comes on quickly when life's trials pile up. In those times, her ability to remain present and to not withdraw into a dissociative state are most apparent. Now that Janice has a more secure foundation, she is working on expanding her capacity to emotionally handle the frustration and fear that are part of such stressful situations.

In each of these junctures and transitions in her life, Janice has been able to form new connections with people who are kind, considerate, and present. That includes finding a new therapist who had the opportunity of building on the connections that began in the earlier therapy. Janice's greatest challenge is being able to maintain her sense of perspective and balance when she is being bombarded by intensely meaningful stimuli. She in effect recognizes that she will always have her own vulnerabilities but that they do not have to prevent her engagement in life.

## Hope and Earned Secure Attachment

Sam and Janice are two examples of individuals who achieved earned secure attachment status through repetitive and continuous secure experiences with therapists, teachers, professors, mentors, friends, and intimate partners. They have experienced many cycles of organization, disorganization, and reorganization of attachment schemas, which allowed the creation of a new earned secure attachment style (Schore, 2003). Children (and adults) can overcome difficult relationships in early life. Relationships with figures of importance in children's lives, which contain repetitively secure interactions, can ameliorate and defuse an earlier, more poisonous relationship with a primary caregiver in early development. Because our brains are capable of new neuronal growth, we can be hopeful about more secure attachment relationships in life leading to the development of an earned secure attachment status that will promote physical and mental well-being. Having the courage to go into these new and different secure relationships is the first step in allowing this change. Taking this risk offers a different outcome relationally from what was experienced in the past. All of this builds the confidence necessary to proceed differently in life and to create more secure relationships.

## References

Ainsworth, M. D. S., Blehar, M. C., Waters, E., & Wall, S. (1978). *Patterns of attachment: A psychological study of the strange situation.* Hillsdale, NJ: Erlbaum.

Beebe, B., & Lachmann, F. M. (1988). The contribution of mother-infant mutual influence to the origins of self-and object representations. *Psychoanalytic Psychology, 5,* 305–337.

Belsky, J. (2005). Social-contextual determinants of parenting. In R. E. Tremblay, R. G. Barr, & R. D. Peters (Eds.), *Encyclopedia on early childhood development.* Montreal: Centre of Excellence for Early Childhood Development.

Bowlby, J. (1958). The nature of the child's tie to his mother. *International Journal of Psychoanalysis, 39,* 350–373.

Bowlby, J. (1969). *Attachment and loss: Vol. 1 Attachment.* New York: Basic Books.

Bowlby, J. (1973). *Attachment and loss: Vol. 2. Separation.* New York: Basic Books.

Bowlby, J. (1982). Attachment and loss: Retrospect and prospect. *American Journal of Orthopsychiatry, 52*(4), 664–678.

Bretherton, I., & Munholland, K. A. (1999). Internal working models in attachment relationships: A construct revisited. In J. Cassidy & P. R. Shaver (Eds.), *Handbook of attachment* (pp. 89–111). New York: Guilford.

Cozolino, L. (2002). *The neuroscience of psychotherapy: Building and rebuilding the human brain.* New York: W. W. Norton.

Egeland, B., Carlson, E., & Sroufe, L. A. (1993). Resilience as process. *Development & Psychopathology, 5,* 517–528.

George, C., & Solomon, J. (1999). Attachment and caregiving. In J. Cassidy & P. R. Shaver (Eds.), *Handbook of attachment* (pp. 649–670). New York: Guilford.

Goldstein, S., & Thau, S. (2004). Integrating attachment theory and neuroscience in couple therapy. *International Journal of Applied Psychoanalytic Studies, 1*(3), 214–223

Karen, R. (1994). *Becoming attached: First relationships and how they shape our capacity to love.* New York: Oxford University.

Kiecolt-Glaser, J. K., & Newton, T. L. (2001). Marriage and health: His and hers. *Psychological Bulletin, 127*(4), 472–503.

Kobak, R. (1999). The emotional dynamics of disruptions in attachment relationships: Implications for theory, research, and clinical intervention. In J. Cassidy & P. R. Shaver (Eds.), *Handbook of attachment* (pp. 21–43). New York: Guilford.

Lewis, T., Amini, F., & Lannon, R. (2001). *A general theory of love.* New York: Vintage.

Lieberman, A. F., Padron, E., Van Horn, P., & Harris, W. W. (2005). Angels in the nursery: The intergenerational transmission of benevolent parental influences. *Infant Mental Health Journal, 26*(6), 504–520.

McEwen, B. S. (1998). Stress, adaptation and disease: Allostasis and allostatic load. *Annals of the New York Academy of Science, 840*, 33–44.

McEwen, B., & Wingfield, J. (2003). The concept of allostasis in biology and biomedicine. *Hormones and Behavior, 43*(1), 2–15.

Pearson, J. L., Cohn, D. A., Cowan, P. A., & Cowan, C. P. (1994). Earned and continuous security in adult attachment: Relation to depressive symptomatology and parenting style. *Development & Psychopathology, 6*, 359–373.

Phelps, J. L., Belsky, J., & Crnic, K. (1998). Earned security, daily stress, and parenting: A comparison of five alternative models. *Development & Psychopathology, 10*, 21–38.

Raphael-Leff, J. (1991). *Psychological processes of childbearing.* London: Chapman and Hall.

Sable, P. (2000). *Attachment and adult psychotherapy.* Northvale, NJ: Jason Aronson.

Schmidt, S., Nachtigall, C., Wuethrich-Martone, O., & Strauss, B. (2002). Attachment and coping with chronic disease. *Journal of Psychosomatic Research, 53*, 763–773.

Schore, A. (1994). *Affect regulation and the origin of the self: The neurobiology of emotional development.* Hillsdale, NJ: Lawrence Erlbaum Associates, Inc.

Schore, A. (2003). *Affect regulation and the repair of the self.* New York: W. W. Norton.

Shaver, P. R., & Mikulincer, M. (2007). Adult attachment strategies and the regulation of emotion. In J. J. Gross (Ed.), *Handbook of emotion regulation* (pp. 446–465). New York: Guilford Press.

Siegel, D. (1999). *The developing mind: How relationships and the brain interact to shape who we are.* New York: Guilford.

Simpson, J. A., Rholes, W. S., & Winterheld, H. A. (2010). Attachment working models twist memories of relationship events. *Psychological Science, 21*, 252–259.

Sroufe, L. A. (1988). The role of infant-caregiver attachment in development. In J. Belsky & T. Nezworski (Eds.), *Clinical implication of attachment* (pp. 18–38). Hillsdale, NJ: Erlbaum.

Thompson, R. A. (1999). Early attachment and later development. In J. Cassidy & P. R. Shaver (Eds.), *Handbook of attachment* (pp. 265–286). New York: Guilford.

CHAPTER 5

# Creating Secure Attachment

## *A Model for Creating Healthy Relationships*

SHEA M. DUNHAM and SCOTT R. WOOLLEY

The yearning for humans to feel safe and securely connected to others is hardwired into their genes and brains (Johnson, 2004a, 2004b, 2007, 2008; Johnson & Greenman, 2006). It is this drive to be intimately attached to others that makes parental and partner relationships so important in people's lives. However, if these relationships are troubled or, even worse, poisonous, it means these attachments can be damaging. When children or adults are emotionally bonded to another, that person represents both the means for comfort and solace as well as a source for potential hurt, fear, and loneliness. When the person children or adults are supposed to turn to for comfort in times of emotional or physical pain is the one doing the hurting, what do they do? In these situations most people react to the attachment figure with varying degrees of either anxiety (becoming hypervigilant about the relationship) or withdrawal (convincing oneself that others are not needed) (Cassidy & Shaver, 2008). Sometimes people combine both anxiety and withdrawal as coping mechanisms.

The authors of each chapter in this book have highlighted the importance of the child–parent relationship for people's intrapersonal and interpersonal health. From an attachment perspective it makes sense to emphasize early attachment figures in understanding relationship health and distress. "The quality of the connection to loved ones and early emotional deprivation is key to the development of personality and to an individual's habitual way of connecting to others" (Johnson, 2008, p. 17).

Poisonous parents, through neglect, criticism, abuse, or through other violation of boundaries, interfere with their offspring's basic ability to be securely dependent on others or attuned to the needs of others. The internal working model of relationships, based on the bond with the poisonous parent, may negatively bias perceptions of the current attachment figure even if the current relationship appears to be safe and comforting (Johnson, 2002, 2004b). Without intervention, these children can become fruits of the poisonous tree—tainting other relationships with the bitter taste of a spoiled bond with caretakers.

Lack of confidence in the emotional bond with attachment figures saps the security from the relationship over time. Each time individuals reach out to an attachment figure in times of emotional turmoil and are not satisfied by the response, it may influence their propensity to seek solace in that relationship. An insecure attachment predisposes people to perceive actions as injurious and to respond to perceived injuries in a maladaptive manner (Cassidy & Shaver, 2008; Johnson, 2002). Depending on the severity of the offense and number of times they occur, children and partners may suffer feelings of abandonment, fear, violation, loneliness, and hurt (Johnson, 2008). People who have had a destructive relationship with their parents need more experiences of positive bonding events over a longer period of time to create a secure attachment relationship, even with a responsive partner (Johnson, 2002, 2004b).

While having poisonous parents makes it more likely that people will struggle in relationships, people can develop secure attachments through relationships other than with parents. Romantic relationships provide fertile ground for sowing the seeds of new attachment models and strategies. Previous chapters in this book have focused on the parent–adult child relationship; in this chapter repairing romantic relationships is discussed. Confronting, repairing, and forgiving attachment injuries in romantic relationships as soon as possible assists in repairing damage to the emotional connection (Johnson, 2008).

## Adult Romantic Relationships and Attachment

When working with couples it is essential for therapists to understand the human condition as it relates to attachment and romantic love. The attachment perspective on romantic love provides a therapist with a frame of reference for understanding what "goes right" and what "goes wrong" in a couple's affectional bond. In addition, attachment theory provides a systemic perspective for understanding and intervening in problematic relationships (Johnson, 2004a, 2008). It helps make sense of the connection between the intrapersonal and interpersonal and the reciprocal effect of historical representations of self and others with current relationships.

Johnson (2004a, 2007) point out several things that attachment theory teaches couples therapists:

1. Everyone has an innate need for emotional connection, and powerful emotions help regulate connections.
2. A secure attachment provides a secure base and is an antidote to anxiety and vulnerability.
3. Relational expectations are created by thousands of interactions that create current representations of relationships and are carried forward into new relationships. These models create views of self and others.
4. Extreme distress and emotional reactions are a typical response to threats to the quality of the emotional connection. A lack of mutual emotional accessibility and responsiveness will trigger separation distress and feelings of abandonment. Intense emotions include anguish and sadness, feelings of abandonment, shame, fear, and loss.
5. The basic strategies for regulating threats to attachment are anxiety, avoidance, and fearful-avoidant.

The original attachment writings, such as those of John Bowlby, focused mainly on the infant–caregiver relationship and how infants were impacted when they were separated from their mothers (Bowlby, 1969, 1973; Hazan & Shaver, 1987). He observed that children with insecure attachments had only a few negative ways to deal with their basic feelings and needs (Johnson, 2008). Later, attachment researchers and authors applied understandings of the child–caregiver bond to romantic bonds (Cassidy & Shaver, 2008). Understanding attachment from a childhood perspective is one part of the puzzle, and understanding adult attachments is the other part of the puzzle, completing a picture that people carry with them about their intimate relationships.

### *When It "Goes Right"*

As two people are getting to know each other, they typically take risks in opening up to each other—sharing their hopes, dreams, fears, hurts, likes, and dislikes—which creates vulnerability. As both people continue, over time, to make themselves vulnerable and to accept the vulnerability of a partner, trust is created, and emotional bonding takes place. The yearning for a secure relationship fuels the desire to continue to risk sharing, connecting, and being together.

Most simply stated, for couples a secure relationship is one where each partner is accessible and responsive (Johnson, 2004b). This simple definition makes secure relationships sound easily attainable, but for some it is difficult. Being accessible and responsive is more than just being around and saying "uh-huh" when a partner makes a bid for attention (Gottman, 1999). Being accessible and responsive includes touch, vocalizations, gazing into each other's eyes, and giving feedback that lets others know they are being listened to with interest. It's not just about being physically present; it's about participating.

Secure relationships predict desirable relationship factors such as trust, commitment, interdependence, and relationship satisfaction (Kirkpatrick & Davis, 1994). At its best, a secure relationship leads partners to feel accepted, validated, and safe. Even when there are incidences of disconnection, partners in secure relationships have the confidence and assurance that they can repair and reconnect. Most importantly, partners feel seen, understood, and valued. The "heart of the matter" is that people feel they matter to their partner. When people believe they matter, they experience feeling unique, irreplaceable, priceless, and precious.

When partners feel confident in an attachment figure's availability and are receptive to a partner's soothing, they are much less likely to succumb to intense or chronic fear in relationships (Hazan & Shaver, 1987). The ability to effectively depend on one another for emotional support and to fulfill the caregiving role is reciprocal and flexible. Each partner is able to successfully move back and forth between receiving and giving care.

People with secure attachment models are able to share emotions without disguising them. They are able to share "true," vulnerable, primary emotions rather than secondary reactive emotions (Greenberg & Paivio, 1997; Johnson, 2004b). For example, a wife is talking to her husband about a very attractive coworker. Instead of saying to her, "You better stop seeing him. What is your problem? Are you cheating on me?" he would say, "This is a bit scary for me. I need to know that he doesn't pose a threat to our relationship." However, even if the husband is reactive, in a secure relationship the wife is able to soothe his fears even when they are stated in a threatening, reactive manner. She's open to reinterpreting and reframing his perspective from "Are you cheating on me?" to "I am scared of losing you because you are so important I can't imagine my life without you. I don't want to imagine my life without you." Even though she may have to reinterpret his words into its underlying meaning, she is able to react in a manner to soothe her husband by reassuring him: "Honey, I don't want you to worry. No one could ever take your place. Everyone may think he is attractive, but he could never be as attractive to me as you are. You are irreplaceable." In a secure relationship, even though partners may briefly lose their cool, they can recover and attune to the need for reassurance, comfort, and connection.

In summary, securely attached partners help each other feel valued and important. Each person feels like the other happily dedicates time, thought, and energy to the other's needs and desires. When misunderstandings happen, as they inevitably will even in the best of relationships, they are able to come back and repair the damage. Each person is able to demonstrate the security of the relationship through words, thoughts, and actions. As the first author's grandmother used to say, "A penny for your thoughts is worthless; a dime for your trouble is worth more." Although words and thoughts are important, it's also about choices and actions that support each person's ability to be vulnerable and to be safe doing so. When there are perceived threats to the relationship, insecure partners may feel they are in emotional solitary confinement; however, the partner has the key, and when things work well the partner quickly frees the other partner. They provide each other amnesty even in the most difficult of times.

*When It "Goes Wrong"*

If primary caregivers were not available or did not respond during critical moments in children's lives, the children may doubt that significant others can be relied upon. This lack of faith in caregivers' availability and responsiveness lessens children's feelings of security and bolsters the belief that any attempt at gaining security will lead to disappointment and hurt. Based on early and ongoing interactions, children create an internal model of attachment that will be carried into adulthood and into their romantic relationships.

Couples that form a pair bond and experience relationship distress show remarkably similar reactions to infants separated from their mothers (Johnson, 2004a). When children are separated from their mothers, they typically go through a series of responses starting with protest, moving onto despair, and ending with detachment (Hazan & Shaver, 1987). Similarly, a lack of responsiveness from a partner may cue separation distress, leading to various versions of the protest, fight, flight, or freeze response (Palmer, 2006). When distress and a lack of soothing responsiveness occur repeatedly in a romantic relationship an interactional pattern emerges. Couples become frozen in negative, interactional cycles usually taking the form of a criticize–pursue response from one partner and a placate–withdraw response from the other partner (Johnson, 2004b; Palmer). Once couple distress becomes the rule rather than the exception, negativity becomes a houseguest that doesn't easily leave (Gottman, 1999). During times of couple distress, high levels of negative affect become an absorbing state and are more compelling than positive affect. "Safety first" becomes the relationship rule, and couples stop risking reaching out to one another and connecting (Johnson, 2004b).

Eventually, gone unchecked, these relationship patterns culminate in physical and emotional distance that may lead to relationship dissolution. Gottman (1999) described couples as "living parallel lives" who are in an extreme state of emotional distance and showed that this state predicts divorce. To maintain a strong connection, partners need to know they are a priority to one another, that they matter, and that their needs, wants, and dreams are represented in their partners' thoughts on a day-to-day basis (Fonagy & Target, 1997; Gottman).

## Emotionally Focused Therapy and Attachment Theory

Although a destructive relationship with parents gives rise to an internal working model skewed toward insecurity, couples nevertheless are not necessarily doomed by their experiences with a poisonous parent. Studies have confirmed that between 26 and 61% of people change attachment styles over time (Scharfe, 2003). The salve for past relationship wounds is attachment relationships that provide a secure base and safe haven. The partner who is receptive and emotionally approachable, has low reactiveness, and is attuned to a partner's needs for caregiving may become a source of earned felt security and a secure attachment figure (Palmer, 2006).

As mentioned earlier, attachment theory offers a map for understanding and intervening with individuals and relationships. It focuses on the role of emotion and attachment in affect regulation and people's patterned ways of connecting with others (Johnson, 2004b). While attachment theory points to the general destination, emotionally focused therapy (EFT) is the navigational system that provides clinicians and clients with a step-by-step route to an engaged, compassionate, trustworthy relationship.

EFT is the leading empirically validated form of couples therapy. Research indicates that between 70 and 73% of treated couples recover from distress and that 90% of treated couples are able to significantly improve their relationships when compared with untreated couples (Johnson, Hunsley, Greenberg, & Schindler, 1999). For example, a 2-year follow-up on a relationship study on distress in the parents of chronically ill children, a population at high risk for divorce, indicated most couples maintain their gains or continue to improve in the 2 years following termination of therapy (Cloutier, Manion, Walker, & Johnson, 2002).

EFT integrates systems therapies with experiential and Rogerian therapies. The focus is on the association between the inner experience and internal working models of attachment of both partners to their relational patterns and the association between relational patterns and their inner experience (Johnson, 2004b). The EFT change process can be broken down into three stages and nine steps to assist in creating a secure bond between partners and to create new responses through a focus on emotion (Johnson, 2004b). The stages are (1) deescalation of negative cycles of interaction (steps 1–4); (2) changing interactional positions and creating engagement (steps 5–7); and (3) consolidation and integration (steps 8–9).

**Stage 1: Cycle Deescalation**

1. Develop an alliance, and do basic assessment.
2. Identify the negative cycle.
3. Access primary emotions and attachment needs.
4. Reframe the problem as the negative cycles.

**Stage 2: Changing Interactional Positions and Creating Engagement**

5. Promote identification and expression of primary emotions and attachment needs.
6. Promote acceptance of the other partner's primary emotions and attachment needs and new responses.
7. Facilitate the expression of needs and wants directly to create emotional engagement and bonding events that redefine the attachment between the partners.

**Stage 3: Consolidation and Integration**

8. Facilitate the emergence of new solutions to old relationship problems.
9. Consolidate new positions and new cycles of attachment behaviors.

The process of change in EFT involves three major shifts or change processes. The first is called cycle deescalation and occurs in Stage 1. It involves getting the couple to recognize their cycle and to fight against the cycle, not against each other. The other two shifts occur in Stage 2 and are called withdrawer engagement and pursuer softening. Withdrawer reengagement involves getting the withdrawer to open up and start engaging in the relationship. Pursuer softening involves getting the pursuer to reach, from a position of vulnerability, to an accessible partner (Johnson, 2004b).

## Attachment Injuries

The most common impasses in EFT involve what are called attachment injuries. Attachment injuries represent major relational and therapeutic gridlock that must be worked through for a couple to reconnect and create secure attachment strategies (Johnson, Makinen, & Millikin, 2001). When an attachment injury transpires, the injured party feels abandoned, betrayed, or that trust has been violated by an attachment figure, typically at a time of crucial need or vulnerability. This abandonment or betrayal is not just a deep hurt; it leads the injured party to call into question the partner's devotion and love and the stability of the relationship (Johnson & Whiffen, 1999; Johnson et al., 2001). An attachment injury is more than a general trust issue; it is specifically related to anxiety and fear around a particular event in which a partner was unavailable and unresponsive (Johnson et al., 2001). Attachment injuries, which occur in all relationships, may be magnified by partners having experienced dangerous and unreliable relationships throughout their lifetimes (Johnson et al., 2001; Makinen & Johnson, 2006).

When partners feel their attachment security is threatened, a set of attachment behaviors are triggered with the goal of protecting the attachment bond. If the attachment behaviors are unsuccessful at eliciting the wanted response from the partner (attachment figure), then a set of predictable responses begins, such as anger, relentless pursuit, withdrawal, or hopelessness, that ends with one or both partners in isolation (Naaman, Pappas, Makinen, Zuccarini, & Johnson-Douglas, 2005). Validation, availability, and receptiveness are keys when a relationship crisis arises.

Anyone in a relationship can be overwhelmed by the powerful attachment protest or withdrawal of a partner, and those with a poisonous parent history may have a lower threshold for becoming overwhelmed. Children of poisonous parents will typically experience multiple attachment wounds and injuries growing up. If those injuries are not repaired, they are likely to impact their working models of attachment and thereby impact their adult intimate relationships. Adult children of poisonous parents may be especially prone to feeling attachment wounds, and it may be more difficult to process them. It is analogous to a damaged ligament or joint; once severely hurt it is more prone to injury again in the future. Nevertheless, even those with poisonous parents can work through current attachment wounds and injuries with a responsive partner. Part of working through attachment issues is understanding one's own and one's partner's habitual attachment strategies and how they play into the negative cycles in the relationship. For those who are insecure, there are three main approaches to addressing relationship distress: anxiety, avoidance, or a combination of both (fearful-avoidant).

### *Anxious Strategies*

People who use anxious attachment strategies tend to become clingy, persistent, and aggressive to connect when they feel insecure. Anxiously attached partners long to be close to feel safe and may overwhelm their partner with the need to be reassured. For example, a husband talks to his wife about going on a mission trip to Africa for a week. The wife begins to cry and says, "Why are people always leaving me?" In the next few days, the wife asks the husband over and over again, "Do you really love me? Why don't you seem like you are going to miss me? Why didn't you ask me to come with you?" The husband again explains that he is going there only for a week to help translate and that there is no funding for her to go with him. Instead of the wife discussing her true feelings about being abandoned and not connected to her husband, she pouts, complains, and gets angry. She becomes hypervigilant, looking for any clue that supports her current activated belief that he doesn't really want or love her and that he is trying to leave her.

*Avoidant Strategies*

Avoidant partners have a hard time believing others are trustworthy, open, receptive, safe, and accepting. They distrust their partners and seek to find out their true motives, often believing that their motives are suspicious in nature. They may fear that if their partner really knew them the partner would not love them. Avoidant partners often define themselves as unlovable. Therefore, avoidant partners will often position themselves in relationships to be self-sufficient and emotionally distant from their partners. For example, a wife comes home after a disastrous work day because her boss reprimanded her. When the wife comes home she goes to her room and says nothing to her husband. He attempts to comfort her by saying, "Honey, don't let them bother you." She doesn't reply. She continues as if nothing has happened. Her husband says, "What can I do to help?" The wife shouts back, "I don't need them, and I don't need you. I can take care of myself. I have always taken care of myself, and this time is no different." The wife's fear is activated, and instead of talking with her husband about how disappointed she is and how lonely she feels she decides to distance from her husband and isolate her feelings to protect herself. In the past she couldn't count on anyone, so she doesn't trust that her husband can be there now and thus does not allow herself to need her husband.

*Fearful-Avoidant Strategies*

Fearful-avoidant partners desire to be close to their partners, but they push their partner away when they come near. They have mixed feelings about relationships—they want them, but they are also fearful of being rejected. They vacillate between being overly concerned about the relationship and distancing to pretend they don't need the relationship. For example, a husband reaches out to his wife, wanting reassurance about himself and their relationship. "I'm a good husband, right? Do you like being my wife?" The wife replies, "Of course you are a good husband. Things are not always perfect, but overall I love being your wife." The husband is immediately hurt, and his wife notices his hurt expression. The wife reaches out to rub his back and reassure him. The husband shrugs his shoulders and walks away. Fearful-avoidant partners can be prone to attachment injuries and tend to deal with them by acting detached.

*Model for Healing Injuries (Interventions)*

Once wounds and attachment injuries occur, regardless of people's attachment strategies, the sooner they are resolved the better. Makinen and Johnson (2006) used task analysis to develop an attachment injury resolution model. Resolving attachment wounds and injuries fosters a cycle of engagement and reconciliation. Their model for resolving attachment injuries consists of identifying the attachment injury, reconnecting with the primary emotions of the injured party, reengaging with the partner (offending party), forgiving, and reconciling. Johnson (2008) expanded on this model in her "Six Steps to Forgiveness" in her book *Hold Me Tight: Seven Conversations for a Lifetime of Love.*

*Step 1* In the first step, injured partners tap into the emotional experience related to the attachment injury and describe the incident's effect on relational trust. The hurt partners have to be able to discuss their pain freely, honestly, and simply. Although the injured partners may be rightfully hurt and angry, they should be specific about the incident rather than taking an opportunity to be contemptuous, criticizing, or cynical (Gottman, 1999). Partners expressing their pain are supported in revealing their vulnerability rather being supported in pummeling a partner with a hammer of, "Let me tell you about every hurt that you have caused." Injured parties express fear, sadness, and grief related to the specific incident and how it influenced the attachment bond.

*Step 2* Following the injured party's description of the incident, with the support of the therapist, the offending partner works on being responsive to the other's vulnerability and takes responsibility for the injury. Taking responsibility when someone understands the depth of hurt is partly possible because of the significance of the relationship. Rather than being symbolic of the offending partner's flaws, the depth of hurt represents the importance of the partner. Along with taking responsibility, the offending partners should be empathetic, express regret, and demonstrate remorse. The partner responsible for the injury has to stay present emotionally without being defensive. This is not the time to defend one's actions or lack thereof. Research has shown that being defensive rarely works because defending is a thinly disguised form of attack (Gottman, 1999). Accepting responsibility acknowledges a partner's pain and sends the message, "I hear you, I see you, and I respect you." This is crucial in restoring safety in the relationship.

*Step 3* After the offending partner accepts responsibility, the injured party asks for the comfort and caring that was not accessible during the time of injury. The couple works together toward changing the emotionally laden history by changing what they do in the present. The injured partner moves from a position of, "Never again will I allow you to hurt me or make me feel like a fool," to a position of "I love you, so I am willing to work on restoring our emotional connection."

*Step 4* The offending partner responds to the request for comfort in a caring, warm manner that tranquilizes the previously traumatic experience. Partners who have caused pain take ownership of the injurious event and sincerely apologize. Offending partners concede how their lack of perceived compassion impacted not only the partner but also the state of the relationship. In this process they can't simply say, "I'm sorry," and explain the pain away. They have to put words into action and help their partner heal in an emotionally engaged manner, which is the opposite of what happened when the injury occurred.

*Step 5* Once the offending party sincerely apologizes, the injured party specifically identifies what is needed to bring closure to the event. In communicating with the injured partner, both partners learn how to respond differently from the way they did in the initial distressing event. This step focuses on restructuring the old incident into an opportunity for emotional connection, buffering against the loneliness, disconnection, and fear the event precipitated.

*Step 6* Finally, the couple moves to a place where they can begin rewriting their story. The new story summarizes the attachment injury event that resulted in the destruction of the couple's trust and emotional connection. The couple connects on a higher level that creates a safe haven for both partners. The couple works together on preventing future attachment injuries. New connecting rituals are created, and the couple approaches each other in a loving, supportive manner. The key to this process is understanding forgiveness as an ongoing procedure rather than a one-time event. Some or all of these steps may have to be repeated. Reminding couples that they may have to revisit an injury more than once will help both partners be patient and realistic about healing attachment injuries.

## Case Example

Mike (24) and Sylvia (23) have been dating for 1 year. Mike is Haitian American, lives with his parents, and was working at a local restaurant while applying to schools to become a physician's assistant. Thus far, Mike's scores have not been high enough to get him into the programs he wants. Sylvia is African American, an auditor for a local bank, makes twice the income Mike does, and is getting ready to move out of her parents' house. She wanted Mike to move in with her so neither was under the watchful eye of their parents.

Sylvia originally contacted the counseling agency for premarital counseling to make sure they were well matched. During counseling Sylvia complained that Mike does not always keep promises. He does not want to disappoint anyone, but when he inevitably disappoints Sylvia she becomes angry and reactive and then becomes cold and distant. To soothe Sylvia, Mike makes additional promises even if it is not something he wants or is ready to do. For example, he knows he is not financially stable and that his parents want him to finish school before he marries. However, he promises Sylvia they can marry soon, because she does not want to wait 3–4 more years to marry because she feels like they can get married and she can support Mike financially until he finishes school and gets a good job. However, he keeps putting off setting a date for the wedding and talks a lot about finances.

Mike acquiesces to Sylvia's demands verbally but then does not follow through because of his own needs, parental expectations, and cultural values. He wants to honor his parents, and there is part of Mike that believes he should be at least an equal contributor to their finances. Sylvia believes that Mike is using the financial issue as a way to drag his feet about getting married. "If we love each other, what does it matter if I support us financially for a few years? Isn't that what people in love do?"

Six weeks ago Sylvia found out she was pregnant. Mike was overjoyed about the prospect of becoming a father, but his parents were not happy because they thought a family should be started after he completed school. Mike was still worried about not having a good job. The couple set a wedding date, and Mike was considering other advanced degrees to pursue that would take less time to earn. A few weeks after setting the wedding date, Sylvia miscarried. Shortly afterward, Mike asked if they could postpone the wedding and them moving in together. Sylvia was devastated and felt like Mike had agreed to marry her only because of the baby and that he was going to eventually leave her. She became so enraged at the perceived betrayal that she told him to "come get all of your shit."

Both members of the couple were struggling with attachment injuries. Sylvia's injury related to fear of abandonment from Mike. He kept backing out of his commitment to her, and when they lost the baby (when she needed him to reassure her most) he let her down. In her mind he fulfilled her worst fear—he abandoned her.

Mike, on the other hand, feels that whenever he is honest with Sylvia about his needs she gets very angry, reactive, and punishing. He feels forced to agree to things that he is not ready to agree to. He worries that if he doesn't agree then she will break up with him. So he appeases her in the short run but then ends up disappointing her anyway when he does not fulfill promises he felt coerced to make. When Sylvia gets upset, at first Mike wants to comfort her, but from his perspective her reaction is so severe he is scared to reach out to her and he feels helpless. He feels nothing he does is going to pacify her. "She gets so angry and then so cold and distant. I feel like I am in solitary confinement, and I have to stay there until she decides to let me out. I don't want to be a prisoner." Sylvia stated she doesn't want to be his jailor but is afraid that he will "try to escape."

When Mike and Sylvia came to session, they stated that they wanted to focus on Mike not following through on moving in with Sylvia. Interestingly, neither had processed the loss of the baby. The first time they discussed emotions related to the loss was in session. The first half of the session was spent discussing her frustration at Mike not moving in with her and his feeling overwhelmed by her angry reaction. Eventually, the therapist moved the conversation to the underlying feelings of loss, fear, and feelings of abandonment.

*Mike:* These last 6 weeks have been filled with the highest of the highs and lowest of the lows. I don't have a job anymore. I quit the restaurant so I could look for a better job and study. I don't want to go back to the restaurant. I want to find financial stability. In the last 6 weeks I found out that Sylvia was pregnant, and I had no job and no insurance.

*Therapist:* (Speaking softly and slowly) Did you tell her what that was like for you? "I don't have the money for an ultrasound."

Mike looks surprised and then begins to rub his face and cry. Sylvia gets out of her seat and sits in his lap and begins to rub his back. Mike begins to sob while holding Sylvia, and Sylvia continues to sit in his lap and rub his back.

*Sylvia:* I never made him feel bad about not having insurance.

*Therapist:* But that didn't stop him from feeling that way.

Mike continues to cry and clings to Sylvia.

*Sylvia:* (whispers) Let it out baby; let it out.

*Therapist:* Mike, what do you want her to know? What do you want to let her know at this moment?

*Mike:* I am not where I want to be. I just feel weak and like I have nothing to offer. I want to give and offer stability. I don't want everything to be on her shoulders. I have tried to let her take all of the responsibility, but I just can't. I can't move forward right now.

I can't have nothing to offer again. I could have possibly prevented bad things from happening if I was where I should be.

*Therapist:* Like preventing losing the baby?

*Mike:* Yes, I fear not being able to give—I don't want to go through this again.... I don't want to.

*Therapist:* So when you suffered that loss you went into problem-solving mode and tried to make some things happen?

*Mike:* Right. Right.

Sylvia, still sitting in Mike's lap, begins to cry.

*Sylvia:* Okay, I understand. I understand where his heart is. I can respect it. I want to respect it. I don't want him feeling like that.

*Therapist:* Did you know that he carried the death on his heart like that?

*Sylvia:* No.

*Therapist:* What about you? What are you carrying on your heart? You don't want to lose him.

*Sylvia:* No.

*Therapist:* The thought of losing him scares you. When you are scared your anger comes out. It's weird. When you love someone like that you sometimes behave in ways that you never thought you would. Because something about Mike does make you feel safe and that scares you a little. That feeling of safety is something that you are not familiar with.

*Sylvia:* Yeah. It scares me sometimes. I don't want to lose him.

*Mike:* Yeah, I am the oldest boy in my family. I am supposed to be the one who takes care of others.

*Therapist:* Yeah, and in some ways Sylvia wants you to take care of her, too.

*Mike:* Yeah.

*Therapist:* But you don't think you can do that right now to the best of your ability, and you don't want to keep letting her down.

*Mike:* Yeah. Even though I want to be with her and I want to live with her, I would rather stay at my parents' house until I can be an equal partner—until I have the ability to take care of her if something goes wrong. I don't want to be separate from her, but I would rather be separate and concentrate on what I need to do than fail her.

*Sylvia:* But I want to take care of you until you finish school.

*Mike:* That's not how I was raised, and I think part of you will resent it in the future. That's great that I can need you and you can take care of me, but I can't do the same. Because that's a true partnership ... both people can take care of each other.

*Sylvia:* But that's what a marriage is. Sometimes one person has to take care of the other.

Sylvia reaches over and puts her hand on Mike's leg. Mike puts his hand over hers and squeezes it.

*Mike:* Yes, for the unexpected that's fine. But we shouldn't go into a marriage where you know you are going to have to take care of the other person. I don't want that, and you shouldn't want that. That doesn't mean I don't want you. I do want you. I want you, I need you, and I want to be able to take care of you when you need me. I don't want to ever feel as helpless as I have in the last few weeks. I couldn't be there for you or for our baby like I should have. (Pause)

*Therapist:* It has been a rough evening. I thank both of you for sharing. In the next week I want the two of you to not focus on decisions. I want you to focus on being honest when the two of you are tempted to push each other away. I want you to look at each other's hearts. Mike, when you look at Sylvia I want you to remember that sometimes her anger is really about her fear. She is afraid of losing you. Sylvia, his fear is not being a provider, not being able to take care of you and be responsive when you need him. You two have been really honest tonight and spoke from your hearts.

Sylvia went back and sat on Mike's lap. They held each other for a minute and murmured softly to one another. Mike wiped away Sylvia's tears, and she wiped away his. They were both vulnerable with each other, and both took care of one another. After a few minutes of holding one another, they both indicated that they were ready to end the session.

During the session Mike was able to describe the incident of losing their baby and the fact that she didn't understand the he was not able to protect her and the baby. He was able to process the event with Sylvia honestly and emotionally. Mike started the process of being vulnerable with Sylvia by expressing his fear of not being able to provide for his family. Initially Sylvia wasn't able to take responsibility: "I never made him feel bad about not having insurance." Later she was able to acknowledge Mike's pain: "I understand. I understand where his heart is. I can respect it. I want to respect it. I don't want him feeling like that." Here Sylvia was telling Mike, "I hear you, I see you, and I respect you." Sylvia is now acknowledging Mike's vulnerability instead of her need for the reassurance of being married or moving in together. In the session Sylvia was able to offer comfort that she wasn't able to offer due to her preoccupation with her own needs for reassurance and safety. Sylvia comforted Mike by sitting in his lap, holding him, and encouraging him to "let it out" and be vulnerable in her presence. Without Sylvia's anger present they began the process of restoring safety in the relationship.

Sylvia's original story was, "Mike doesn't love me enough to commit to me." So when Mike did or said something that triggered her fear of losing him she cried out in an angry protest and pushed him away if she didn't get the response she needed. Since she expressed anger, Mike tended to respond to this emotion with his own fear instead of responding to her fear, which is what she really needed soothed. After processing Mike's pain, she understood that his fear was not related to commitment. Rather, his fear was about not being a good partner who could contribute to the relationship and be what she wanted, needed, and deserved. She saw that his fear was rooted in his love for her, which made all the difference.

## Conclusion

Poisonous parents impinge, negatively, on children's internal working model of relationships. Although an insecure attachment style makes having healthy, adult relationships more difficult, individuals can alter their attachment strategies through experiences with trustworthy, responsive individuals. Nevertheless, regardless of how secure a relationship is, attachment injuries will occur. Understanding attachment needs, how to repair events that damage attachment, and forgiving one another is an important part of maintaining a secure relationship and is a major component of EFT. Emotionally focused therapy is a powerful, empirically validated approach for healing distressed relationships in the present and helping people deal with the effects of poisonous relationships from the past. This model assists couples, families, and individuals in healing relational wounds and developing long-lasting, secure relationships. More information about EFT can be found at www.iceeft.com.

## References

Bowlby, J. (1969). *Attachment and loss: Vol. 1, Attachment.* New York: Basic Books.

Bowlby, J. (1973). *Attachment and loss: Vol. 2, Separation: Anger and anxiety.* New York: Basic Books.

Cassidy, J., & Shaver, P. R. (Eds.). (2008). *Handbook of attachment: Theory, research,* and *clinical applications,* 2nd ed. New York: Guilford Press.

Cowen, N. J., Muir, E., & Lojkasek, M. (2003). The first couple: Using watch, wait, and wonder to change troubled infant–mother relationships. In S. M. Johnson & V. E. Whiffen (Eds.), *Attachment processes in couple and family therapy* (pp. 215–233). New York: Guilford Press.

Cloutier, P. F., Manion, I. G., Walker, J. G., & Johnson, S. M. (2002). Emotionally focused interventions for couples with chronically ill children: A 2-year follow-up. *Journal of Marital and Family Therapy, 28*(4), 391–398.

Fonagy, P., & Target, M. (1997). Attachment and reflective function: Their role in self-organization. *Development and Psychopathology, 9,* 670–700.

Gottman, J. M. (1999). *The marriage clinic: A scientifically based marital therapy.* New York: W. W. Norton.

Gottman, J. M., & Silver, N. (1998). *The seven principles for making marriage work: A practical guide from the country's foremost relationship expert.* New York: Three Rivers Press.

Greenberg, L. S., & Paivio, S. C. (1997). *Working with emotions in psychotherapy.* New York: Guilford Press.

Hazan, C., & Shaver, P. (1987). Romantic love conceptualized as an attachment process. *Journal of Personality and Social Psychology, 52*(3), 511–524.

Johnson, S. M. (2002). *Emotionally focused couple therapy with trauma survivors: Strengthening attachment bonds.* New York: Guilford Press.

Johnson, S. M. (2004a). Attachment theory: A guide for healing couple relationships. In W. S. Rholes & J. A. Simpson (Eds.), *Adult attachment: Theory, research, and clinical implications* (pp. 367–387). New York: Guilford.

Johnson, S. M. (2004b). *The practice of emotionally focused couple therapy,* 2nd ed. New York: Brunner-Routledge.

Johnson, S. M. (2007). A new era for couple therapy: Theory, research, and practice in concert. *Journal of Systemic Therapies, 26*(4), 5–16.

Johnson, S. M. (2008). *Hold me tight: Seven conversations for a lifetime of love.* New York: Little, Brown.

Johnson, S. M., & Greenman, P. S. (2006). The path to a secure bond: Emotionally focused couple therapy. *Journal of Clinical Psychology, 62*(5), 597–609.

Johnson, S. M., Hunsley, J., Greenberg, L., & Schindler, D. (1999). Emotionally focused couples therapy: Status & challenges. *Clinical Psychology: Science & Practice, 6,* 67–79.

Johnson, S. M., Makinen, J. A., & Millikin, J. W. (2001). Attachment injuries in couple relationships: A new perspective on impasses in couples therapy. *Journal of Marital & Family Therapy, 27*(2), 145–155.

Johnson, S. M., & Whiffen, V. E. (1999). Made to measure: Adapting emotionally focused couple therapy to partners' attachment styles. *Clinical Psychology: Science and Practice,* 6(4), 366–381.

Johnson, S. M., & Williams-Keeler, L. (1998). Creating healing relationships for couples dealing with trauma: The use of emotionally focused marital therapy. *Journal of Marital & Family Therapy, 24*(1), 25–40.

Kirkpatrick, L. A., & Davis, K. E. (1994). Attachment style, gender, and relationship stability: A longitudinal analysis. *Journal of Personality and Social Psychology, 66,* 502–512.

Makinen, J. A., & Johnson, S. M. (2006). Resolving attachment injuries in couples using emotionally focused therapy: Steps toward forgiveness and reconciliation. *Journal of Consulting and Clinical Psychology, 74*(6), 1055–1064.

Naaman, S., Pappas, J. D., Makinen, J., Zuccarini, D., & Johnson-Douglas, S. (2005). Treating attachment injured couples with emotionally focused therapy: A case study approach. *Psychiatry: Interpersonal and Biological Processes, 68*(1), 55–77.

Palmer, G. (2006). Couple attachment: Love does have something to do with it. *Family Therapy Magazine, 5*(5), 21–23.

Schachner, D. A., Shaver, P. R., & Mikulincer, M. (2003). Adult attachment theory, psychodynamics, and couple relationships. In S. M. Johnson & V. E. Whiffen (Eds.), *Attachment processes in couple and family therapy* (pp. 18–42). New York: Guilford Press.

Scharfe, E. (2003). Stability and change of attachment representations from cradle to grave. In S. Johnson & V. Whiffen (Eds.), *Attachment processes in couple and family therapy* (pp. 64–84). New York: Guilford Press.

CHAPTER 6

# Couples Relationships

LEN SPERRY

Much of this book focuses on the parent–child and parent–adult child relationship. Why is this relationship so important, and what are other key relationships in one's life? For children, the parent–child relationship is the building block for individual and relational health. Views of oneself and expectations for relationships are born from early caretaker relationships. For adults, the mechanism for testing one's view of self and others is often romantic relationships. Adults whose parents had a poisonous pedagogy (discussed in Chapter 1) learn how to love and be loved in ways, without intervention, that are likely to be damaging to adult, romantic relationships and one's sense of self. While the parent–child relationship is pivotal for early development, the couple subsystem provides fertile ground for testing and revising views of oneself, relationships, and the larger world.

Adult children of poisonous parents are likely to have unrealistic expectations for the relationship, to have less flexibility to negotiate relationship transitions, and to have exaggerated reactions to desires for dependence and independence than individuals who had healthier relationships with their parents. Individuals may pursue romantic relationships to fulfill their desires for connection, stability, and balance that were unmet by their parents. Although these couples may want to do things differently than their own parents, children of poisonous parents are prone to having poisonous relationships with their partners and children.

Romantic relationships can bring out the best and worst in people. Needs and patterns of getting them may become exaggerated, especially in poisonous couples. Couples' tolerance for variation in getting needs met may be problematic, particularly after the "honeymoon" phase of the relationship ends. How easily needs can be fulfilled, or even if they can, depends on how couples navigate their relationship transitions. Successfully moving through transitional stages relies on their emotional and cognitive flexibility, their ability to balance needs for independence and dependence, and their ability to maintain clear boundaries between themselves as couples and other systems. A comprehensive picture of a couple integrates a developmental, individual, and systemic perspectives. Consequently, the clinician must have the capacity to intervene both with individual symptoms and with system dynamics.

In addition to assessing and intervening in the couple dynamics, as mentioned already, the clinician needs to address past and future familial patterns. On the surface, coupling is the joining of two individuals, but coupling actually represents the merging of two individuals and their various relationships, histories, expectations, and hopes for the future. From a systemic perspective, the couple unit is one small subsystem among a large interconnected family system. The couple bridges at least two families of origin and their rules, relationships, and cultures. When the romantic relationship, whether it is brief or long term, results in children, it is also one of the devices for passing relational patterns and quality of relationships to the next generation.

In this chapter, the conditions and circumstances that prompt the development and maintenance of a toxic or poisonous relationship (hereafter referred to as "couples toxicity" and "poisonous couple") between both partners in a committed couple's relationship are considered. Left unchecked, such couples toxicity can severely impact the couple's relationship, the parent–child relationship, and the subsequent relationships of the partners' adult children. Unless an antidote can be created to counteract couples toxicity, that couple's relationship (and other familial relationships) is doomed to suffer and ultimately fail. This chapter begins with a description of various models for understanding the phenomenon of the poisonous couple. This couple is situated and distinguished from other couples in which toxicity is limited or not present.

Accordingly, the poisonous couple is examined from several frameworks, including developmental stages and levels of competence or functionality. Then, the chapter moves on to describe a number of intervention strategies that can modify this relational dynamic. Case material illustrates key points in the discussion. Unlike other chapters in this book, which focus primarily on parent–child relationships, this chapter focuses largely on partner–partner relationships.

### Understanding the Poisonous Couple

This section describes five explanatory models for conceptualizing poisonous couple relationships: (1) intimacy deficits; (2) four horsemen (i.e., predictors of toxicity and divorce); (3) psychopathology; (4) parental alienation; and (5) systemic dynamics. Each of these is described briefly in this section.

#### *Intimacy Deficits*

Marriage involves a close intimate relationship. It is a relationship in which the partners strive to know and trust one another and share deep personal information without fear of ridicule or reprisal. Psychological safety is the precondition for intimacy, and unless partners make it safe for the other to be themselves mature intimacy is impossible (Hendrix, 1988/2008). Because mature intimacy demands trust, deep sharing, and vulnerability, relatively few couples experience mature intimacy as an ongoing, sustained state. The reality is that most couples experience it only episodically and imperfectly, if at all (Welwood, 2005). In this section three different views of intimacy deficits are reviewed: mature versus immature intimacy; marital stages; and couples competence.

*Mature Versus Immature Intimacy* Welwood (2005) distinguishes mature or perfect love and intimacy from immature love and intimacy. Distinguishing between mature and immature intimacy is useful for understanding the type of intimacy expected in couples relationships versus other familial relationships. Mature intimacy is marked by mutuality—an ability for both people to appropriately meet the emotional needs of the other. For example, husband–wife relationships are capable of mature intimacy, whereas mother–child relationships are not. A child should not be expected to meet the emotional and psychological safety needs of a parent.

As noted previously, ongoing trust, psychological safety, vulnerability, and deep sharing characterize mature intimacy, whereas a deficit in one or more of these or the inability to sustain them is reflective of immature intimacy. Beavers (1985) added that equal and mutual sharing of power is characteristic of mature intimacy. Obviously, couples relationships can be characterized by immature intimacy, despite their capacity to relate maturely. Again, very few couples experience sustained, mature intimacy, and poisonous couples are certainly not capable of such intimacy.

*Marital Stages* A developmental model of the four stages of a marital relationship has been described by Sperry (1978; Sperry & Carlson, 1991; Sperry, Carlson, & Peluso, 2006). These stages are described in terms of the developmental process of growth from the symbiotic-like quality of new relationships through other stages requiring considerable growth and differentiation of both partners in terms of intimacy. Four stages distinguish various points on this developmental journey: dependence, counterdependence, independence, and interdependence. Most couples begin at the first and quickly move to the second, where they may become stuck for a long time and may not proceed beyond this stage without significant personal and relational growth, often requiring effective therapy to continue on this journey. It is at this stage that toxicity is most evident and that poisonous couples are liable to remain stuck.

*Dependence* In this stage, which spans first attraction to the end of the honeymoon, both individuals seek a sense of mutual completeness, symbiotic striving, and total happiness, which they wrongly and blindly assume is achieved simply by being in the presence of the other. In the beginning the myth that a partner "completes me" provides a sense of security, but as that person fails to live up to the fantasy each partner becomes disillusioned. Both poisonous and couples with little toxicity begin in the dependence stage, but poisonous couples may be using the dependence stage as a way to heal hurts from the parental relationship. In addition, the potential loss of a "perfect partner" may be more devastating for couples who do not have strong connections to family members or friends. As one or both relinquish their allegiance to this myth, the relationship shifts to the next stage.

*Counterdependence* Also called negative independence, the counterdependence stage is marked by disillusion, discontent, and discord. Here couples alternate between blaming and relinquishment of personal responsibility. Couples reflect their discontent directly by demanding, fighting, and competing with each other or more indirectly with passive aggressiveness or leading lives of unhappiness and quiet desperation. Efforts at autonomy are in stark conflict with mutuality, and thus infidelity, divorce, and separation are common at this stage.

*Independence* The independence stage, also called positive independence, is marked by the recognition that demands for mutual completeness and total happiness are unrealistic. The fantasy of mutual completeness is replaced by acceptance that growth in autonomy, self-knowledge, self-disclosure, and self-differentiation are necessary for growth and intimacy. This is a transitional stage in which the need for autonomy and mutuality are recognized but only tentatively met.

*Interdependence* The interdependence stage is marked by the integration of autonomy and mutuality. Both partners develop and express a heightened sensitivity to the rhythmic pattern of pain and joy in a relationship and can more easily forgive and risk sharing their deepest fears and longing. Needless to say, relational satisfaction is high as both partners grow and develop the uncompleted parts of their selves and have no need for the symbiotic striving that characterized their initial attraction to one another.

*Couples Competence* The Global Assessment of Relationship Functioning (GARF) scale is a clinician-rated instrument for assessing couple and family functioning on a continuum from optimal to severely disturbed (American Psychiatric Association, 2000). In his book *Successful Marriage*, Beavers (1985) described five levels of competence among couples, similar to the five ranges of functioning of GARF. These levels range from the severely disturbed, borderline, midrange, and adequate to the optimal level of competence. He noted that partners typically come from families with about the same degree of distance, trust, and toleration of intimacy. Furthermore, he noted that individuals tended to marry partners who had similar family rules regarding distance and intimacy. These levels of couples functioning are briefly described along with a notation of the emotional climate dimension of GARF at the corresponding range of functioning.

*Severe* Among couples rated as severe, coherence and hope were the primary deficiencies, although enmeshment, lack of gratification, nonexistent choice, and unresolved ambivalence also characterized these couples. Couples with enmeshed styles tended to deny the need for warmth and closeness, whereas those with more detached styles tended to deny anger and a desire for separateness. Beavers noted that being loving meant both partners believed they had to think and feel the same way. Psychosis was occasionally an issue in severely disturbed marriages, and in addition to medication couples work focused on relationships, communication, boundaries, and choice. Triangulation, particularly involving the couple, a parent, or a child, was ordinarily tenacious and persistent in these couples (Beavers & Hampson, 2003). Little, if any, sense of attachment, commitment, or concern about partners' welfare is noted in the corresponding range of GARF (American Psychiatric Association, 2000).

*Borderline* The most difficult couples to treat, comprising about 40% of Beaver's (1985) practice and usually having had several previous treatment experiences, were borderline couples. These couples were identified with an extreme concern with control, often of a bizarre nature. Borderline couples with detached styles were unlikely to remain in treatment after a crisis was settled, whereas those with enmeshed styles tended to be involved in more intensive treatment, and a central issue in therapy was the power struggle (Beavers & Hampson, 2003). Significant ongoing, unresolved conflict and sexual dysfunction is noted on the corresponding range of GARF (American Psychiatric Association, 2000). Most poisonous couples are likely to be rated in the borderline and severe range and are less likely to be rated in the midrange or higher levels of functioning.

*Midrange* Beavers (1985) noted that the midrange group comprised about 40% of the couples in his practice and were the easiest and most gratifying to treat. As with other types of couples, the midrange couples with detached styles seldom needed long-term treatment, whereas those with more enmeshed styles were less demoralized. He also noted that these couples had more successful experiences with intimacy than severely disturbed or borderline couples. With these couples, Beavers tied the control issue to the intimacy issue and helped the individuals to see that intimidation was a method that ultimately reduced and eliminated any possibility of intimacy (Beavers & Hampson, 2003). Pain, anger, or emotional deadness interferes with couples enjoyment, and troublesome sexual difficulties are noted in the corresponding range of GARF (American Psychiatric Association, 2000).

*Adequate* Unlike couples at the preceding three levels of functioning, adequate couples are able to reasonably communicate and deal with their problems, although some conflicts remain unresolved without disrupting couples and family functioning. If they seek out couples therapy it is typically situationally specific (e.g., death in family, job loss; Beavers & Hampson, 2003). Caring, warmth, and sharing are mixed with frustration or tensions, with some reduced or problematic sexual activity noted in the corresponding range of GARF (American Psychiatric Association, 2000).

*Optimal* Couples at the optimal level rarely seek couples therapy because of their level of differentiation and competence. These couples have the capacity to experience intimacy on an ongoing basis (Beavers & Hampson, 2003). Optimism, caring, warmth, and sharing are present, and satisfactory sexual relations are noted on the corresponding range of GARF (American Psychiatric Association, 2000).

In terms of intimacy, the differences between mature and immature intimacy have been distinguished, four stages of couple relational development described, and five levels of couple functioning explained. Poisonous couples are incapable of mature intimacy, become predictably stuck at the second stage, and probably function in the borderline and severe levels of couple functioning.

*Four Horsemen*

Anger is commonly believed to be the root cause of unhappy and poisonous relationships. Yet research concludes that it is not conflict itself that is the problem but how it is handled (Gottman, 1999). For example, venting anger constructively can, in fact, clear the air and rebalance a relationship. However, conflict becomes problematic when it is characterized by the presence of the so-called four horsemen of the apocalypse: criticism, contempt, defensiveness, and stonewalling (Gottman & Silvers, 1999).

*Criticism* Criticism involves attacking a partner's personality or character rather than focusing on the specific bothersome behavior. Airing disagreements are healthier than attacking a partner's personality. This is the difference between saying, "I'm upset that you didn't take out the trash," and, "I can't believe you didn't take out the trash. You're just so irresponsible." Research indicates that women are more likely to use this horseman during conflicts (Gottman & Silvers, 1999).

*Contempt* Contempt is one step up from criticism and involves tearing down or being insulting toward the partner and is an unmistakable indicator of disrespect and disgust. Examples include putting down one's spouse, eye rolls, sneering, and mockery. It is the most corrosive of the four horsemen and is seldom, if ever, found in healthy marriages. Gottman's research indicates that contempt is the single best predictor of divorce (Gottman, 1999).

*Defensiveness* Adopting a defensive stance in the midst of conflict may be a natural response, but it comes at the price of diminishing the relationship. When partners are defensive, they often experience a great deal of tension and have difficulty tuning in to what is being said. Examples of defensiveness include denying responsibility, making excuses, or meeting one complaint with another (Gottman, 1999).

*Stonewalling* Partners who stonewall simply refuse to respond. While occasional stonewalling can be healthy, stonewalling as a typical way of interacting, especially during conflict, can be destructive to the marriage. Ongoing stonewalling diminishes a marriage rather than enriches it. Research indicates that men tend to engage in stonewalling much more often than women (Gottman, 1999).

All couples engage in these types of behaviors at some point in their marriage, but when the four horsemen take permanent residence, the relationship is increasingly likely to fail. Gottman's (1999) research reveals that the chronic presence of these four factors in a relationship predicts, with about 85% accuracy, which couples will eventually divorce. When attempts to repair the damage done by these horsemen are met with repeated rejection, the likelihood of divorce increases to more than 90% (Gottman, 1999). It may be especially important to target these behaviors in couples who have had poisonous parents. Children of poisonous parents are likely to use extreme coping mechanisms under distress. They will use aggressive, disparaging methods such as criticism and contempt or distancing, self-protective methods such as defensiveness and stonewalling.

*Psychopathology*

Psychopathology in one partner can be useful in understanding couples toxicity. The diagnoses in the *Diagnostic and Statistical Manual of Mental Disorders,* 4th edition, text revised (*DSM-IV-TR;* American Psychiatric Association, 2000) of psychosis, paranoid personality disorder, borderline personality disorder, narcissistic personality disorder, antisocial personality disorder, and histrionic personality disorder have been observed in one partner when couples toxicity is manifest (Andritzky, 2006; Gardner, 1998, 2006). While some poisonous partners may meet the diagnostic criteria for one or more of these disorders, most partners do not. Accordingly, the psychopathology model provides only limited explanatory power in understanding this phenomenon.

*Parental Alienation Syndrome*

Parental alienation syndrome (PAS) can be a viable explanation for couples toxicity. Richard A. Gardner, MD, described PAS as a diagnostic entity (2001a). It is defined as "…a disorder that arises primarily in the context of child-custody disputes. Its primary manifestation is the child's campaign of denigration against the parent, a campaign that has no justification. The disorder results from the combination of indoctrinations by the alienating parent and the child's own contributions to the vilification of the alienated parent" (Gardner, 2001b, p. 61). Initially, Gardner described the mother as the alienator in 90% of PAS cases but later found that both parents were equally likely to alienate. He also notes that accusations of sexual abuse are not present in the vast majority of cases of PAS (Gardner, 2001a).

Parental alienation syndrome is characterized by a cluster of nine symptoms observed in the child (Gardner, 1998):

- A campaign of denigration against the targeted parent and may include a false sex abuse accusation
- Weak, frivolous, or absurd rationalizations for the deprecation
- Lack of ambivalence about the targeted parent
- Strong assertions that the decision to reject the parent is theirs alone
- The independent thinker phenomenon

- Reflexive support of the favored parent in the conflict
- Lack of guilt over the treatment of the alienated parent
- Use of borrowed scenarios and phrases from the alienating parent
- The spread of the animosity to the extended family and friends of the alienated parent

"While the diagnosis of PAS is based on the assessed level of the *child's* symptoms, the court's decision for *custodial transfer* should be based primarily on the *alienator's* symptom level" (Gardner, 2006, p. 9). Such symptoms include severe psychopathology, episodes of hysteria, and frequency of complaints to the police and child protective services agencies (Gardner).

Three levels of severity of PAS have been described: mild, moderate, and severe. The number and severity of the nine symptoms displayed increase through the different levels, and treatment and management recommendations differ according to the severity level of the child's symptoms. Gardner (2006) contends that any change in custody should be based primarily on the symptom level of the alienating parent. In mild cases, there is some parental programming against the targeted parent, but typically there is little or no disruption of visitation, and court-ordered visitations are usually not recommended. In moderate cases, there is more parental programming and greater resistance to visits with the targeted parent. Accordingly, the recommendation is usually that primary custody remains with the programming parent if the brainwashing is expected to stop, but, if not, that custody is transferred to the targeted parent. Furthermore, individual therapy with the child is recommended to stop alienation and remediate the damaged relationship with the targeted parent. In severe cases, children will display most or all of the symptoms and typically will refuse to visit the targeted parent. This may include threats to run away or commit suicide if the visitation is forced. Here the recommendation is removal of the child from the alienating parent's home into a transition home before moving into the home of the targeted parent. Also, individual therapy for the child is recommended (Gardner, 2006).

PAS is not currently a diagnosis in *DSM-IV-IR*, nor is it an ICD-9 code (International Classification of Diseases, 9th revision). However, there is considerable effort to achieve these designations. A special issue of the *American Journal of Family Therapy* titled "Proposal That Parental Alienation Be Accepted as a Diagnosis" (Bernet, von Boch-Galhaus, Baker, & Morrison, 2010) makes a reasonably compelling case for PAS being included as a *DSM-V* diagnosis.

### *System Dynamics*

Conceptualizing poisonous couples relationships in terms of immature intimacy, contempt, psychopathology in one spouse, or PAS can be useful but provides only limited clinical value in understanding couples toxicity because the explanation largely involves individual dynamics. On the other hand, conceptualizing toxicity in terms of systemic dynamics provides greater clinical value since a marital relationship is a system (and is embedded in a larger family system). Since systemic perspectives can be integrative, such a view can encompass some or all of the features of the previous other four models. Couples toxicity does not arise and manifest in a vacuum but rather as an interactive phenomenon encompassing individual dynamics as well as systemic dynamics. These family, or systemic, dynamics include homeostasis, circularity–reciprocity, boundaries, myths, scapegoating, and interlocking psychopathologies.

*Homeostasis* In systems language, homeostasis identifies the manner by which systems regulate and maintain sufficient balance to ensure their survival. Healthy as well as maladaptive interactions are regulated in the family system. Families can remain in balance in the face of dramatic symptoms such as violence, substance dependence, or depression. However, situations such as parental separation and divorce often stress a system such that prior balance cannot be maintained. Nevertheless, parents struggle to form a new postseparation or postdivorce system, and attain a new sense of balance that incorporates past PAS, psychopathology, and intimacy issues.

*Circularity* Circularity refers to the reciprocal influence and manner in which specific behaviors or issues exert an interactive impact on all members of a system. Reciprocity defines the interactive component of circularity by which one member's behavior will not only impact the other members but also will elicit an emotional or behavioral reaction from each. For example, a father may say to his daughter, "I'm sorry you had to put up with your mother's outbursts during your visit with her." The daughter might reciprocate by saying, "And she yelled at me when we went to the store, and I started to cry I was so scared."

*Boundaries* Boundaries are the invisible lines that separate members from one another. Boundaries range from being too diffuse to excessively rigid. When boundaries are too diffuse, family members can become overinvolved or enmeshed with another, such as when external figures like grandparents are allowed to become too intrusive or involved. Boundaries can be excessively rigid, and members become insufficiently connected or disengaged from one another. Ideally, boundaries are balanced between these two extremes as well as flexible. Sometimes, a coalition (i.e., a boundary that separates or excludes one or more members from another) may form as a protection against a perceived enemy. For example, following marital separation, a mother and daughter may form a coalition against the husband/father. This not only creates distance from the husband/father but also creates a negative perception of him.

*Myths*

Myths refer to central themes involving beliefs about life that are shared by all members. These shared beliefs can be adaptive or maladaptive. For example, a common PAS myth shared by mother and child is, "Daddy is a bad man, and we cannot trust him anymore. So we need to stick together to protect ourselves from him."

*Scapegoating* Scapegoating is a process in which anger or aggression is displaced onto another, usually less powerful family member because the scapegoater believes it is too dangerous to directly confront a member who is considered to be more powerful. For example, if the marital relationship is difficult or unstable, a child may be scapegoated to redirect partner stress, or the scapegoating is directed toward the alienated parent instead of a child.

*Interlocking Pathologies* It is not uncommon to observe that the psychopathology of one marital partner complements or interlocks with the other partner's psychopathology or that it may have antagonistic effects. It has been observed that "the greater the potential pathology of the inducing parent, the greater will be the intensity, power, and insidiousness of the PAS" (Andritzky, 2006, p. 232). Similarly, some forms of psychopathology may be shared by both partners (Ackerman, 1956). The *DSM-IV-TR* (American Psychiatric Association, 2000) lists one such shared disorder, shared psychotic disorder 297.3, also known as *folie a deux*. When this psychotic disorder exists in a marriage, a delusion develops in one partner after the other partner has an already-established delusion. Interlocking personality disorders are not uncommon in poisonous couples.

For example, one partner may meet diagnostic criteria for histrionic personality disorder while the other meets diagnostic criteria for the obsessive compulsive personality disorder (Sperry & Maniacci, 1998). Until the mid 1980s, the most common interlocking relational pattern presenting for couples therapy involved an obsessional partner having conflict with a histrionic partner. The dynamics of the histrionic pattern are the opposite of the obsessive-compulsive pattern and so was the basis of the individuals' attraction to each other in the dependence relational stage. Not surprisingly, this interlocking pattern set the stage for significant relational conflict as the couple moved into the counterdependence stage (Sperry & Maniacci).

In sum, a systemic explanation of couples toxicity can offer a more comprehensive and clinically valuable explanation than any of the previous individual-oriented explanations. Largely because the systemic explanation integrates much from the other models, this understanding provides a broadened perspective for planning specific clinical interventions.

## Assessment of the Poisonous Couple

The assessment of couples toxicity can be reasonably straightforward or quite difficult and perplexing because of the complexity of dynamics involved. However, guided by the previously described models, the clinician can effectively assess the presenting situation. The clinician who is likely to be successful in effecting positive change will need to undertake a comprehensive assessment. Such an assessment will evaluate couples with regard to both individual dynamics as well as systemic dynamics.

To begin the assessment, the clinician can conduct a systematic evaluation of individual dynamics. This includes an evaluation of couples' intimacy (mature vs. immature); their stage of development; their level of functioning; the presence of the four horsemen (i.e., criticism, contempt, defensiveness, stonewalling); psychopathology; and (if couples have children) the presence of PAS symptoms and level of severity.

With regard to systemic dynamics, the clinician can evaluate factors such as homeostasis, circularity, boundaries, myths, scapegoating, and interlocking pathologies. Since these system dynamics are interrelated, identifying one often leads to the identification of others. For example, *scapegoating* evolves to relieve stress and conflict by directing emotional reactions away from one part of the system to another. Whatever the problematic situation, one partner focuses attention on a particular behavior or trait of the other partner. This scapegoating can "pull" children, in-laws, and others into an evolving *myth*, no matter how unsubstantiated, that the other partner is the cause of marital discord or family problems and of the partner's *psychopathology* or emotional symptoms and reactions, including the four horsemen. Through the dynamics of *circularity*, the partner forms a coalition with one of the children or extended family members. These individuals begin to internalize and share among themselves the anger, hurt, alienation, and disaffection toward the other partner. These feelings and attitudes become a "reality," which serves to rebalance or establish a new *homeostasis*. Subsequently, new *boundaries* are established. These boundaries effectively close off the system to outside feedback that contradicts the new myth that has evolved. The result is that the other partner is perceived as bad, untrustworthy, and the cause of the couple's or family's problems and demise.

## Treatment Challenge

The treatment challenge with poisonous couples involves reducing symptomatic distress and minimizing relational discord in the short term. In the long term, the challenge involves neutralizing the transmission of the toxic couples effect from one generation to the next. The intervention strategies described in the next section can be useful with both short-term and long-terms goals, particularly the short-term ones.

## Intervention Strategies

Clinicians who work with poisonous couples are advised that certain strategies that may work in other situations are unlikely to be successful. The first ineffective strategy involves trying to undermine coalitions formed with children or extended family members. Efforts to question and challenge the *myth* and the related beliefs of the offending partner are likely to only reinforce the myth and those beliefs. The second ineffective strategy involves trying to challenge the offending partner in a direct confrontation or power struggle. Like the first ineffective strategy, such direct confrontations only complicate and reinforce maladaptive system dynamics.

Instead, based on the comprehensive assessment, the clinician would do well to develop an integrative case conceptualization based on both individual and system dynamics. This conceptualization recognizes that both individual and system dynamics have led to the current situation and that both sets of dynamics must be considered in the change process. This conceptualization will also recognize that interlocking pathologies are likely to be embedded in the structure of couples' relationships and interactions while symptomatically being expressed and that these interlocking pathologies define the homeostasis or balance of the relationship system. Furthermore, the clinician must have the capacity to provide multiple levels of intervention simultaneously (i.e., working directly with individual symptoms) while working directly with system dynamics.

Following are some intervention strategies that may be useful in working with poisonous couples. They have been adapted from Everett (2006). These interventions are largely systemic in focus, given that couples toxicity is engendered primarily by system dynamics, which are complicated by individual dynamics.

### *Get Inside Couples' Closed Boundaries*

This strategy is based on the premise that as long as the system's boundaries remain closed to feedback and intervention, change efforts will be ineffective. The strategy is to meet with offending partners and listen to their story in a nonjudgmental fashion. This permits the clinician access to the inner workings of the system's closed boundaries, albeit for a short time. Needless to say, while inside those boundaries, it is essential that the clinician does not challenge the system's myths. The goal is to understand this closed system.

*Challenge the System's Closed Boundaries by Involving Other Family Members*

This strategy is based on the premise that the clinician cannot easily be the target for offending partners if the clinician is just one of many individuals in the session. Therefore, the strategy is to invite several family members including extended members, such as aunts, uncles, or parents, to broaden the closed system's boundaries. Many or all of these members will share the myth and will feel compelled to share with the clinician how bad the other partner has been. By remaining neutral and objective, it is less likely that the clinician will be perceived as a threat in the early stage of treatment.

*Clarify Situations and Reframe Scapegoating*

This strategy is based on the premise that the system's boundaries will close immediately if the clinician challenges and confronts directly. The clinician's power and influence will be negated by the use of directive methods, even if there is a court order for treatment. Instead, the strategy is to use indirect and subtle methods. These include the use of clarification, request for additional information, as well as reframing and redefining situations. With reframing, the goal is to actively block scapegoating messages and challenge their irrationality.

*Divide and Conquer Using Appropriate Tactics*

This strategy is based on the premise that if the level of hostility is too high to risk meeting with all parties involved, it is better meeting with subsystems, even if it means seeing the partners separately for a few sessions. Assuming a couple has more than one child and that it possible to meet with the children, it can be quite useful to meet with them separately to observe the strength of the myth and the extent of scapegoating among them. Because one of the children may not fully support the myth, the clinician must intentionally look for this, because this small degree of nonsupport may be a potential therapeutic opening for change among these children. While any such change is likely to be undone by the parent/partner afterward, the fact remains that some ambivalence regarding the myth has been interjected. As a result, the extent of scapegoating may be delimited. Because meeting separately with the children can be perceived as a serious threat by one of the parents/partners, the clinician needs to be particularly sensitive to this possibility and not force the issue but frame the request in such a way that reduces the perceived threat.

*Case Example*

This case illustrates the reciprocating dynamics of a poisonous couple on each spouse as well as their child. These reciprocating dynamics are both individual and systemic. A brief discussion of recommendations is also included.

The Simpsons have separated and have become locked in a custody battle. Jeff is a 36-year-old accountant, and Samantha, age 35, is a public health nurse. Both have begun new live-in relationships. Their 8-year-old daughter, Amy, has witnessed many of the couple's fights over the years. In school she is functioning below her intellectual potential and does not relate well to her classmates. As part of the child custody evaluation, an individual evaluation of each family member is completed along with an extensive family evaluation. Jeff is requesting primary custody of Amy and is open to liberal visitation by the child's mother.

The individual evaluation of Jeff indicates a moderate level of disturbance and an overly controlled, ruminative, and obsessive-compulsive personality disorder from which his underlying resentment periodically breaks through. His relational style is to sidestep dealing with ambivalent and hostile feelings by pushing them away or avoiding any awareness of them. However, after seething long enough he can erupt in an angry, toxic manner.

The individual evaluation of Samantha indicates a high level of disturbance along with diagnoses of anxiety disorders in the context of histrionic and narcissistic personality dynamics. Despite the appearance of putting up a good front, there are indications that she is grief stricken about an emotional loss. Her relational style is marked by charm, entitlement, and hostility. She is fearful of rejection and needs constant reassurance that she is the superior, effective person she strives to be. Unfortunately, this self-focus interferes with her ability to extend herself toward her daughter as her daughter evolves into an increasingly independent person. The potential violence of her verbal and, sometimes, physical outbursts are at a level to be potentially damaging for a child. The ubiquitousness of her underlying hostility means that her relationships with adults and children are likely to be more superficial and that she is likely to put others off. Finally, she has not developed a workable problem-solving style in that she vacillates and is unsure about which way is better for herself.

The individual evaluation of Amy indicates that she identifies her family as her father, her father's new partner, and her paternal grandmother. Remarkably, Amy does not include her mother in her family drawing. In addition, Amy is a very angry youngster, and her anger and related distress are so pervasiveness that it impairs her ability to think clearly. As a result, her decision making is inconsistent. She also suffers from poor reality testing accompanied by distortions in her ways of thinking about the world. Furthermore, her sense of personal worth is very poor, and her need for safety is significant.

The family evaluation was similarly revealing. The overriding feature of this family is their hostility and toxicity. In terms of stage of marital development, Samantha and Jeff appear to be stuck at the counterdependence stage. At the time of the evaluation, their level of relational competence is assessed at the borderline level. In terms of the "four horsemen," Jeff primarily uses defensiveness and stonewalling, whereas Samantha primarily uses criticism, contempt, and defensiveness. Prominent among systemic dynamics are boundary violations, particularly by Samantha, and scapegoating by both spouses. Furthermore, interlocking pathologies are clearly evident in this couple. They manifest the prototypic interlocking personality disorder presentation of the obsessive-histrionic pattern.

Samantha has not only a temper but also a ubiquitous toxic quality underlying her relationships, despite an overt orientation to charm others. This readiness to break through her social, other-oriented exterior is made worse by her inadequate controls over expression of feelings, particularly anger. Her anger seems matched by her daughter's marked hostility, also characterized by lack of adequate controls, even in comparison with other 9-year-olds. Flare-ups, which have a long history between mother and daughter, have become increasingly frequent since the parental breakup. It is likely that Amy's fear of abandonment, stimulated when the mother left, significantly fuels these flare-ups, even though the mother has returned to visit regularly. Despite Samantha's action in leaving the family home, her sense of loss and accompanying loneliness is probably related to her frayed connection to her daughter. She cannot acknowledge her ambivalence at not having more contact with her daughter and, hence, fights in a custody "battle" for her, precipitating this evaluation. Were she not to fight so strongly she would need to confront her ambivalence about her daughter, manage her anxiety, and deal with the guilt for, in many ways, rejecting her daughter. Jeff, as father, does not have the same problem of ubiquitous anger that his wife displays. Rather, he holds in all feelings, including anger, until, rarely, the provocation is strong enough that he can explode. He can pick Samantha's most extreme behavior to righteously express his own and thereby not have to look at his own role in the family conflict. The mix of anger between them has developed and serves to maintain a cyclical fight dynamic.

A concern that needs to be addressed is that her mother views Amy as very disturbed, seeing her as acting out and acting in, with depression and probably high anxiety. This relationship between mother and daughter is reinforced by the fact that Amy does not include her mother in her family drawing. Interestingly, her father does not see a disturbance in Amy. Their different views of Amy may reflect their different relationships with her. That is, mother–daughter relationships may reflect conflict and difficulty, whereas the relationship with her father may be relatively free of problems. Amy was traumatized and responded with her fearfulness by identifying with her aggressive mother even while being very angry with her. Amy's anger overwhelms her, disrupting her thinking process, particularly when confronted with her mother's anger or in the wake of it. Amy's reaction generalizes to others. She is hyper alert, wary, and mistrustful and does not easily mix with other children. This standoffish attitude means that she cannot benefit from the day-to-day feedback from peers so necessary for adequate development. Accordingly, her personality and relational development appear to be noticeably arrested.

In short, Jeff and Samantha are a characteristically poisonous couple. Not only has their toxic relationship significantly affected their daughter, but it has also negatively affected each other. Not surprisingly, treatment was deemed necessary and was recommended. The recommendation included individual play therapy for Amy to handle her trauma. Likewise, individual therapy was indicated for Samantha to help her manage her anger more constructively, and couples therapy was indicated for Jeff and Samantha to work on their relationship. Only then would it be reasonable for mother, daughter, and father to meet with a family therapist to rework the child's trauma with them and establish a working coparenting relationship. In the meantime, the recommendation was for the father to continue to have primary physical custody and the parents to have joint legal custody.

## Concluding Note

Poisonous couples are a reality of daily life. Their impact is significant both to themselves and to other family members in both the short term and long term. These couples are likely to be the most challenging type of clients that most clinicians will ever work with therapeutically. The prognosis for working with such couples is viewed by many as limited to somewhat guarded. Nevertheless, clinicians who possess a framework for understanding this particular constellation of individual dynamics and relational or systemic dynamics are in a better position to assess such couples, to develop a case conceptualization, and to plan and implement treatment interventions than clinicians without such a framework. Accordingly, this chapter has emphasized the value of having a comprehensive framework for understanding couples toxicity.

## References

Ackerman, N. (1956). Interlocking pathology in family relationships. In S. Redo & G. Daniels (Eds.), *Changing concepts of psychoanalytic medicine* (pp. 135–150). New York: Grune & Stratton.

American Psychiatric Association. (2000). *Diagnostic and statistical manual of mental disorders*, 4th ed., text rev. Washington, DC: Author.

Andritzky, W. (2006). The role of medical reports in the development of parental alienation syndrome. In R. Gardner, R. Sauber, & D. Lorandos (Eds.), *The international handbook of parental alienation syndrome: Conceptual, clinical and legal considerations* (pp. 195–208). Springfield, IL: Charles C. Thomas.

Beavers, R. (1985). *Successful marriage: A family systems approach to couples therapy*. New York: Norton.

Beavers, W., & Hampson, R. (1990). *Successful families: Assessment and intervention*. New York: Norton.

Beavers, W., & Hampson, R. (2003). Measuring family competence: The Beavers system model. In F. Walsh (Ed.), *Normal family processes*, 3rd ed. (pp. 549–580). New York: Guilford.

Bernet, W., von Boch-Galhaus, W., Baker, A., & Morrison, S. (2010). Parental alienation, DSM-V and ICD-11. *American Journal of Family Therapy, 38*, 76–187.

Everett, C. (2006). Family therapy for parental alienation syndrome: Understanding the interlocking pathologies. In R. Gardner, R. Sauber, & D. Lorandos (Eds.), *The international handbook of parental alienation syndrome: Conceptual, clinical and legal considerations* (pp. 228–241). Springfield, IL: Charles C. Thomas.

Gardner, R. (1985). Recent trends in divorce and custody litigation. *Academy Forum, 29*(2), 3–7.

Gardner, R. (1998). *The parental alienation syndrome*, 2nd ed. Cresskill, NJ: Creative Therapeutics, Inc.

Gardner, R. (2001a). Parental Alienation Syndrome (PAS): Sixteen years later. *Academy Forum, 45*(1), 10–12.

Gardner, R. A. (2001b). Should courts order PAS children to visit/reside with the alienated parent? *American Journal of Forensic Psychology, 19*(3), 61–106.

Gardner, R. (2006). Introduction. In R. Gardner, R. Sauber, & D. Lorandos (Eds.), *The international handbook of parental alienation syndrome: Conceptual, clinical and legal considerations* (pp. 5–11). Springfield, IL: Charles C. Thomas.

Gottman, J. (1999). *The marriage clinic: A scientifically based marital therapy*. New York: Norton.

Gottman, J., & Silvers, N. (1999). *The seven principles for making marriage work: A practical guide from the country's foremost relationship expert*. New York: Three Rivers Press.

Sperry, L. (1978). *The together experience: Getting, growing, and staying together in marriage*. San Diego, CA: Beta Books.

Sperry, L., & Carlson, J. (1991). *Marital therapy: Integrating theory and technique*. Denver, CO: Love Publishing.

Sperry, L., Carlson, J., & Peluso, P. (2006). *Couples therapy: Integrating theory and technique*, 2nd ed. Denver, CO: Love Publishing.

Sperry, L., & Maniacci, M. (1998). The histrionic-obsessive couple. In J. Carlson & L. Sperry (Eds.), *The disordered couple* (pp. 187–206). New York: Brunner/Mazel.

Welwood, J. (2005). *Perfect love, imperfect relationships: Healing the wound of the heart*. Boston, MA: Trumpeter.

CHAPTER 7

# Father–Son Relationships

MELANIE H. MALLERS, MATT ENGLAR-CARLSON,
and JON CARLSON

> Fathering is the single most creative, complicated, fulfilling, frustrating, engrossing, enriching, depleting endeavor of a man's adult life.
>
> **Psychiatrist Kyle Pruett, Yale Child Study Center**

The difficult relationship between fathers and sons has been the subject of Greek tragedy (e.g., Oedipus the King, Antigone, Hippolytus; Gregory, 2005), Shakespearean drama, and of course, real-life pain, longing, and heartbreak (Chethik, 2001). William Shakespeare depicted the father–son relationship when he wrote about Polonius and his son Laertes in *Hamlet*. Laertes is a young man, desperate to leave his father in Denmark and make it on his own in France. When news of Polonius's death reaches Laertes, he returns immediately home to avenge his father's death. Though Laertes sought individuation and personal freedom in his life, he still was compelled to keep his loyalty to his father, something Shakespeare depicted is a behavior that a son must always do. Symbolically, the story reminds us that the father–son relationship is one often grounded on intense respect, and although some sons may hate or not even know their fathers they must learn to respect such position, for they may one day become a father and become, perhaps, as the Latin proverb implies, just like one's father.

This chapter discusses the unique and intricate relationship that exists between fathers and sons, one that oftentimes has detrimental outcomes for men's identities and for men's abilities to establish healthy, close relationships with others, in particular with their own sons. In so doing, we trace the historical and cultural context of fatherhood, one that has in part shaped the development of poisonous relationships among many fathers and sons today. Such poisonous relationships are often characterized by fathers who are dismissive, controlling, and emotionally or physically unavailable and by sons who are left struggling with their own notions of masculinity, sense of self, feelings of loss and anger. The notion of poisonous father–son relationships is also encapsulated by the disconnect that many fathers and sons experience due to varying constructs of what constitutes good parenting. Many fathers today therefore struggle with learning to forgive and reconcile their personal feelings about their dads while concurrently learning to be effective and healthy fathers to their own sons. Throughout this chapter, we use several historical and contemporary quotes related to father–son relationships as well as vignettes (where identifying information and demographics have been altered in order to maintain confidentiality) from actual fathers and sons to highlight the salient role of fathers on their sons' development. Finally, we also provide direction for potential solutions that will empower men to reconnect with their fathers or sons and, in so doing, recreate their own sense of self.

## Historical and Contemporary Constructs of Fatherhood

> I was frightened of my father and I am damned well going to see to it that my children are frightened of me.
>
> **King George V (1865–1936)**

Historical notions of fatherhood in part shape expectations and beliefs about what constitutes good or healthy father–son relationships. Over the course of American history, this concept has shifted dramatically (Lamb, 2000), and it continues to evolve today. But traditional notions of fatherhood have insidiously poisoned how men and their sons interact, leaving a residue of unresolved pain and suffering for many men today. For example, from the mid-19th century through the Great Depression, the father primarily fulfilled the role of "breadwinner" in which good fathers met their family obligation by earning the majority if not all of the family income (Lamb, 2004). Many fathers spent little time at home and placed little priority on nurturing their children. Beginning in the 1930s and 1940s fathers continued to be breadwinners, but their role was extended to that of a sex-role model and genial playmate, especially for their sons. During this time, "good" fathers exemplified traditional masculine traits of emotional stoicism, remaining calm under pressure, independent, and demonstrating sacrifice and hard work. There continued to be little emphasis on valuing the development of emotional expression among young boys;

instead, the emphasis was on rearing boys to have strength and power and to display dominance. In the 1950s and early 1960s, popular culture reflected sociological reality by exalting the virtuous father as the financial support for the family and the disciplinarian to his children, while his role as a source of emotional support was further downplayed. As few women were employed outside the home, mothers represented the "homemakers" who cared for and raised the children on a day-to-day basis (Goodnough & Lee, 1996). Mothers were portrayed as individuals who had the most contact with the children and therefore were traditionally seen as the primary source of childhood emotional support.

Interestingly, as women's participation in the labor force has risen (Hochschild & Machung, 1989), the extent and expectation of father involvement and responsibility in childcare has increased (Cabrera, Tamis-LeMonda, Bradley, Hofferth, & Lamb, 2000; Pleck, 1997), and the emphasis on fathers as the "good provider" has diminished (Christiansen & Palkovitz, 2001). The women's movement of the late 1960s ushered in shifts in the role and expectations of fathers. By the beginning of the 1970s, fathers were defined as good if they were the new "nurturant" father who actively participated in childcare duties. Today, the ideal image of father is that of coparent and one who shares equally in the household, financial, and caregiving responsibilities (Lamb, 2004; Pleck). The new father is expected to provide day-to-day physical and emotional care to his children as well as serve as an equal partner of the mother to compensate for her "lost time" as part of the labor market (Yeung, Duncan, & Hill, 2000). The resulting impact on many fathers is that being active, nurturing, supportive, and emotionally available are now central components of fatherhood and are often portrayed as the measure by which "good fathers" are assessed (Lamb, 2000). Interestingly, recent discourse around fathering is in fact challenging traditional notions of fatherhood and is acknowledging that becoming a father is one of the most profound experiences, not only to one's personal identity but also as it relates to the impact a father has on his sons. Both popular press and scholarly literature are expressing concern about men in contemporary society. Television shows (e.g., *The Cosby Show, Family Ties, Parenthood, Rosanne*) and movies (e.g., *The Pursuit of Happyness, Sleepless in Seattle*) portray fathers as warm, loving, involved, and competent. And current theorists writing in the field of new psychology of men have noted problems with traditional notions of masculinity and are calling for a reconstructed masculinity (Brooks & Silverstein, 1995; Levant, 1992; Levant & Kopecky, 1995; Silverstein, Auerbach, & Levant, 2002) that also places emphasis and attention on rearing boys to have greater emotional expressiveness. Indeed, current research shows that, for today's dad, being a good father is an important factor in their definition of success (Bond-Zielinski, 2007) and successful outcomes for their children (Brotherson & White, 2007). Thus, despite dominant cultural narratives that emphasize the role inadequacy of many fathers (Hawkins & Dollahite, 1997), an alternative narrative has emerged that emphasizes the many ways that fathers care for the next generation and supports men in their roles as fathers (see Oren & Oren, 2010). As Joseph Campbell (2008) implies, true men today are "not the physical self visible in the mirror, but the king within" (p. 315).

However, despite current emphasis on establishing high-quality father–son relationships and equitable notions of masculinity, there lies at the intersection of historical and traditional constructions of fatherhood many adult sons who struggle with resolving their own personal demons about masculinity as well as with how to be effective and competent dads themselves. That is, many men harbor memories about being ridiculed, shamed, embarrassed, ignored, and punished by their fathers for not meeting their expectations of masculinity and success and consequently are confused about how to connect with their own sons.

## The Fathers They Became

Many men who were reared throughout the middle to the end of the last century were exposed to fathers who adhered to a strict and rigid ideology of boyhood and masculinity. The result is a generation of many boys who grew into men yearning for deep and authentic connection with their fathers. As Pittman (1993) writes, "Life for most boys and for many grown men is a frustrating search for the lost father who has not yet offered protection, provision, nurturing, modeling, or especially, anointment" (p. 129). In fact, many men today struggle with issues of loss, including emotional and physical emptiness; many also experience pain and confusion about the way they were treated by their fathers and have guilt for disappointing their father's expectations. Below are two reflections on how not meeting expectations impacts adulthood.

> I grew up idolizing my dad. He was the family provider, and I looked to him as my role model in life. He told me time and again that I could do anything I wanted to in life if I set my mind to it. As a young child I was fascinated with dinosaurs, I memorized the scientific names, their characteristics, habitat, and diets. Looking back I was on my way to potentially becoming a paleontologist. At dinner one evening—I must have been 8 or 9 years old—I distinctly remember my dad asking me what I wanted to do when I grew up. I responded, study dinosaurs. My dad said, "You don't make any money in that line of work." His statement confused me because it was contrary to the message of following my dreams and aspirations. I not only

> stopped studying dinosaurs that day, but I also learned it was important to make money over doing something I love; in the years since then I have questioned if what I am doing for work is practical.
>
> In 2004, I reached a milestone in my life by graduating from college with a BA degree. For me one of the most exciting aspects of graduating was the fact that I was the first of my father's children to graduate from college. Both of my older brothers had dropped out of high school, in spite of my dad's strong emphasis on the importance of education. I thought for sure that I would make my dad proud by reaching this goal. I studied in Ohio, so my family flew out from California for commencement. The ceremony was memorable, and many of my close buddies graduated with highest honors, something I did not accomplish. After the ceremony ended, I excitedly greeted my family, diploma in hand and head held high. To my painful surprise, the first words out of my father's mouth were, "So where's your summa cum laude?" He said it jokingly, but the damage was done and many painful memories of never feeling good enough for my dad were reawakened.

Erickson (1996) refers to this loss as father hunger and argues that it can lead to barriers in developing intimacy and healthy self-esteem. Having unresolved father hunger can also impede a man's ability to develop and sustain intimate relationships (Bartholomew, 1990; Byng-Hall, 1991) as the hungry son may acquire "a sense of self as the kind of person who is abandoned and the son of a father who would abandon" (Herzog & Sudia, 1971, p. 30). This undoubtedly leads one to question his value and significance to intimate others. One 47-year-old father of a 5-year-old son commented, "I sometimes feel a slap in the face, like, wow, I am a father? I am a husband? How can that be? How can anyone need me so much?" If left unaddressed or unfulfilled, father hunger can lead to chronic emotional and relational problems, including feelings of incompetency, powerlessness, and low self-worth. A social worker reflected:

> A client of mine tells of a time when he was 6 years old and doing homework after school. He asked his father, an alcoholic, the difference between a noun and a verb. His father became irate. He picked him up and threw him against the wall. To this day, my client still experiences a great deal of shame, which affects his marriage and career.

Emotional or physical abandonment can also lead to experiences and feelings of shame and stigma, which oftentimes prohibit men from accessing their full range of needs and emotions (Schenk & Everingham, 1995). Shame, a feeling of worthlessness coupled with a core sense of inadequacy, can also permeate all aspects of a person's life and, when internalized, can impair one's core foundation of identity (Kaufman, 1985; Lansky, 1992). It can also lead to intense anger. Unfortunately, research indicates that long-term, unresolved anger can increase a man's risk of cardiovascular disease and other health problems (Chang, Ford, Meoni, Wang, & Klag, 2002). Emotionally, though, what a man loses is his relationships with himself and his ability to find his real feelings and needs that have been hidden within his script of masculinity.

The impact of growing up with a poisonous father–son relationship is deeply rooted and often difficult to change; for men it makes knowing and wondering about themselves a personal battle. For many men, the battle is lifelong. Boys without bonds to their fathers may become more desperate about their masculinity and may begin to idealize and worship the absent father and create a fantasy image that is never met (Corneau, 1991); others may use hypermasculine role models such as those of Rambo and the Terminator to meet their needs for guidance and to "cauterize their emotions about its absence" (Erickson, 1996, p. 39). Others may live within a "mask of masculinity" (Pollack, 1998, p. xxii) and hide behind unresolved grief and anger:

> I could feel the tears within me, undiscovered and untouched in their inland sea. Those tears had been with me always. I thought that at birth, American men are allowed just as many tears as American women. But because we are forbidden to shed them, we die long before women do, with our hearts exploding or our blood pressure rising or our livers eaten away by alcohol because that lake of grief inside us has no outlet. We, men, die because our faces were not watered enough.
>
> **Pat Conroy, *Beach Music***

Unfortunately, father loss is especially insidious because traditional men's socialization does not encourage the expression of emotions; thus, grieving becomes almost impossible. Bly (1990) stated, "Grief is the doorway to a man's feelings. But men don't know what they are grieving about." Emotionally abandoned sons have intense feelings related to their fathers and often have responses of, "I'll never be like him," and even reject the importance of not only their father but also of all fathers. The truth, however, is nicely articulated by Pittman (1993), who wrote, "Present or absent, dead or alive, real or imagined, our father is the main man in [our] masculinity" (p. 107).

This creates a catch-22 for the many men who grew up without fathers or who had poor quality relationships with their fathers: These men are in need of something they can never have.

## Different Definitions and Expectations of Fatherhood

> You don't have to deserve your mother's love. You have to deserve your father's.
>
> **Robert Frost**

Many men today struggle with emotionally connecting with their fathers because notions of fatherhood have so dramatically evolved, with fathers and sons potentially have differing views and expectations of the fatherhood role. For example, a second-generation Japanese American father noted:

> My dad and I are different, from different times. He used to come home from work and was greeted at the door with a drink and a kiss from his wife (my mom). He would sit down in his favorite chair, newspaper in hand. We all knew that he was to be left undisturbed by his wife and children, for this was his time to relax after a long day at work. Me? Well, when I come home I often get handed a toddler with a dirty diaper. Without hesitation, I just grab the baby wipes and the box of diapers. I play dolls with my daughter and then video games with my son until dinner. Somewhere in there I give baths, read stories, put the kids to bed, and at some point catch up with my wife. The difference between us is just one generation, but our lives seem so different.

A lack of shared reality regarding what constitutes healthy parenting can exacerbate any ill feelings and make the process of understanding and empathizing with one's father even more of a challenge. It also further hinders the ability to satiate ones' need for father affection and, as such, further impairs the grieving process. As a result, men may hold onto their anger toward their fathers and consequently toward themselves. As discussed already, boys and men need to know that their father, or some father, loved them; they need to know ultimately that they were worthy of such love.

The quest to gain a father's approval and affection has been depicted in the classic science fiction saga *Star Wars*. For men of a certain generation, one of the more difficult father–son relationships (to say the least) is that of Luke Skywalker and Darth Vader. The centerpiece of the film is the father–son relationship that unfolds first as Darth Vader attempts to oppress his son and finishes in redemption as he saves his son and kills himself in the process. Luke, as the beacon of goodness and strength, fights to reclaim his father because it benefits the galaxy but also (one must assume) because it is a lifelong quest to belief that is his father is good and thus feels something for his son.

## The Cycle of Poison

A historical father–son disconnect also causes some men to struggle with transitioning into fatherhood themselves. Few men today indicate they have had satisfactory models of fatherhood (Daly, 1993). Caretaking and childcare experiences seem to prepare fathers to be more involved (Gerson, 1993; Pleck, 1997), yet for most men caring for siblings was not a major responsibility; thus, they are novices when they become a parent. Shapiro (2001) noted, "When a man becomes a father, he is faced with many issues for which he is a complete rookie" (p. 408). Given that there is little guidance to help shape or guide men who are transitioning into fatherhood, most men therefore rely on their constructions of fatherhood as defined by their own dads. Ironically, while fathers tend to parent more like their fathers than like their mothers (Losh-Hesselbart, 1987), few fathers report learning to parent from their own fathers (Hofferth, 1996). A father of a 5-year-old described his process:

> My father worked a lot. He would come home, eat dinner, and then go to bed. It was a rare occasion that he would get on all fours and play with us. When I had my son, I wanted to be involved and play with him, but I wasn't sure if it looked silly. I did not know what exactly to do. I knew I wanted children (because my mom was so loving), but I did not know how to be a father or what that meant.

While the meaning and practice of fatherhood are often related to men's experiences with their own fathers (Cowan & Cowan, 1987; Herzog, 1979), it is further complicated by the fact that this is intertwined with lingering notions of gender identity and related expectations of masculinity (Daly, 1993; Lytton & Romney, 1991; Witt, 1997). Though there is growing emphasis on cultivating the emotional world of boys, there is still great fear among fathers that their boys need to be tough and aggressive, competitive, independent, strong, and focused on external success (Brody & Hall, 2000; Fivush & Buckner, 2000; Gilligan, 1982; Jordan, Surrey, & Kaplan, 1991; Pollack, 1998; Zahn-Waxler, Cole, & Barrett, 1991). An adult man put his boyhood in that context, noting:

> I can remember a time in my past when my father became bothered that as a 4th grader I had never been in a fight. I can remember him sending me outside to pick a fight with another kid that lived across the street and was in my class. I told this boy, James, that my dad said that I needed to get in to a fight because I hadn't done it yet. To my surprise, neither had James. We stood in the street for over 2 hours talking about what we should be doing and who should do it first. Finally, as it grew dark, we agreed to punch each other in the arm and trade baseball cards. That was my first and only fight.

In other words, many fathers today are struggling with parenting their sons in a manner that promotes masculinity but does not impose rigidity. They are confused about how to teach their sons to become "real" boys, but, without healthy guidance, may ignite a vicious cycle of poisonous father–son relationships. Without more healthy role modeling from their own dads, they may become fathers who themselves reinforce such beliefs and lessons to their own children.

The lack of healthy modeling is exacerbated by the fact there remains a historical, scholarly, and cultural residue that suggests that fathers are inconsequential to their children's development. Early media images of fathers portrayed men as irrelevant and incompetent (Mackey, 1996), and early research studies examining parenting received in childhood, for example, focused solely on the relationship with the mother (e.g., Bowlby, 1982). In fact, in previous decades it was suggested that children could be raised as well without fathers as with them (Horn, 1997). When fathers were mentioned, their contribution to their children's welfare was often limited to financial support or to the effects of inadequate or absent fathering (Hawkins & Dollahite, 1997; Marks & Palkovitz, 2004). As a consequence, a father's presence has been minimized both in more recent research and in clinical research, having relatively little understanding of the meaning and saliency of father–son relationships. Media and lay literature have reinforced this with relatively fewer parenting-related resources, community programs, support services, and social policies for men. May (2002) cited Pruett (2000) in declaring that:

> The images of fatherhood today are rather mixed, even tattered. There is formidable mythology about men being deadbeat dads, absentee fathers, derelict in carrying out their fatherly responsibilities. There is a residual of the old belief that men are still to do the 3 P's: provide, protect, and procreate, and maybe barbecue on the weekend. Television and movies have often contributed to the portrayal of fathers as stupid, macho, sex-crazed, beer drinking, hormonally driven womanizers—insensitive buffoons and eternal adolescents. There is a pervasive male mystique that says … they [men] are unemotional, rational, power-driven, highly competitive…. We know this is not true, but unfortunately, many men have bought into the mystique and the results are not very pretty.

And, as mentioned already, many new fathers today struggle with how to rear their sons and report feeling ambiguous about their role as a father (Fagan & Iglesias, 1999). This further ignites unresolved issues toward men's fathers as it may serve as a reminder that they were not provided with necessary tools for survival.

The lack of ability to parent or, rather, the lack of confidence in one's efficacy to parent may result in many new fathers who do not embrace their role and who do not involve themselves in their sons' lives. This can have detrimental outcomes for boys today. As discussed in *Real Boys*, Pollack (1998) suggests, "many boys are deeply troubled" (p. xxiii) and live in a "gender straitjacket" (p. xxiv) due to conventional expectations of manhood and masculinity that boys should be stoic or express only anger; be tough, confident, and take risks; achieve power; and not express a full range of emotions. The fear is, of course, that boys will otherwise be effeminate or sissy-like. Many male models of masculinity, both old and contemporary, such as John Wayne, Clint Eastwood, and Sylvester Stallone, are expressionless, emotionless, and dominant (Sandborn, 2007), and superheroes, including Batman and the Lone Ranger, mask their true feelings. Not surprisingly, more and more boys today are suffering from depression, loneliness, eating disorders, and other psychological problems (e.g., Kindlon & Thompson, 1999; Kiselica, Englar-Carlson, & Horne, 2008). For example, healthy forms of competition are essential to successful male development (Gurian, 1997), and some of the happiest moments for fathers are when they are teaching or competing with their sons (Larson & Richards, 1994); likewise, sons want to test their psychological and physical strength against their father and make Dad proud when they "win." However, to maintain their own notions of masculinity and to teach their sons to be masculine, many fathers are unwilling to relinquish their control and status over their son. The irony of this is that while fathers want their sons to do well and have a better life than they had, they are reluctant to give up control and power. As a result, sons continue to struggle with impressing their fathers and inevitably becoming wounded when they do not.

May (2002) noted, "For fathers it is an old game being played by new rules." But many fathers are poisonous to their sons because they never learned that the rules, or the game for that matter, could change. That is, they have not yet learned that they can let go of their control over their sons and instead find a healthier, balanced way of fathering. The result is that they perpetuate the pattern they learned, and if their sons become fathers one day they may inadvertently start the cycle again. In fact, fathers who remember that their own fathers had been high in expressing anger and low in expressing love themselves have children who are rated as more aggressive and hyperactive in kindergarten (Cowan, Cohn, Cowan, & Pearson, 1996).

Men who grew up with and continue to have poisonous father–son relationships may also not recognize their own relevance in their children's lives. In this sense, poisonous parenting is demonstrated by not being a present fatherly figure or, if there is some contact, not taking the responsibility to actually *be* a parent. A literary example comes from Mary Shelley's

*Frankenstein* in the relationship between Victor (the creator) and the creature. The creature's lack of guidance and Victor's refusal to take responsibility for his creation ultimately lead to the horrible suffering of everyone involved. Of course a more critical form of neglectful parenting comes in the form of father absence and not being physically present at all in their son's lives.

Some fathers voluntarily, even before their children are born, or following a divorce, become a nonresident and uninvolved father. According to the National Fatherhood Initiative (2006), more than 30% of general population births occur out of wedlock. Further, due to this and high rates of divorce, there is a large percentage of fathers who are not involved with their children. Such absence can have a lasting impact on one's development and overall well-being as well as pose detrimental outcomes to male offspring. For example, fatherless children are five times more likely to live in poverty than children living with both parents (U.S. Census Bureau, 2002). Children in father-absent families are also reported to have lower educational achievements, more aggression, and less self-regulation (Honig, 2008), early childbearing, difficulty with psychological adjustment, aggression, and risk-taking behavior (Cabrera et al., 2000; Pope & Englar-Carlson, 2001), and increased risk for mental health problems, including suicidal risk and psychiatric-related problems, and other risky behaviors. Additionally, violent criminals are overwhelmingly males who grew up without fathers (Gurian, 1997; Heimer, 1996; Ryan, 1996; Stanton, Oei, & Silva, 1994; U.S. Department of Health and Human Services, 1993).

Such outcomes are in sharp contrast to boys who were reared with competent, nurturant, and involved fathers. Current literature shows that children who have strong emotional bonds with their fathers experience significant benefits. For example, infants of highly involved fathers are more cognitively competent (Allen & Daly, 2002; Radin, 1981). Men whose fathers were involved in raising them tend to be more involved with their own children, take more responsibility with their own children, show more warmth, and closely monitor behavior and activity (Pleck, 1997). Children with involved fathers are more confident, are better able to deal with frustration, have higher grade point averages, and are more likely to mature into compassionate adults (U.S. Department of Health and Human Services, 2006). Children with involved fathers also have better emotional development and greater ability to cope with stress (e.g., Amato, 1986; Biller & Solomon, 1986; Clarke-Stewart, 1978; Radin, 1982) as well as better social competence and relationships with others (Easterbrooks & Goldberg, 1990). Father involvement also protects children and adolescents from engaging in delinquent and maladaptive behaviors including drug use (see Allen & Daly for a review). Fathers also can serve as sensitive, supportive, and gently challenging companions for children in their attempts to move beyond the family to explore the world (Grossman et al., 2002; Marsiglio et al., 2000). Recent research also shows that the influence of having an involved and nurturing father persists across adulthood. It has been shown, for example, that father involvement during childhood protects against psychological distress and emotional responses to daily stressful events during middle adulthood (Horn Mallers, Charles, Neupert, & Almeida, 2010).

## Becoming a Father: Impact on Identity

> Fathers represent another way of looking at life—the possibility of an alternative dialogue.
>
> **Louise J. Kaplan, *Oneness and Separateness: From Infant to Individual* (1978)**

One way for men to resolve some of their own fathering conflicts is to first recognize that they play a powerful role in their son's life. It may help contemporary fathers who grew up having a poor relationship with their own father to know that they are as capable as mothers of being competent and nurturant caregivers (Bronstein & Cowan, 1988; Silverstein & Auerbach, 1999) and can have strong and intense bonds with their children (Fox, Kimmerly, & Schafer, 1991; Hanson & Bozett, 1991). And when they do, the benefits to their children are extraordinary. That is, fathers should know that they play a unique and critical role in their sons' development (e.g., Lamb, 2004; Nord, Brimhall, & West, 1997; Tamis-LeMonda, Shannon, Cabrera, & Lamb, 2004). They should also know that this does not have happen in some grandiose, superhero way (a notion that may scare off many men who feel inadequate) but often through the simple interaction of play and contact. Bowlby (1969, 1982) posited that a child's secure attachment to one's father is through vigorous, physical play, including rough-housing, talking, and recreational activities (Jacklin, DiPietro, & Maccoby, 1984; Lamb, 1997). This play-based interaction has been shown to serve as catalysts for children to take initiative in unfamiliar situations and to explore, take chances, and overcome obstacles. In accordance, research has shown that children of involved fathers have greater problem-solving capacity, social competence, social efficacy, and interpersonal cognition in peer interaction (see Liu, 2008) and are more likely to demonstrate greater tolerance for stress and frustration as well as be more resourceful and skillful when presented with a problem (Biller, 1993; Easterbrooks & Goldberg, 1990). Involved fathers can "open their children up to the world."

Indeed, fathers should also know that they matter to their sons because of the distinct differences in the psychological development between boys and girls. Beginning early on, even by the age of 3, teachers state that boys are more troublesome than girls and report that common "boy behaviors" of shouting, attention seeking, aggression, silliness, and running about are negative traits. Sadly, "our society takes some of the most impressive qualities a boy can possess—their physical energy, boldness, curiosity, high action level—and distorts them into punishing, dangerous definitions of masculinity" (Kindlon & Thompson, 1999, p. 15). As Gurian (1997) points out, nurtured competition, for example, is crucial to healthy male development and self-image. That is, boys need to compete and need to feel tested in their physical and interpersonal world. As Geppetto exclaimed, "Pinocchio! Oh Pinocchio! You're a boy! A real boy!" Fathers, compared with mothers, can uniquely guide boys to *be* and *feel* real. Interestingly, some studies have shown that while the father–son relationship is more important to boys' development of masculinity than is the mother–son relationship (e.g., Biller & Borstelmann, 1967), recent findings indicate that is it not masculinity per se that drives positive developmental outcomes for sons but rather provision of warmth, acceptance, and closeness from fathers to their sons (Lamb, 1997). Fathers who grew up without a dad or who had poor quality father relationships may take comfort in knowing that their involvement with their own sons again does not have to be overly powerful but through simple day-to-day sharing of their lives.

Luckily, many fathers today are willing to take on the struggle and learn what it means to be a nurturing and an involved role model to their sons. It is important to note the importance of fathers being involved and available with their sons as opposed to just being around. Father involvement tends to have the most beneficial effects when the father–child relationship is supportive (Amato & Rezac, 1994). Responsive fathering (e.g., warmth, attentive, sensitive) and participation during specific activities with children are important (Doherty, Kouneski, & Erickson, 1998). Generative fathering is used to describe fathering that responds readily and consistently to a child's developmental needs over time. Dollahite and Hawkins (1998) described generative fathering as "a non-deficit perspective of fathering rooted in the proposed ethical obligation for fathers to meet the needs of the next generation" (p. 110). The model builds on Erikson's concept of generativitiy in life span developmental theory and also incorporates a contextual emphasis, suggesting that good fathering is "generative work." Fathering thus becomes a way for men to provide and protect their children but also a means to contribute to the development of a new generation of men. Being a "good" father becomes an important aspect of identity for many men and a way of contributing to social welfare.

For many men, becoming a father clearly has consequences for their lives and identity (Palkovitz, 2002). Some research suggests that fatherhood may lead men to question what is important in life and help fathers clarify values and set priorities (Palkovitz; Parke, 1995; Snarey, 1993). Strauss and Goldberg (1999) note that the transition to parenthood is also an impetus for change in self-concept and in reorganizing one's inner psychological sense of self. Becoming a father can thus be a time for growth by resolving old issues (Antonucci & Mikus, 1988; Cowan, 1988) and for reinventing fatherhood or at least trying to become the father one always wanted. Palm (1993) reflected:

> During the past summer, while I was walking around Washington, D.C., looking at the sights with my 10-year-old son, he reached over and grabbed my hand. I squeezed his hand but felt embarrassed and uncomfortable. Would his peers (and mine) stare at us and make comments as we walked down the street? It was apparent to me that he didn't seem concerned. Holding my hand was his way of saying, "I'm glad we're here together," a gesture that was much easier than words. Over the next few days, I became more comfortable holding hands with my son and in the process examined my feelings of discomfort. I traced them to my childhood, when I could hear the voices of my 10-year-old peers taunting me if I showed affection toward my parents. I also remembered homophobic messages about boys holding hands. I wanted to feel close to my son, but first I had to confront some of the barriers to emotional intimacy that resulted from my socialization as a male. He was reaching out to me, and I had to dig within myself to understand and overcome my reluctance to accept his simple, innocent gesture of affection. Our children often challenge us to look at ourselves through our relationships with them in new ways that help us to grow beyond our old selves.

Interestingly, it is often through having children that men can begin to reexamine their attitudes about their own fathers. Fatherhood can give men a new beginning to resolve hurt feelings, to learn what emotional intimacy is all about, and as such, begin to understand their personal value, especially to their own sons. Bergman (1991) describes traditional male socialization as a process that oftentimes leads men away from learning how to be with or nurture others. Being a father today, though, holds many opportunities to grow and learn in ways that are typically stunted by male socialization.

Indeed, fathers who are involved in their children's lives can learn alongside their children about how to establish and maintain healthy and intimate relationships. The process of attachment between father and child is the context for reciprocal learning (Ambert, 1992). Diamond (2007) writes that fatherhood is an essential event for both the son's and the father's development whereby "both achieve a deep and lasting understanding of what it means to be a man" (p. 198). A 48-year-old father of two boys explained his experiences:

> J. August Strindberg, the troubled Swedish playwright and novelist, said, "That is the thankless position of the father in the family … the provider for all, and the enemy of all." As I reflect upon my own relationship with my dad I can see how this resonates with my own conceptualization of him—a provider and sometimes my enemy. So what does this mean to me as I reflect upon my own role as father to my two sons? For me, being a father means trying to teach my sons how to be men in a world that is constantly confused on what a man is supposed to be. It means teaching them how to love others when men are most often encouraged to dominate others. It means teaching them that the positions of servant and leader are not necessarily diametrically opposed to one another. It means loving their mother in such a way that they know that their family foundation is a firm one—no matter how difficult. And last, for me it means taking the best of what my father taught me and trying to leave the worst behind, all the while forgiving myself when the worst comes out of my mouth or from my heart. In short, being a father means hard work driven by a love explained in another quote, this one from the writer Elizabeth Stone: "Making the decision to have a child is momentous. It is to decide forever to have your heart go walking around outside your body."

While children learn to trust that their needs will be met, fathers can also learn about caring, nurturing, listening, and expressing affection in new ways as well as begin to redefine for themselves what masculinity and fatherhood mean. Further, other research indicates a bidirectional, dynamic relationship may exist where fathers affect children's health and children affect fathers' health (Garfield, Clark-Kauffman, & Davis, 2006). Children may affect fathers' health by their very presence in a father's life. Palkovitz (2002), in a qualitative study of 40 fathers, found that involved fathers readily acknowledged and could provide examples of the ways that their children contributed to who they were as a developing person.

For many men, becoming a father today means having a second chance for overcoming their socialized views of themselves. Phelps (2008, p. 86, as cited in Honig, 2008) highlights in a winning entry from a Father's Day contest in which wives nominate the "Best Dad Ever": Two examples highlight that process:

> In our world, a normal dad plays golf, watches sports, goes four-wheeling with buddies, and works late. My husband, Michael, does

> none of these things. He says our children are his life. He is truly an angel among dads. I have never seen a father who is as gentle as he is. He has never raised his voice or his hand to them. His childhood was filled with hitting, yelling, and throwing, and he is determined that his children never know violence. I suffer from depression, severe sometimes; my husband just picks up the slack—without complaining. He sleeps in our baby's room and takes care of her all night so I can sleep. Then he goes to work early so he can come home early and help me with our kids. His work is stressful. He is a religious educator for high school students, some of whom are special needs kids. He never brings his work home or complains. Our children have emulated his unfailing optimism and hardworking nature. His favorite pastime truly is playing with the kids and reading to them. All you have to do is look at our children to know what kind of father he is. They are the most respectful and helpful children I have ever known. For these and many other reasons, I believe he is the best dad in the world.

An example from a 40-year-old father of a 6-year-old reflects on how he is changed since becoming a father:

> My son likes to come sit with me, stick his cold feet under my legs, and ask to eat my sandwich and drink my milk. My wife does the same. Even though they each have their own lunch, they want mine. They say it tastes better when it is Daddy's. My dad never shared with me. At first I was frustrated they [son and wife] did this. Now I know it means I am a father.

Being a father can also mean improving overall well-being. Fatherhood may act in similar ways to marriage by reducing health-risk behaviors (e.g., smoking, alcohol use, dangerous activities) by serving as a signal to men that they have someone to live for, thus encouraging more healthy and responsible behaviors. Further, the presence of children in a man's life often encourages fathers to become more involved in community and service-oriented organizations, establish more frequent contacts with extended kin, get more involved in church and faith-based community activities, and show greater attachment to their jobs or career (Kaufman & Uhlenberg, 2000; Knoester & Eggebeen, 2006). A father of two young boys described his experience of change, noting:

> Now that I am a father, I see the big picture. I feel more mature. I feel more gratitude. Not just with my son, but also at work. Even little things like replacing the water cups for our clients is something I see the value in. They appreciate it; they appreciate me.

It is important to note that the positive impact of children on fathers is mostly found for those fathers living with their children. Once fathers step away from co-residence, the power of fatherhood often dissipates (Eggebeen & Knoester, 2001).

## Antidotes to Father–Son Poison

> The father who would taste the essence of his fatherhood must turn back from the plane of his experience, take with him the fruits of his journey and begin again beside his child, marching step by step over the same old road.
>
> **Angelo Patri**

Fathers who want to change can begin their journey of redefining themselves. Through this, a man learns to have real power, one that does not bully or dominate but that allows him to take care of himself and others. Helping professionals can guide their clients, whether the client is the hungry son or the struggling father, by helping understand some of the cultural, societal, and psychological forces that make it hard for men, including fathers and sons, to create real, meaning connections. From this discussion, a new conversation can emerge that challenges rigid norms and roles between fathers and sons and provides the potential for change. Inherent in this process is not only understanding the significance fathers have in their own sons' lives but also reconciling their own personal father-related issues. Reconciliation is, in essence, creating a healthy balance between two opposing forces. Katz (2002) notes that there is not one model of healthy father–son balance, but there are shared qualities, including awareness and satisfaction in sharing a close relationship together, appreciation for the relationship, sense of trust and safety, sharing emotional availability, and recognition of unavoidable life challenges.

Engaging in grief work may also be a critical aspect of resolution, especially for sons who were physically abandoned or who are feeling emotionally abandoned (Balcom, 1998). Delving into a son's relationship history can highlight that a series of losses have occurred and that successful, finalized mourning is essential. Through loss of the actual father or through the ideal or fantasized father, experiencing and expressing anger, sadness, and shame in nonviolent ways (either toward self or others) is often necessary. That is, all losses need to be resolved for people to emerge whole, strong, and capable of intimate relationships (Erickson, 1996). Some helping professionals may wish to attempt reunification between client and father during a supervised session or, if not possible, to assist the client in verbalizing unspoken wishes about the father. Clients can be guided to examine: What do you want to say to your father? Are there things you always wanted to ask your father? Share with your father? A sense of completion and closure can often be obtained by role playing these conversations using psychodramatic, Gestalt, or other active techniques and may assist the son to speak his real voice (Balcom).

Many boys often learn to hide sadness and fear and may grow into men who constrain emotional expressiveness (especially in relation to their own emotionally stoic fathers). Whereas the empirical evidence on sex difference in emotionality concludes that men's and women's emotional behavior is more similar than different (Wester, Vogel, Pressly, & Heesacker, 2002), men may experience more difficulty in expressing emotions because they have been socialized to say less or because they have a more limited capacity to express themselves in certain contexts, not because there is a lack of emotional arousal in men (Robertson, Woodford, Lin, Danos, & Hurst, 2001). It is important to note that the very act of expressing emotions may not necessarily be healthy for men (Wong & Rochlen, 2005). Whereas expressing emotions to another can often reduce distress if the feelings are validated, men can also feel vulnerable and threatened when they are not (Kennedy-Moore & Watson, 2001). Developmentally, many boys may have felt shamed or hurt (especially from other boys, men, and fathers) when they expressed more tender emotions; thus, the process of emotional expression creates a conflict where the desire to express emotions becomes paired with fears or wounds of shame. Helping professionals can assist with resocializing men to be aware and expressive of a fuller range of emotions, including hurt, tenderness, and warmth (Levant, 1992), all of which can lead to greater emotional relatedness, both internally and with others. This can also help working through layers of hurt and disconnection between fathers and sons. For helping professionals, there are multiple ways to facilitate safe emotional expression. Emotions can be expressed verbally, nonverbally (writing), linguistically, and through physiological means (Wong & Rochlen). Changing the mode of expression can be a helpful intervention to provide expressive outlets for men (Englar-Carlson, 2006).

The ability to access emotions may be especially critical during the birth of a first son, when many fathers who are transitioning into fatherhood struggle with mourning their own father loss, bonding with their new baby, all the while being attentive to their spouse (Berger, 2010). These struggles may lead new fathers to feel distanced from the birth experience and the new baby rather than an active participant in the new parenting process. It may also be essential when a father is parenting an adolescent, a time when many fathers withdraw. In general though, helping professionals can work with fathers and help them to redefine emotionality as part of their own masculinity (Silverstein et al., 2002).

Helping professionals can also serve as teachers and broaden their clients' notions of father involvement and parenting. Given that most men have not taken a parent education class and lack preparation for involved parenting (Palm, 1993), many men need to learn that being a father is more than just bringing home the paycheck or playing sports together; it is helping their growing sons to regulate their emotions and achieve a sense of mastery. It can be expressed during routine physical care (e.g., bathing, preparing meals, taking children to doctor's appointments), talking and listening, engaging in shared interests, and monitoring activities as well as through affection and encouragement. Such activities, as indicated earlier, do not need to be momentous or extravagant but simply unfold even during the most mundane and simple day-to-day life events. From a child's perspective, such events seem big and special anyway, as noted by a 5-year-old boy in reference to what he likes most about his dad: "I like when my dad looks for bugs with me or wrestles with me." And during these moments, the father can learn to attend to his own inner world and begin to focus on growing more empathic, vulnerable, and trusting. As Keen (1991) stated, "Men have much to mourn before they can be reborn" (p. 136).

A primary, related challenge fathers may face is the lack of "comprehensibility" of their children. As mentioned already, many fathers lack parenting and empathic skills and do not always know how to relate to their sons. Helping professionals can assist their clients with alleviating anxiety and overcoming feelings of inadequacy as a father by building good parenting skills and tapping into their thoughts and feelings of what they wanted from their own father. Additionally, men can learn from their children, and helping professionals can show their clients that by *being* a dad they can *learn to be* a dad. Through fathering, men overcome their fears and instead improve their listening skills and empathic skills, delay gratification, redefine goals and values, understand sexism and its impact on children, deepen and intensify feelings, and learn the feeling of connection (Palm, 1993). It can be quite healing to remove the mask of masculinity. As Darth Vader stated upon his death, "Luke … help me take this mask off … and look on you with my own eyes."

## References

Allen, S., & Daly, K. (2002). *The effects of father involvement: A summary of the research evidence.* Newsletter of the Father Involvement Initiative–Ontario Network. Retrieved from http://www.ecdip.org/docs/pdf/IF%20Father%20Res%20Summary%20(KD).pdf

Amato, P. R. (1986). Father involvement and the self-esteem of children and adolescents. *Australian Journal of Sex, Marriage & Family, 7,* 6–16.

Amato, P. R., & Rezac, S. J. (1994). Contact with non-resident parents, interparental conflict, and children's behavior. *Journal of Family Issues, 15*, 191–207.
Ambert, A. M. (1992). *The effect of children on parents*. New York: The Haworth Press.
Antonucci, T. C., & Mikus, K. (1988). The power of parenthood: Personality and attitudinal changes during the transition to parenthood. In G. Michaels & W. Goldberg (Eds.), *The transition to parenthood: Current theory and research* (pp. 62–84). New York: Cambridge University Press.
Balcom, D. A. (1998). Absent fathers: Effects on abandoned sons. *Journal of Men's Studies, 6*, 283–296.
Bartholomew, K. (1990). Avoidance of intimacy: An attachment perspective. *Journal of Social and Personal Relationships, 7*, 147–178.
Berger, R. (2010). Increasing clinical and contextual awareness when working with new fathers. In C. Z. Oren & D. C. Oren (Eds.), *Counseling fathers* (pp. 187–206). New York: Routledge.
Bergman, S. (1991). *Men's psychological development: A relational perspective*. Work in Progress No. 48, The Stone Center, Wellesley College, Wellesley, MA.
Biller, H. B. (1993). *Fathers and families*. Westport, CT: Auburn House.
Biller, H. B., & Borstelmann, L. J. (1967). Masculine development: An integrative review. *Merrill-Palmer Quarterly, 13*, 253–294.
Biller, H. B., & Solomon, R. S. (1986). *Child maltreatment and paternal deprivation*. Lexington, MA: Heath.
Bly, R. (1990). *Iron John*. New York: Addison-Wesley.
Bond-Zielinski, C. (2007). *The involved father. Family and consumer sciences fact sheet #3451*. Published by Ohio State University Extension.
Bowlby, J. (1969). *Attachment and loss, Vol. 1. Attachment*, 2nd ed. New York: Basic Books.
Bowlby, J. (1982). Attachment and loss: Retrospect and prospect. *American Journal of Orthopsychiatry, 52*, 664–678.
Brody, L. R., & Hall, J. A. (2000). Gender, emotion, and expression. In M. Lewis & J. M. Haviland-Jones (Eds.), *Handbook of emotions*, 2nd ed. (pp. 338–349). New York: Guilford Press.
Bronstein, P., & Cowan, C. (1988). *Fatherhood today: Men's changing role in the family*. New York: John Wiley & Sons.
Brooks, G. R., & Silverstein, L. B. (1995). Understanding the dark side of masculinity: An interactive systems model. In R. Levant & W. Pollack (Eds.), *A new psychology of men* (pp. 280–336). New York: Basic Books.
Brotherson, S. E., & White, J. M. (Eds.). (2007). *Why fathers count: The importance of fathers and their involvement with children*. Harriman, TN: Men's Studies Press.
Byng-Hall, J. (1991). The application of attachment theory to understanding and treatment in family therapy. In C. Parkes, J. Stevenson-Hinde, & P. Marris (Eds.), *Attachment across the life cycle* (pp. 199–215). New York: Routledge.
Cabrera, N. J., Tamis-LeMonda, C. S., Bradley, R. H., Hofferth, S., & Lamb, M. E. (2000). Fatherhood in the twenty-first century. *Child Development, 71*(1), 127–136.
Campbell, J. (2008). *The hero with a thousand faces*, 3rd ed. Novato, CA: New World Publishers.

Chang, P. P., Ford, D. E., Meoni, L. A., Wang, N. Y., & Klag, M. J. (2002). Anger in young men and subsequent premature cardiovascular disease: The precursors study. *Archives of Internal Medicine, 162,* 901–906.

Chethik, N. (2001). *Fatherloss: How sons of all ages come to terms with the death of their dads.* New York: Hyperion.

Christiansen, S., & Palkovitz, R. (2001). Why the "Good Provider" role still matters: Providing as a form of paternal involvement. *Journal of Family Issues, 22,* 84–106.

Clarke-Stewart, K. A. (1978). And daddy makes three: The father's impact on mother and young child. *Child Development, 49,* 466–478.

Corneau, G. (1991). *Absent fathers—lost sons.* New York: Shambhala Publications.

Cowan, C. P., & Cowan, P. A. (1987). Identifying the antecedents and understanding the barriers. In P. W. Berman & F. A. Pedersen (Eds.), *Men's transition to parenthood: Longitudinal studies of early family experience* (pp. 145–174). Mahwah, NJ: Lawrence Erlbaum Associates.

Cowan, P. (1988). Becoming a father: A time of change, an opportunity for development. In P. Bronstein & C. P. Cowan (Eds.), *Fatherhood today: Men's changing role in the family* (pp. 13–35). New York: Wiley.

Cowan, P. A., Cohn, D. A., Cowan, C. P., & Pearson, J. L. (1996). Parent's, attachment histories and children's externalizing and internalizing behaviors: Exploring family systems models of linkage. *Journal of Consulting and Clinical Psychology, 64,* 53–63.

Daly, K. (1993). Reshaping fatherhood: Finding the models. *Journal of Family Issues, 14*(4), 510–530.

Diamond, M. J. (2007). *My father before me: How fathers and sons influence each other throughout their lives.* New York: W. W. Norton & Company, Inc.

Doherty, W., Kouneski, E., & Erickson, M. (1998). Responsible fathering: An overview and conceptual framework. *Journal of Marriage & the Family, 60*(2), 277–292.

Dollahite, D. C., & Hawkins, A. J. (1998). A conceptual ethic of generative fathering. *Journal of Men's Studies, 7,* 109–132.

Easterbrooks, M. A., & Goldberg, W. A. (1990). Security of toddler–parent attachment: Relation to children's sociopersonality functioning during kindergarten. In M. Greenberg, D. Cicchetti, & E. M. Cummings (Eds.), *Attachment in the preschool years: Theory, research and intervention* (pp. 221–244). Chicago, IL: University of Chicago Press.

Eggebeen, D. J., & Knoester, C. (2001). Does fatherhood matter for men? *Journal of Marriage and Family, 63,* 381–393.

Englar-Carlson, M. (2006). Masculine norms and the therapy process. In M. Englar-Carlson & M. A. Stevens (Eds.), *In the room with men: A casebook of therapeutic change* (pp. 13–48). Washington, DC: American Psychological Association.

Erickson, B. (1996). Men's unresolved father hunger: Intervention and primary prevention. *Journal of Family Psychotherapy, 7,* 37–62.

Fagan, J., & Iglesias, A. (1999). Father involvement program effects on fathers, father figures, and their Head Start children: A quasi-experimental study. *Early Childhood Research Quarterly, 14*(2), 243–269.

Families and Work Institute. (2008). Times are changing: Gender and generation at work and at home. Retrieved on July 30, 2010 from http://familiesandwork.org/site/research/reports/Times_Are_Changing.pdf

Fivush, R., & Buckner, J.P. (2000). Gender, sadness and depression: The developmental of emotional focus through gendered discourse. In A. H. Fischer (Ed.), *Gender and emotion: Social psychological perspectives* (pp. 232–253). Cambridge, England: Cambridge University Press.

Fox, N., Kimmerly, N. L., & Schafer, W. D. (1991). Attachment to mother/attachment to father: A meta-analysis. *Child Development, 62*, 210–225.

Garfield, C. F., Clark-Kauffman, E., & Davis, M. M. (2006). Fatherhood as a component of men's health. *Journal of the American Medical Association, 296*, 2365–2368.

Gerson, K. (1993). *No man's land: Men's changing commitment to family and work.* New York: Basic Books.

Gilligan, C. (1982). *In a different voice: Psychological theory and women's development.* Cambridge, MA: Harvard University Press.

Goodnough, G. E., & Lee, C. C. (1996). Contemporary fatherhood: Concepts and issues for mental health counselors. *Journal of Mental Health Counseling, 18*(4), 333–346.

Gregory, J. (Ed.). (2005). *A companion to Greek tragedy*, 2nd ed. New York: Wiley.

Grossman, K., Grossman, K. E., Fremmer-Bombik, E., Kindler, H., Scheuerer-Englisch, H., & Zimmermann, P. (2002). The uniqueness of the child-father attachment relationship: Father's sensitive and challenging play as a pivotal variable in a 16-year longitudinal study. *Social Development, 11*, 307–331.

Gurian, M. (1997). *The wonder of boys. What parents, mentors and educators can do to shape boys into exceptional men.* New York: Putnam, Inc.

Hanson, S. M., & Bozett, F. W. (Eds.). (1991). *Fatherhood and families in cultural context.* New York: Springer.

Hawkins, A. J., & Dollahite, D. C. (1997). Beyond the role-inadequacy perspective of fathering. In A. J. Hawkins & D. C. Dollahite (Eds.). *Generative fathering: Beyond deficit perspectives* (pp. 3–16). Thousand Oaks, CA: Sage.

Heimer, K. (1996). Gender, interaction, and delinquency: Testing a theory of differential social control. *Social Psychology Quarterly, 59*, 39–61.

Herzog, E., & Sudia, C. (1971). *Boys in fatherless families.* Washington, DC: U.S. Government Printing Office. DHEW Publication No. [OCD] 72-33.

Herzog, J. M. (1979). Patterns of expectant fatherhood. *Dialogue: A Journal of Psychoanalytic Perspectives, 30*, 55–67.

Hochschild, A., & Machung, A. (1989). *The second shift: Working parents and the revolution at home.* New York: Viking.

Hofferth, S. (1996). Childcare in the United States today. *The Future of Children: Financing Child Care, 6*(2), 41–61. Los Altos, CA: Center for the Future of Children, The David and Lucile Packard Foundation.

Honig, A. S. (2008). Supporting men as fathers, caregivers, and educators. *Early Child Development and Care, 178*, 665–687.

Horn, W. F. (1997). You've come a long way, Daddy. *Policy Review, 84*, 24–30.

Horn Mallers, M., Charles, S., Neupert, S., & Almeida, D. M. (2010). Perceptions of childhood relationships with mother and father: Daily emotional and stressor experiences in adulthood. *Developmental Psychology, 46*(6), 1651–1661.
Jacklin, C., DiPietro, J., & Maccoby, E. (1984). Sex-typing behavior and sex typing pressure in child/parent interaction. *Archives of Sexual Behavior, 13*(5), 413–425.
Jordan, J. V., Surrey, J. L., & Kaplan, A. G. (1991). Women and empathy: Implications for psychological development and psychotherapy. In J. V. Jordan, A. G. Kaplan, J. B. Miller, I. P. Stiver, & J. L. Surrey (Eds.), *Women's growth in connection: Writings from the Stone Center* (pp. 27–50). New York: Guilford Press.
Kaplan, L. J. (1978). *Oneness and separateness: From infant to individual.* New York: Simon and Schuster.
Katz, S. (2002). Healing the father-son relationship: A qualitative inquiry into adult reconciliation. *Journal of Humanistic Psychology, 42*, 13–52.
Kaufman, G. (1985). *Shame: The power of caring.* Cambridge, MA: Schenkman Publishing.
Kaufman, G., & Uhlenberg, P. (2000). The influence of parenthood on the work effort of married men and women. *Social Forces, 78*(3), 931–947.
Keen, S. (1991). *Fire in the belly: On being a man.* New York: Bantam Books.
Kennedy-Moore, E., & Watson, J. C. (2001). How and when does emotional expression help? *Review of General Psychology, 5*, 187–212.
Kindlon, D., & Thompson, M. (1999). *Raising Cain: Protecting the emotional life of boys.* New York: Ballantine Books.
Kiselica, M. S., Englar-Carlson, M., & Horne, A. (2008). A positive psychology perspective on helping boys. In M. S. Kiselica, M. Englar-Carlson, & A. Horne (Eds.), *Counseling troubled boys: A guidebook for professionals* (pp. 31–48). New York: Routledge.
Knoester, C., & Eggebeen, D.J. (2006). The effects of the transition to parenthood and subsequent children on men's well-being and social participation. *Journal of Family Issues, 27*, 1532–1560.
Lamb, M. E. (Ed.). (1997). *The role of the father in child development*, 3rd ed. Hoboken, NJ: John Wiley & Sons Inc.
Lamb, M. E. (2000). The history of research on father involvement: An overview. *Marriage and the Family Review, 29*, 23–42.
Lamb, M. E. (Ed.). (2004). *The role of the father in child development*, 4th ed. Hoboken, NJ: Wiley.
Lansky, M. (1992). *Fathers who fail: Shame and psychopathology in the family system.* Hillsdale, NJ: Analytic Press.
Larson, R. W., & Richards, M. H. (1994). Family emotions: Do young adolescents and their parents experience the same states? *Journal of Research on Adolescence, 4*(4), 567–583.
Levant, R. (1992). The new father roles. In B. Wainrib (Ed.), *Gender issues across the life cycle* (pp. 56–66). New York: Springer.
Levant, R. F., & Kopecky, G. (1995). *Masculinity reconstructed: Changing the rules of manhood—at work, in relationships, and in family life.* New York: Dutton.

Liu, Y. L. (2008). An examination of three models of the relationships between parental attachments and adolescents' social functioning and depressive symptoms. *Journal of Youth and Adolescence, 37*, 941–952.

Lytton, H., & Romney, D. M. (1991). Parents' differential socialization of boys and girls: A meta-analysis. *Psychological Bulletin, 109*, 267–296.

Mackey, W. C. (1996). *The American father: Biocultural and developmental aspects.* New York: Plenum Press.

Marks, L., & Palkovitz, R. (2004). American fatherhood types: The good, the bad, and the uninterested. *Fathering 2*(2), 113–129.

May, J. (2002). *Opening doors for men in childcare settings.* Retrieved from http://www.fathersnetwork.org/772.html

National Fatherhood Initiative. (2006). *The father factor: How father absence affects our youth.* Gaithersburg, MD: Author.

Nord, C. W., Brimhall, D. A., & West, J. (1997, October). Fathers' involvement in their children's schools. Washington, DC: U.S. Department of Education, National Center for Education Statistics.

Oren, C. Z., & Oren, D. C. (Eds.). (2010). *Counseling fathers.* New York: Routledge.

Palkovitz, R. (2002). *Involved fathering and men's adult development: Provisional balances.* Hillsdale, NJ: Erlbaum.

Palm, G. F. (1993). Involved fatherhood: A second chance. *Journal of Men's Studies, 2*, 139–155.

Parke, R. D. (1995). Fathers and families. In M. Bornstein (Ed.), *Handbook of parenting: Status and social conditions of parenting* (pp. 27–63). Mahwah, NJ: Lawrence Erlbaum Associates Publishers.

Pittman, F. (1993). *Man enough: Fathers, sons, and the search for masculinity.* New York: G.P. Putnam's Sons.

Pleck, J. H. (1997). Paternal involvement: Levels, sources, and consequences. In M. E. Lamb (Ed.), *The role of the father in child development*, 3rd ed. (pp. 61–103). New York: Wiley.

Pollack, W. S. (1998). *Real boys: Rescuing our sons from the myths of boyhood.* New York: Random House.

Pope, M., & Englar-Carlson, M. (2001). Fathers and sons: The relationship between violence and masculinity. *Family Journal: Counseling and Therapy for Couples and Families, 9*(4), 367–374.

Radin, N. (1981). The role of the father in cognitive, academic and intellectual development. In M. E. Lamb (Ed.), *The role of the father in child development*, 2nd ed. (pp. 379–427). New York: Wiley.

Radin, N. (1982). Primary caregiving and role-sharing fathers of preschoolers. In M. E. Lamb (Ed.), *Nontraditional families: Parenting and child development* (pp. 173–204). Hillsdale, NJ: Erlbaum.

Robertson, J. M., Woodford, J., Lin, C., Danos, K. K., & Hurst, M. A. (2001). The (un)emotional male: Physiological, verbal, and written correlates of expressiveness. *Journal of Men's Studies, 9*, 393–412.

Ryan, G. (1996). Trends in a national sample of sexually abusive youths. *Journal of the American Academy of Child Adolescent Psychiatry, 35*, 17–25.

Sandborn, C. (2007). *Becoming the kind father: A son's journey.* Gabriola, BC, Canada: New Society Publishers.

Schenk, R., & Everingham, J. (Eds.). (1995). *Men healing shame: An anthology.* New York: Springer.
Shapiro, J. L. (2001). Therapeutic interventions with fathers. In G. R. Brooks & G. E. Good (Eds.), *The new handbook of psychotherapy and counseling with men: A comprehensive guide to settings, problems, and treatment approaches* (pp. 403–423). San Francisco: Jossey-Bass.
Silverstein, L. B., & Auerbach, C. F. (1999). Deconstructing the essential father. *American Psychologist, 54,* 397–407.
Silverstein, L. B., Auerbach, C. F., & Levant, R. F. (2002). Contemporary fathers reconstructing masculinity: Clinical implications of gender role strain. *Professional Psychology, Research and Practice, 33,* 361–369.
Snarey, J. (1993). *How fathers care for the next generation: A four-decade study.* Cambridge, MA: Harvard University Press.
Stanton, W. R., Oei, T. P. S., & Silva, P. A. (1994). Sociodemographic characteristics of adolescent smokers. *International Journal of the Addictions, 7,* 913–925.
Strauss, R., & Goldberg, W. A. (1999). Self and possible selves during the transition to fatherhood. *Journal of Family Psychology, 13,* 244–259.
Tamis-LeMonda, C. S., Shannon, J. D., Cabrera, N. J., & Lamb, M. E. (2004). Fathers and mothers at play with their 2- and 3-year-olds: Contributions to language and cognitive development. *Child Development, 75,* 1806–1820.
U.S. Census Bureau. (2002). *Children's living arrangements and characteristics.* P20-547, Table C8. Washington, DC.
U.S. Department of Health and Human Services. (1993). *Survey on child health.* Washington, DC: National Center for Health Statistics.
U.S. Department of Health and Human Services. (2006). Promoting responsible fatherhood. Retrieved on September 1, 2010, from http://fatherhood.hhs.gov/
Wester, S. R., Vogel, D. L., Pressly, P. K., & Heesacker, M. (2002). Sex differences in emotion: A critical review of the literature and implications for counseling psychology. *Counseling Psychologist, 30,* 630–652.
Witt, S. (1997). Parental influence on children's socialization to gender roles. *Adolescence, 32,* 253–259.
Wong, Y. J., & Rochlen, A. B. (2005). Demystifying men's emotional behavior: New directions and implications for counseling and research. *Psychology of Men & Masculinity, 6,* 62–72.
Yeung, W. J., Duncan, G. J., & Hill, M. S. (2000). Putting fathers back in the picture: Parental activities and children's adult outcomes. *Marriage and Family Review. Special Issue: Fatherhood: Research, Interventions, and Policies, Part I, 29,* 97–113.
Zahn-Waxler, C., Cole, P. M., & Barrett, K. C. (1991). Guilt and empathy: Sex differences and implications for the development of depression. In J. Garber & K. A. Dodge (Eds.), *The development of emotion regulation and dysregulation* (pp. 243–272). Cambridge, England: Cambridge University Press.

CHAPTER 8

# Disconnection and Parenting

## *A Relational–Cultural Perspective*

JUDITH V. JORDAN

The mother–daughter relationship has received considerable attention in clinical and developmental discourse, some celebratory, but much pathologizing. Over the years, critiques of this relationship have often taken the form of mother blaming, particularly by psychodynamic and psychoanalytic theorists (Caplan, 1989). Texts, popular magazines, and parenting books put forth the message that a good mother should hold herself primarily responsible for raising healthy, well-adjusted children (Thurer, 1994), while at the same time mothers are often seen as the source of all their children's ills (Surrey, 1990). Most developmental theories emphasize the power of the maternal relationship for the child, a bias that, until recently, has downplayed the influence of genetic factors, differences in brain structure, sibling or peer influences, paternal input, and effects of the larger social milieu in sculpting a child's development (Harris, 1998).

The notes of child guidance clinics are filled with references to the ways mothers have damaged and failed their children (both sons and daughters). One example of this is an early explanation for the etiology of the borderline personality. Kernberg's (1967) primary notion was that mothers failed borderline individuals in the rapprochement period of development. However, as we learned later, sexual abuse, most often by a father or male relative, typically created the trauma, instability, and personal suffering that led to "borderline personality." Still, the mental health system continually and erroneously pointed the finger of blame at the mother, as therapists continued to ignore the cultural problem of widespread physical and sexual violence against girls and women until victims themselves insisted on being heard.

While the responsibility of mothers should not be overestimated, the importance of the mother–child relationship should also not be underestimated. For daughters, especially, this relationship is indeed critical, but when we burden mothers with unrealistic expectations about their ability to singlehandedly determine children's futures we set them up for failure. We also set them up for blame when their children struggle or suffer. Finally, we fail to acknowledge the importance of the psychological and social context within which mothering occurs and that can profoundly affect a mother's capacity to mother effectively (Caplan, 1989; Coll, Surrey, & Weingarten, 1998). The mother–daughter relationship is especially fraught. Mothers bring up their daughters in a patriarchal context that subtly and sometimes harshly gives the message: We (females) are not valued; you will live in a world defined by others; our relationship itself will be demeaned.

Relational–cultural theory (RCT) looks at the mother–child relationship as an ongoing relationship that is shaped by and that responds to social context, meets multiple needs, and changes and grows over time rather than as something that needs to be repudiated or permanently characterized as toxic or "poisonous" (Jordan, Kaplan, Miller, Stiver, & Surrey, 1991; Jordan, 2009). While this relationship can be challenging and even destructive, in many cases both mothers and their children, especially daughters, are capable of developing empathic and viable ways of being in relationship together.

## Relational–Cultural theory

Relational–cultural theory focuses primarily on relationships and working with the disconnections that happen in relationships (Jordan, 2009; Jordan et al., 1991; Miller, 1976; Miller & Stiver, 1997). We listen for the relational images that drive current expectations for relationships. These images are often formed in the earliest relationships with caregivers and contain constructions like, "If I express my needs with my mother, she will be annoyed and abandon me." While relational images continue to be formed throughout the life span, it is natural to assume that many of the core relational images are constructed early in life with the mother. Over time, these images become overgeneralized and limiting. Part of the work of therapy is to reexamine (emotionally as well as intellectually) the rigidity and inappropriateness of these expectations in one's current life ("Yes, your mother might have had trouble with your needs when you were a toddler, but in fact your partner and your best friend are very, very responsive to your needs"). These relational images actually get enacted in the therapy relationship where their distortions can be corrected. Therapy can rework empathic failures and acute disconnections in such a way that the client begins to question the absolute certainty with which she held these old images.

In addition to working with personal disconnections and relational images, RCT therapists also help people appreciate the power of context in their lives. We acknowledge that cultural images can create isolation and pain for people. Thus, the pain of racism, heterosexism, and sexism creates real pain that resides in and shapes all our primary relationships. In fact, we now know that the pain of social exclusion is registered in the same part of the brain (the anterior cingulate) as physical pain. Social pain—the pain of marginalization or exclusion—is real pain, but too often it is overlooked and treated as not important. Relational–cultural theory therapists not only validate the pain created by these social forces (shaming people, excluding people, casting people in a negative light) but also validate the difficulty of the job of mothering in a context that offers inadequate support for mothers. As Vasquez notes, "we must guard against our tendency to apply psychotherapy in a manner that encourages our clients to adapt to unhealthy environments, rather than empowering them to change those environments or leave them" (Vasquez, as cited in Comas-Diaz & Greene, 1994, p. 129). We do not assume that the client's problems arise only from intrapsychic forces or the pain arising in nuclear families, but rather we work with the entire context of her life and relationships.

## The Power of Context: How Social Forces Shape Motherhood

The context within which mothers and daughters live casts a large shadow on the relationships they develop. Racist and sexist oppression creates treacherous footing for most girls and women in their efforts to create growth-fostering relationships. It has been suggested that clinicians, parents, and society "enlarge our understanding of the sufferings of individual mothers to include the historical and cultural contexts that shape their daily lives" (Freire, as cited in Coll et al., 1998, p. 9). These cultural factors are intricately bound to personal development (Comas Diaz & Greene, 1994; Jordan, Walker, & Hartling, 1993). Mothers who are marginalized by society face particular obstacles in feeling good about themselves as mothers. For example, immigrant mothers have to cope with the disruptive nature of migration and often lose the support of an extended family network. Furthermore, homeless mothers fear they are bad mothers because they cannot provide a home for their children and struggle with the "stink of blame from a society that views poor mothers and their poverty with suspicion and fear" (Coll et al., 1998, p. 62). In a culture that places a premium on blood relations, adoptive mothers must also resist being defined as lesser. Note that it is another instance of ways mothers are demeaned in this culture.

Ethnic and cultural traditions further complicate things for mothers facing the expectations of mainstream White America. In African American families, mothering may be carried out by people other than biological mothers, which can be a strength but may also be looked at askance by others. "The kinship network within African American families can provide children with alternative role models, both mothers and children with emotional safety valves, and mothers with respite from child care" (Greene, 1994, p. 14; Collins, 1971; Troester, 1984). African American mothers also carry a special responsibility to help their daughters and sons survive in a racist and oppressive culture; this often involves paying special attention to differentiating safe and unsafe environments (Greene, 1990a) and a necessary vigilance about social innuendo and power dynamics. This requires careful attention and hypervigilance at all times when operating in the larger, dominant culture, looking beneath the surface for possible messages of danger. Asian American mothers socialized in Confucian, gender-specific cultures face the daunting task of raising their daughters in an American culture characterized by ideals of personal autonomy and self-definition. Complications sometimes arise in these mother–daughter relationships as daughters attempt to redefine their own identities (Suh, 2007).

Heterosexist bias also complicates the lives of many mothers and daughters. Lesbian mothers face assumptions that undermine the very validity of their families. "Lesbian mothers, like unmarried heterosexual women, often mother under the burden of tremendously negative ideas about the effects of 'father absence'" (Benkov, 1998). In sharing their "coming out" stories, many lesbian daughters specifically address their concern about the impact of their disclosures on their mothers (Rosen, 1992). As Rosen notes, "The relational experience of lesbian daughters and their mothers is an extraordinarily complicated one to navigate in a culture that rests firmly on the foundation of sexism and heterosexism" (p. 9). Rosen goes on to write that the strictures and judgments of the surrounding culture create enormous pain for mothers and daughters trying to stay connected through this process. She notes, "It is the sense of failure that becomes contained in the mother–daughter relationship that is in need of reframing, such that the empathic failures of the culture are not erroneously felt as either individual or relational failures" (p. 10).

### Reframing Poisonous Relationships or Relational Toxicity as Chronic Disconnection

Relational–cultural theory posits that all people grow primarily through and toward relationships throughout the life span (Jordan, 2009; Jordan et al., 1991). The desire for connection is central to all people, and the need for connection throughout life is fundamental. Healthy relationships are characterized by a feeling of zest, clarity, creativity, and productivity; a sense of worth; and a desire for more connection (Miller & Stiver, 1997). The traditional developmental narrative that suggests we start out dependent and needy and move toward autonomy and independence does all of us a disservice. It exaggerates the attainment of certainty, control, autonomy, and invulnerability, and it downgrades the value of emotional response, creating unattainable standards for how an adult should function. Because these standards for human "maturity" are impossible to attain, they make us enormously vulnerable to shame. One must be careful in using the term *poisonous parenting* not to abdicate societal responsibility in setting up unrealistic expectations for parents and children or in turning a blind eye to oppressive values that unfairly target marginalized groups. We need to cast a critical eye toward the culture that fosters destructive relationships rather than characterizing individual parent–child connections as "toxic" or "poisonous."

Although RCT does not ordinarily use the term poisonous to describe relationships, some relationships are clearly destructive or not conducive to growth. Growth-fostering relationships are characterized by "five good things": an increase in energy; sense of worth; clarity about oneself and the other person; the capacity to act creatively in the world; and a desire for more connections with others. One can describe the goals of the ideal, nurturing, mothering relationship in similar terms: to raise children who embody these "five good things." By contrast, what is generally termed poisonous can be seen in the RCT model as akin to chronic disconnection, stagnation, decrease in energy and vitality, and a diminished sense of worth. Relationships that are not open to growth and change for both people are limiting. When relationships are unrelentingly characterized by chronic disconnection, lack of mutuality, and frank destructiveness, therapists assist clients in moving from them. Rather than suggesting that clients "stand on their own two feet" and "go it alone," however, RCT assists them in finding more growth-fostering opportunities in other relationships. While some relationships are "workable" and people can find their way to more empathic mutuality, some are simply hurtful. People need to discern which relationships are healthy and which are not. If in the mother–daughter relationship there is nothing but pain and disconnection, the therapist will help clients see the very real limitations of both the mother and the relationship. We do psychoeducation around what constitutes a healthy relationship, we encourage gaining perspective on the mother's limitations, and we help clients realize that they are not the source of the chronic disconnection. In other words, we help clients take appropriate responsibility, but we also acknowledge the responsibility the mother bears.

Relational–cultural theory describes the ways chronic disconnection can arise out of the parent–child relationship. If children cannot represent their experience fully to a parent, they begin to keep aspects of themselves out of the relationship. In particular, when children are hurt by the parent and attempt to convey that pain to the parent and are met with indifference, inattention, or, worse, anger, attack, and denial, they will learn that they cannot be authentic about their experience. These experiences create secrecy and shame that impact not only the mother–daughter relationship but also other relationships as well. Feeling themselves ineffective in finding an empathic response from the parent, daughters often blame themselves. Over time, when they repeatedly encounter either nonresponsiveness or wounding, they learn that they do not "matter" (Jordan, 2009). Rather than moving forward in a relationship that supports their growth and distinctiveness—that is, a relationship that would encourage them to move into the world in a confident and creative way—they begin to move into chronic disconnection from themselves and from others. Chronic disconnection leaves individuals feeling isolated, beyond the pale of human caring, immobilized. If such a state may sound like the consequences of having a toxic or poisonous mother, it is important to note that the focus here is on the failure of relationships, failures that may have many causes, not simply the failure of individuals.

On the other hand, if acute disconnections are responsively repaired, trust and competence increase, along with the feeling that this relationship supports "who I am and who I can be" in other relationships, providing the underpinning for growth, expansion, and increasing vitality. This occurs when a daughter can tell her mother about the hurt that has occurred and the mother responds with empathy and concern, making it clear that the child's distress matters to her and she wants to understand. This kind of response contributes to positive relational images and a strong sense of connection.

It is important to note, however, that while some of this responsiveness depends on the parent's own psychological state and capacity for empathic response, many other factors impact the movement of disconnection and reconnection. For instance, a woman who is feeling marginalized and oppressed in her home by her partner may not have the patience to listen to the pain of her child. A single mother who is exhausted from working two jobs may not be as acutely attuned as she would like to be. A mother who is preoccupied with becoming a partner in a high-powered law firm may feel it is a sign of weakness if she tries to generate "quality" time with her child.

Mothers who feel alone and unsupported in the very challenging job of mothering may wonder how on Earth they can know if they are doing well by their children. Relational–cultural theory is thus deeply committed to working for social justice as a means of alleviating these pressures and transforming our culture into one that makes it possible for mothers to be as responsive to their children as they can. RCT also supports exploring the grief that occurs in such relationships where neither mother nor daughter can bring her full experience into the relationship.

## Healing the Wounds of Patriarchy

When asked what percent of families are dysfunctional, Jean Baker Miller once responded, “In a patriarchal culture all families are dysfunctional” (Miller, personal communication, 1990; Stiver, 1990). Western and Westernized, patriarchal cultures emphasize the independent, autonomous self. The separate self model shapes the ideals for maturity that are privileged in this culture, generating a developmental model suggesting that “healthy” development leads to increasing independence from the mother, an increasing ability to stand on one’s own, a desire to be free of the encumbrances of others’ demands on us, and a firmer sense of boundedness and self-control. The mandate of mothering in this cultural system is to shape dependent, helpless babies of both sexes into independent beings. This is to be done within the context of a nuclear family embedded in a patriarchal culture in which fathers are expected to go off to work while mothers remain primarily responsible for raising children. Although gender arrangements in parenting and partnering are certainly shifting, it is still the rare family where the father assumes primary responsibility for child care (Pollack, 1998). Mothers are particularly warned against raising sons who are “tied to their apron strings.” Girls are initially allowed more emotional dependence, but as they traverse adolescence they are encouraged to transfer their earlier dependence on parents to male partners.

In contrast to these traditional family models, RCT suggests that “the optimal conditions for healthy development arise in those families which create a high degree of mutuality between parents and between parents and children. This mutuality encourages growing children to be expressive of their feelings and needs, so that they can feel heard and can become more and more authentic in their interactions with others” (Stiver, 1990, p. 1). Mothers who have been socialized not to listen to their own female voices and wisdom must pay special attention to listening to the truth telling of their daughters (whose voices are also being ignored by the broader culture). Mothers must fight their own internalized silencing as females to support their daughters’ voices. In this model, dysfunctional families are those that interfere with, rather than foster, growth-enhancing experiences for children. In looking at families, RCT focuses on the quality of empathy, movement of relationship, validation, patterns of disconnections and reconnections, and relational resilience. In this context, authentic, growth-fostering relationships within the family pave the way for children in adolescence to expand their relational world to peers and others in the broader world.

Most descriptions of adolescent development emphasize upheaval and separation from parents (Dickerson & Zimmerman, 1992, 1993). The Separate Self model is especially privileged when it comes to understanding adolescents: "Achieving separation, the wider culture would have it, is the gold standard of success for adolescents" (Caplan, 1989, p. 2). Thus, Blos (1979) speaks about a second individuation process during which adolescents attain a distinctly separated self, with firm demarcations between self and others. With regard to adolescents, a mother's involvement is easily defined as intrusion, her care as invasion of privacy, and her sense of responsibility as overprotection (Surrey, 1990). If mother–daughter closeness remains through adolescence, it is often pathologized as "regressive." Only those behaviors, attitudes, and feelings that support separation are considered legitimate (Lazarre, 1991).

The literature particularly emphasizes struggles between mothers and daughters. Conflict is seen as the consequence when daughters attempt to separate from mothers (Kaplan, Klein, & Gleason, 1985). Rather than viewing conflict as contributing to separation, however, one could see conflict as a way of elaborating the continuity of connection to significant others. As Kaplan notes, "The ability to engage in conflict, without losing touch with the more basic affirming aspects of these connections, is an important part of healthy development" (Kaplan et al., p. 3). Studies indicate that many college-age girls see their mothers as their best friends and confidants (Kaplan et al.). Perhaps we need to move away from the picture of adolescents as leaving or separating from their family and instead see adolescence as a period of reworking and finding new paths to closeness. This process can include open acknowledgment of differences and an increasing ability to negotiate the inevitable conflict at the heart of all authentic and mutual relationships.

Considering adolescence as a time of renegotiating and reconfiguring relationships rather than as a time of separating out from relationships also helps us reconceptualize earlier developmental milestones. Developmental psychologists missed the mark when they labeled the early childhood period of increased mobility, when the child becomes capable of physically moving away from the mother, as "separation" (Mahler, Pine, & Bergman, 1975). Rather, it can be understood as a period when the toddler is developing more complex and differentiated ways to connect. Similarly, the physical separation that commonly occurs when children go to college or get a job tends to be translated into emotional separation rather than seen as a renegotiation of relationship. This step has been mislabeled for toddlers, seeing locomotion away from the mother as proof of separation/individuation rather than as a sign of being able to negotiate more complicated relationships from varying physical distances. Developmental psychologists tend to repeat this bias error in descriptions of adolescence.

A major force in adolescence is increasing pressure for both boys and girls, but especially girls, to accommodate to prevailing cultural values and approved gendered behaviors. While boys are put in gender straitjackets at a much earlier age, this is the point at which girls run into the culture's need to define them as pleasing partners, nondominant and accommodating. Carol Gilligan (1982) notices that adolescent girls begin to lose their voices, become inauthentic and out of touch with themselves, and experience major drops in self-esteem as they realize they have to find their place in a male-defined world.

Gilligan has addressed the dilemmas that mothers and daughters face during the daughter's adolescence (Gilligan, Rogers, & Tolman, 1991). She noted especially the pressures on girls to become inauthentic in relationships, to stop knowing what they know. Preadolescent girls are increasingly exposed to the unequal distribution of power between the sexes. In their struggles to resist that knowledge and the prevailing values and dictates of what a good girl should be, they often challenge the choices their mothers have made, seeing the ways a patriarchal system disenfranchises and disempowers their mothers. However, unlike prevailing theories that emphasize the separation of girls from their mothers in adolescence, Gilligan and Rogers (1993) noted the ability of girls and their mothers to stay in authentic, loving connection. They suggested that these ongoing powerful relationships between mothers and daughters provide "the key to the transformation of society and culture" (p. 133). They also note that powerful cultural pressures push girls and their mothers to move apart and surrender or demean these potentially transformative female bonds. One crucial step in fighting these pressures is to find ways to support mothers and daughters in positively transforming their relationships.

## Empathy for Mothers and Others

Finding a place of empathic resonance with our clients is almost universally hailed as beneficial for them, but theories differ on the centrality of empathy to the healing process. Some approaches see it as "useful" to the establishment of the therapeutic alliance (Greenson, 1967), whereas others regard it as the key to therapeutic growth (Jordan, 2009). In RCT, mutual empathy is at the core of major change; mutual empathy shifts relational images and thus develops the capacity to be present with one's environment in an authentic and open way. In the resonant process of the therapist being empathic with clients and clients seeing their impact on the therapist, we find the key to letting go of old, inflexible, limiting expectations of oneself, the other person, and the relationship. Through this empowering movement, restricting images from the past begin to shift, and people can be more present in current relationships where empathic, genuine response is possible. Slowly clients are able to take small risks to let go of the strategies of disconnection and survival that have limited them. They can move into the vulnerability necessary to be emotionally affected in the present. Incremental acts of courage in the context of a supportive and responsive relationship begin to open up new possibilities. Courage develops in relationship and is sustained in relationship. Therapists support the courage of their clients in coming into more authenticity, which includes registering hurt and injustice, and they support the relationships in their clients' lives that "encourage" them.

When the therapist is empathically misattuned or fails clients in some way, there is an acute disconnection, usually reminiscent of some earlier disconnection that clients may have experienced as wounding or even traumatic. Unlike the original scenario, where the disconnection may not have been reworked, in this situation clients ideally are able to address the hurt, while the therapist listens to their protest and responds empathically with caring and concern for the hurt feelings. This forges a stronger and more resilient relationship and begins to help clients move out of the prison of old images, fears, and expectations. It is easier to evoke a therapist's empathy when clients are addressing an injury incurred at the hands of another person; when the therapist is the cause of the pain, it can be more difficult, but it is also crucial to relationship building. The therapist must practice just "being present" and experiencing the impact of clients' pain. This is easier said than done, but when it happens then healing happens.

Relational–cultural therapists work to broaden clients' experience of empathy. We work to stimulate the development of self-empathy, bringing an empathic and compassionate attitude to bear on clients' current and past experience. Though this may require self-forgiveness, it helps people gain a better, contextualized view of themselves. In the case of childhood sexual abuse, we help clients realize the helplessness, dependency, and fear of the young child who was silenced by the older, bigger sexual predator. Rather than feeling shame for not having alerted people or better protecting themselves, clients begin to appreciate how impossible it would have been for them to defend themselves in that situation.

We also help clients access their empathic and compassionate responses toward others. It is important to validate the anger and outrage that clients sometimes feel toward adults who have hurt or wounded them, including mothers, but developing empathy for the other and the other's emotional landscape and history can often open up ways to see that the wounding they received was not about them at all. Children's first reactions to being mistreated are often to examine and blame themselves: "What did I do wrong? What could I have done differently? Was it something about me that made my mother hate me or attack me in that way?" When a therapist can carefully help clients see the mother's woundedness or pain (not to let the mother "off the hook" but to understand her relational failures more accurately), it is often extremely relieving and freeing. However, this can be complicated and tricky territory.

## Case Examples

The following case vignettes explore some of the issues daughters bring to therapy regarding their relationships with their mothers. While their presenting complaints about the mother–daughter relationship were filled with anger at the mother, each of these women struggled with a sense of having failed her mother in some profound way. Initially, the therapist needed to empathize with the client's anger and disappointment with the mother, but eventually she also had to help the client transcend this anger to get to a place of empathy with the mother's limitations. None of the clients were in a place of needing to sever the relationship with mother, but each of them needed to protect themselves from the destructive aspects of the relationship. With the therapist and with partners and friends they were able to gain perspective on the wounding that was occurring while they continued to value those aspects of the relationship that were growth fostering.

### *Molly*

Molly was a very bright 30-year-old woman who came to therapy because she had felt depressed for the last 2 years. She had recently married, had a high-powered job, and was contemplating starting a family. She had been in therapy before, several years prior to contacting me. She commented in the second session that she thought she had a lot of issues with her mother and wanted to work on them. She described her mother as a cold, demanding, unavailable woman whom she characterized as "narcissistic." In contrast, she saw her father as warm, funny, and charming; her only problem with him was that he had been a "workaholic" and rarely at home. Molly's mother, too, was rarely home. Apparently, she was very involved in her church and the social functions that she helped coordinate, which often left Molly home with four older brothers. One of these brothers was "strange." He occasionally threatened her with a pen knife and snuck into her room to stare at her. She sensed that he might have molested her sexually but had no clear memory of it. When she reported these events to her mother, she was told that she should be nice to him because "he couldn't help it." But Molly never had a clear sense of why he couldn't help it and what was wrong with him. She just knew that she was scared and no one seemed to care.

I was very moved by her story, and the first time she told it I teared up and shuddered, commenting that it sounded terrifying, lonely, and awful. She looked closely at my face. She described the memories as being like a "living nightmare." We revisited these living nightmares many times, with increasing memories of sexual abuse by this brother. She also had nightmares of being tortured, from which she would wake up screaming.

Molly struggled with the question of why her mother hadn't been there for her. Inevitably she decided it was because she was bad or disappointing. She would routinely go through a litany of her failures: she wasn't smart enough, she was socially awkward, she wasn't as pretty as her mother wanted her to be, she secretly hated her brother and her mother knew it, and she was too fat. At the bottom of all this terror and neglect, she felt, was her badness. We worked toward self-empathy, an appreciation of how young and innocent she had been when her brother had terrorized her. We noted that she had tried to protest, but no one had listened. She had trouble holding on to self-empathy, but with encouragement and reminders of her childhood vulnerability, which contrasted with her current ability to speak the truth clearly and be listened to, Molly grew into increasing trust and authentic presence.

We also helped her access her anger toward her mother for not protecting her. However, even as she became more comfortable with that anger, she continued to blame herself mercilessly. At one point, when she was directing her anger and disappointment toward her mother while also blaming herself, I suggested that maybe her mother had some limitations that made it hard for her to do a better job as a mother. Molly grew very angry at me, asking if I was trying to talk her out of her experience. Whose side was I on, hers or her mother's? I realized I had unskillfully made it sound like I was sympathizing with her mother, not her. I agreed with her disappointment in me, acknowledging that I had sounded too forgiving of her mother and that I understood how bad that felt to her. I further apologized for suggesting that perhaps her mother had her own woundedness. Then I backed off from this line of understanding, realizing I had indeed made an empathic error. At that point Molly was not served by focusing on an empathic understanding of where her mother was coming from.

Weeks later, Molly brought up this conversation and asked if I had been trying to get her to be nice to her mother and forgive her. I said that really wasn't my intent. I pointed out that although Molly so often saw her mother's poor mothering as the consequence of something defective in Molly, maybe if she could see that her mother was actually responding not to some lack in Molly but to some wound of her own, it might free Molly from personalizing her neglect. She listened quietly but cautiously. Several days later she said that she had been going through some old photo books that included pictures of her mother as a young girl. She noted that her mother's father used to beat her mother's mother and the kids. He had left the family when her mother was 8. When her mother's mother got very sick, her mother had been sent to live with an alcoholic uncle and aunt where she was also physically abused. Molly's usual tone when speaking about her mother became slightly softer. She said, "I guess she didn't have much to build on in the parenting department." This conversation marked a shift in the therapy. Molly began to talk more about how limited her mother was rather than how bad she herself was. She began to notice her own strength and resilience in dealing with her mother's failures. As her empathy for her mother grew, her empathy for herself also deepened. Eventually she came to see that her mother had been particularly devalued as a female in her family of origin and that abuse was an expected part of being female. Boys—not girls—were to be protected and cherished (including abusive boys).

*Sharon*

Sharon is another accomplished, appealing young woman who came to therapy to work on self-doubt and strong negative feelings about her mother. A psychiatric nurse, Sharon was armed with a full diagnosis of her mother, borderline personality disorder. She spoke with great pain and shame about how difficult it was to deal with her mother. The shame arose because she felt she should be doing a better job of managing her feelings about her mother. When I asked if she would like to have her mother join us for a session or two, she laughed heartily and said her mother would never step inside a therapist's office. She described her mother's mixed messages ("Come here, go away"), her tendency to undercut her daughter and compete with her, the endless induction of guilt, and how her mother knew just the right way to push her into self-doubt.

I responded empathically to Sharon's sense that her mother had been disappointed with her and kept mixing up her sense of closeness and distance. At the same time, I was impressed with the strategies Sharon had developed to stay alive and real in this relationship. She used a lot of self-talk to question her overwhelming emotional response of despair. Her intellect would remind her that she was being given many complicated and mixed hidden messages, delivered in a sweet and syrupy tone. Her emotional response would take her to self-doubt ("I'm way overemphasizing how bad she is"; "I think she's right; my hypersensitivity is the problem here"). At times she would find herself panicking.

We talked together about how many skills she had developed to deal with the shifting winds of closeness and what felt like abandonment by her mother. When I asked her if she would like to understand a little of what might be going on in her brain, she was very interested. I find using explanations of the neurobiology of relationship is often helpful to clients and helps them move out of shame-and-blame constructions of relational experience. I suggested that the anterior cingulate cortex (ACC) registered the distance from her mother as dangerous and was trying to help her out. Together, the ACC and the amygdala were trying to protect her from isolation and abandonment. The amygdala would send off urgent messages of danger, bypassing the cortex's sorting and screening ability. At that point she would feel overwhelmed and ashamed that she was "so sensitive" (her mother's words) and out of control. The images of the different parts of the brain working to keep her safe and healthy somehow made it easier for her to move through her uncertainty and fear to anchor herself in her very real ability to understand both her mother's and her part in these episodes. In fact, she could see her mother's difficulty in being vulnerable and getting her needs met. She was more able to quiet her highly aroused amygdala panic response, and she came to see that she (and her brain) were doing the best they could to stay in some balance in these interactions. Over time, she was able to spend more time with her mother, but she was also able to discern when her mother was putting out confusing messages of connection and retaliatory disconnection; she could see that her pain was not about her own "hypersensitivity" but that her mothers' actions were triggering her brain to protect herself. Rather than escalating toward panic and shame, Sharon used her discernment to protect herself and appropriately distance herself from these confusing and hurtful messages. While the mother was not actually in the room in either of these therapies, the relationship with her was often the focus of the work. As I work with the absent–present mother, I often feel like I, too, become more empathic with these mothers. Living in a culture that idealizes the mother in so many ways has its impact on therapists as well as clients. And working with someone who has been wounded in that early relationship evokes strong reactions in therapists as well. My immediate response in hearing about this pain is to feel sad and angry for my client; I feel protective, and it is easy to demonize the injuring party. But the real work for me as a therapist is to move beyond my own reactivity and my own relational images of what a "good" mother–daughter relationship should be and help the client contextualize that relationship. Eventually the client must grieve the limitations of that relationship and construct appropriate, current protective strategies to maintain a positive sense of worth and to recover a sense of clarity and vitality.

### *Cara*

Cara was a 40-year-old woman who grew up in an extremely dysfunctional family. Living in a rundown house in an otherwise upper-middle-class community, Cara and her family were the butt of neighborhood slurs: "the crazy Wilsons." Cara's mother was schizophrenic, periodically taken away by police for random community violations and occasionally awakening her three children in the middle of the night to go visit Jesus at the railroad station. Her father was explosively angry and overwhelmed. As an adult, Cara tried hard to stay connected with her mother and was very protective of her in her therapy work. She felt that most therapists were "mean" to mothers.

As an adult, Cara lived at some distance from her parents but sent them money and tried to visit them on holidays. However, when her mother said she wanted to move in with Cara, Cara felt endangered and guilty. She did not want to turn her mother away, but she felt that she would sacrifice her own life if she went along with this plan. She felt scared and stuck. She and I began to work on how she might safeguard the caring connection she had with her mother at the same time as she protected her own hard-won life and space. We did not vilify her mother or insist that Cara had to separate from her, but we did suggest that she needed to alter the nature of the connection. We also worked on shoring up connections with friends so that Cara felt acknowledged and supported by others as she traversed this new territory with her mother.

Like my clients, I sometimes feel angry, sad, or reactive to the ways mothers have hurt their daughters. Some mothers are destructive in an ongoing way with their daughters, in which case it is necessary for therapists to help clients understand their situations and grasp that sometimes it is not possible to make peace or find a way to a growth-fostering relationship, no matter how much they may desire it. It is important, then, for the daughter to begin to find ways to protect herself. She must disconnect from a destructive, nongrowth-fostering relationship to stay connected with herself and preserve the possibility of connecting with other people. She can best effect this healthy disconnection if she is moving to connect with people in other growth-fostering relationships.

### *Images of Motherhood*

Miller noted that dominant groups "tend to protect the advantages, rewards and spoils of disconnection by erecting barriers to change. They usually create a social structure and culture based on fear: fear of economic suffering, social ostracism, political deprivation, and more" (Jordan, 2010b, p. 142). Patricia Hill Collins (1990) introduced the concept of *controlling images,* which are created by dominant groups about themselves and subordinate groups. As she noted, "These images are always false but exert a powerful influence and act to hold each group in its place, that is, they act against change" (p. 199). She further stated that we take in these images about others and ourselves, sometimes without fully being conscious of the power they exercise in our expectations.

Our culture has strong controlling images for the role of mothering. Filled with the maternal instinct, mothers are supposed to be all-loving, empathic, responsive, strong in the service of others, tireless in their devotion to others' needs, patient, even-tempered, and selfless. At the same time, they must be supportive and loving partners who are interesting, sexy, and attentive, and today they are supposed to make a substantial economic contribution to the family as well. While they receive idealizing appreciation once a year on Mother's Day (and occasionally in idealizing advertisements or magazine articles), the actual challenges of the job are meant to be kept invisible, as mothers seamlessly carry out their work. But when children struggle or run into trouble in the wider world, the first accusing glance is cast at mothers. Perhaps motherhood, not psychoanalysis, is the "impossible profession" (Greenson, 1966).

Paying attention to the destructive consequences of unexamined power arrangements in nuclear families may prove more fruitful to the study of the mother–daughter relationship than looking at the particular wounds that occur between individual mothers and daughters, although both are necessary. It is not that the pain created in these very important relationships is not important. As a therapist I am dedicated to trying to assist my clients to become free from the suffering that has arisen in hurtful relationships with mothers, fathers, or anyone else who has been of importance to them. However, too often we forget to look at the larger picture of cultural disconnection and the trauma inflicted by a culture built on relationships based in fear, dominance, and unequal power and stratification. Until we reexamine the cultural arrangements involved in raising children, sifting through those that promote growth and relatedness and those that create immobilization and isolation, we will be patching and band-aiding where we should be rebuilding and reconstructing. As Martin Luther King, Jr., noted, "Compassion is not throwing a coin at a beggar, it is changing the whole social structure that creates beggars" (King, 1987). Paulo Freire (1989) wrote that "the pursuit of full humanity cannot be carried out in isolation or through individualism but only in fellowship and solidarity" (p. 71). Healing in the mother–daughter relationship depends on being dedicated to respecting women, devoting energy to building growth-fostering relationships in the culture at large, and realizing that the personal is the political. We must change the societal structures that demean and disempower women as we also enter into healing relationships with those already wounded by these dysfunctional systems.

## References

Altheide, D. (2002). *Creating fear: News and the construction of crisis.* New York: Aldine de Gruyter.

Benkov, L. (1998). Yes, I am a swan: Reflecting on families headed by lesbians and gay men. In C. Garcia-Coll, J. Surrey, & K. Weingarten, (Eds.), *Mothering against the odds* (pp. 113–133). New York: Guilford.

Blos, P. (1979). *The adolescent passage.* New York: International Universities Press.

Bradshaw, C. (1994). Asian and Asian American women: Historical and political considerations in psychotherapy. In L. Comas-Diaz & B. Greene (Eds.), *Women of color: Integrating ethnic and gender identities in psychotherapy* (pp. 72–113). New York: Guilford Press.

Caplan, P. (1989). *Don't blame mother: Mending the mother–daughter relationship.* New York: Harper.

Coll, C., Surrey, J., & Weingarten, K. (Eds.). (1998). *Mothering against the odds: Diverse voices of contemporary mothers.* New York: Guilford Press.

Collins, P. H. (1990). *Black feminist thought.* New York: Routledge.

Comas-Diaz, L., & Greene, B. (1994). *Women of color: Integrating ethnic and gender identities in psychotherapy.* New York: Guilford.

Dickerson, V., & Zimmerman, J. (1992). Families with adolescents: Escaping problem lifestyles. *Family Process, 31,* 341–353.

Dickerson, V., & Zimmerman, J. (1993). A narrative approach to families with adolescents. In S. Friedman (Ed.), *The new language of change: Constructive collaboration in psychotherapy* (pp. 226–250). New York: Guilford Press.

Eisenberger, N., & Lieberman, M. (2003). *Why it hurts to be left out: The neurocognitive overlap between physical and social pain.* Unpublished manuscript, Department of Psychology, University of California, Los Angeles.

Eisenberger, N., & Lieberman, M. (2004). Why rejection hurts: A common neural alarm system for physical and social pain. *Trends in Cognitive Sciences, 8,* 294–300.

Friere, P. (1989). *The pedagogy of the oppressed.* New York: Continuum.

Gilligan, C. (1982). *In a different voice.* Cambridge, MA: Harvard University Press.

Gilligan, C., & Rogers, A. (1993). Reframing daughtering and mothering. In J. van Mens-Verhulst, K. Schreurs, & L. Woertman (Eds.), *Daughtering and mothering: Female subjectivity reanalysed* (pp. 125–134). London, England: Routledge.

Gilligan, C., Rogers, A., & Tolman, D. (Eds.). (1991). *Women, girls and psychotherapy: Reframing resistance.* Binghamton, NY: Harrington Park Press.

Greene, B. (1990a). Sturdy bridges: The role of African American mothers in the socialization of African American children. *Women and Therapy, 10,* 205–225.

Greene, B. (1990b). What has gone before: The legacy of racism and sexism in the lives of Black mothers and daughters. *Women and Therapy, 9,* 207–230.

Greene, B. (1994). African American Women. In L. Diaz & B. Greene (Eds.), *Women of color: Integrating ethnic and gender identities in psychotherapy.* New York: Guilford.

Greenson, R. (1966). That "impossible" profession. *Journal of the American Psychoanalytic Association, 14,* 9–27.

Greenson, R. (1967). *The technique and practice of psychoanalysis.* New York: Hallmark Press.

Harris, J. (1998). *The nurture assumption.* New York: Free Press.

Hill, R. (1971). *The strengths of Black families.* New York: National Urban League.

Jordan, J. (Ed.). (1995). *Women's growth in diversity.* New York: Guilford.

Jordan, J. (2009). *Relational–cultural therapy.* Washington, DC: American Psychological Association.

Jordan, J. (2010a). Commitment to connection in a culture of fear. In J. Jordan (Ed.), *The power of connection: Recent developments in relational–cultural theory.* New York: Routledge.

Jordan, J. (Ed.). (2010b). *The power of connection: Recent developments in relational–cultural theory.* New York: Routledge.
Jordan, J., Kaplan, A., Miller, J., Stiver, I., & Surrey, J. L. (1991). *Women's growth in connection: Writings from the Stone Center.* New York: Guilford Press.
Jordan, J., Walker, M., & Hartling, L. (Eds.). (2004). *The complexity of connection.* New York: Guilford.
Kaplan, A., Klein, R., & Gleason, N. (1985). Women's self-development in late adolescent. *Work in Progress, 17.* Wellesley, MA: Stone Center Working Paper Series.
Kernberg, O. (1967). Borderline personality organization. *Journal of the American Psychoanalytic Association, 15,* 641–685.
King, M. L. (1987). *The words of Martin Luther King, Jr. selected by Coretta Scott King.* New York: Newmarket Press.
Lazarre, J. (1991). *Worlds beyond my control.* New York: Dutton.
Mahler, M., Pine, F., & Bergman, A. (1975). *The psychological birth of the human infant.* New York: Basic Books.
Miller, J. (1976). *Toward a new psychology of women.* Boston, MA: Beacon Press.
Miller, J., & Stiver, I. (1997). *The healing connection.* Boston, MA: Beacon Press.
Polikoff, N. (1990). This child does have two mothers: Redefining parenthood to meet the needs of children in lesbian-mother and other nontraditional families. *Georgetown Law Journal, 78,* 459–575.
Polikoff, N. (1996). The deliberate construction of families without fathers: Is it an option for lesbian and heterosexual mothers? *Santa Clara Law Review, 36*(2), 375–394.
Pollack, W. (1998). *Real boys: Rescuing our sons from the myths of boyhood.* New York: Random House.
Robinson, T., & Ward, J. (1991). "A belief in self far greater than anyone's disbelief": Cultivating resistance among African American female adolescents. In C. Gilligan, A. Rogers, & D. Tolman (Eds.), *Women, girls and psychotherapy: Reframing resistance* (pp. 87–104). Binghamton, NY: Harrington Park Press.
Rosen, W. (1992). On the integration of sexuality: Lesbians and their mothers. *Work in Progress, 56.* Wellesley, MA: Stone Center Working Paper Series.
Stampp, K. (1989). *The peculiar institution: Slavery in the ante-bellum South.* New York: Vintage Books.
Stiver, I. (1990). Dysfunctional families and wounded relationships, part 1. *Work in Progress, 41.* Wellesley, MA: Stone Center Working Paper Series.
Suh, S. (2007). Too maternal and not womanly enough: Asian-American women's gender identity conflict. *Women and Therapy, 30*(3–4), 35–50.
Surrey, J. (1990). Mother-blaming and clinical theory. In J. P. Knowles & E. Cole (Eds.), *Motherhood: A feminist perspective* (pp. 83–88). New York: Haworth Press.
Thurer, S. (1994). *The myths of motherhood: How culture reinvents the good mother.* New York: Houghton Mifflin.
Vasquez, M. J. T. (1984). Power and status of the Chicana: A social–psychological perspective. In J. L. Martinez & R. H. Mendoza (Eds.), *Chicana psychology* (2nd ed.; pp. 269–287). New York: Academic Press.
Ward, J. (2000). *The skin we're in: Teaching our children to be emotionally strong, socially smart, and spiritually connected.* New York: Free Press.
White, B. (1971). *Human infants: Experience and psychological development.* Englewood Cliffs, NJ: Prentice-Hall.

CHAPTER 9

# Addressing Poisonous Parenting Within the African American Community

## *A Systems Approach*

JENNIFER I. DURHAM

Addressing poisonous parenting should not be done without considering the nature of poison. Plainly stated, poison is a substance that is harmful to an organism. It is important to note that what makes the substance harmful is variable. It can be something developed in nature that once exposed to an organism immediately and quickly begins impeding functions that support life. It can do this slowly and cause impairment over time. Like alcohol, a substance may be relatively harmless in low dosages but can evolve into poison when experienced in greater quantities or before an organism is mature enough to diffuse it properly. It can also be something that has been created for a benevolent purpose but when taken incorrectly becomes harmful or lethal. Such is the case with poisonous parenting and the African American community. A poison is understood and defined only within the context it is experienced. This chapter examines how the context of African American families and the race-based challenges they face shape poisonous parenting and presents strategies for the treatment of African American adults who have been exposed to poisonous parenting. Although not all poisonous parenting within the African American community is related to race-based issues, the extensive nature and scope of race cannot be ignored in the lives of people of African descent and is the focus of this chapter.

There is significant diversity within the African American community. Not only is there variance with respect to socioeconomic status, religion, education, racial identity, and culture, but there are also differences with respect to family systems. African Americans are raised in two-parent households, one-parent households, extended family constellations, and foster care situations. Clinicians should be cautious about relying on stereotypes when working with clients of African descent. Research presented on African American issues raised in this chapter should be used as guideposts rather than absolutes.

## African American Families and a Systems Approach

In the groundbreaking work of Boyd-Franklin (1989) a multisystems approach is suggested when working with African American families. She asserts that to effectively treat African American families it is imperative that the clinician be able to conceptualize and intervene on a multisystemic level. These systems may include individuals, subsets of family members, extended family, ethnic groups, church groups, or, in the case of poor families, social service organizations. Although the focus of this chapter is on African American adults rather than families, a parenting relationship exists within a system. To understand the nature and dynamics of the poisonous parenting relationship, clinicians must be able to understand and perhaps intervene at a systems level. The multisystems approach also provides a framework to conceptualize and work intergenerationally.

## Parenting Styles

As stated earlier, what makes something harmful depends on the context of the interaction. Styles of parenting and techniques provide a framework with which to describe and assess parenting but can be viewed as harmful only when considered with respect to dosage, health of the system, and timing. Only after these considerations can something be viewed as poisonous.

In her work on parenting styles, Baumrind (1989, 1991b) describes three basic styles of parenting. She reports that the parents of the most capable children demonstrate a demand for maturity and discipline while employing reasoning techniques, warmth, and support. She refers to these parents as authoritative. This style differs from what Baumrind labeled as authoritarian parenting. This style is characterized by a demand for obedience that uses coercion as an enforcement technique. Authoritarian parenting also includes minimal communication between parent and child, and little attention is given to the viewpoints of the child. Research has found that children of authoritarian parents are not as competent in social and academic settings as children raised by authoritative parents. These children also tend to be anxious and irritable (Grusec, 2002).

Permissive parenting is the third style described by Baumrind (1989, 1991b) and is made up of two subcategories. The first is permissive-indulgent, which includes high levels of permissiveness with little demands for discipline and mature behavior, accompanied by high levels of nurturing and warmth. The second category, permissive-rejecting, also includes low demand for disciplined mature behavior but is not accompanied by warmth or responsiveness. Research has found that children raised with permissive-rejecting parenting are the least competent and more prone to behavioral problems (Baumrind, 1991a).

## Race-Based Stressors and Poisonous Parenting

Since parenting styles are embedded within a family system, it is imperative to explore poisonous parenting from a systems perspective. Although all families face stressors, race-based stressors, such as discrimination and racism, have been noted to impact African American family systems and add to the historical residue of oppression and tragedy in the African American community (Boyd-Franklin, 2003; Kelly, 2003). Unlike their Caucasian counterparts, research indicates that economic disparities and racism have resulted in significant stressors on the systems that are raising African American children (Boyd-Franklin, 2003; Boyd-Franklin & Franklin, 1998; Franklin, 2004; Kelly, 2003; Kelly & Floyd, 2001, 2006; La Taillade, 2006).

Tucker and Mitchell-Kernan (1995) demonstrated that poor access to economic resources and higher levels of poverty within the African American community can negatively impact some couples' relationships. It can be suggested that discord within the couple relationship may have an influence on one's availability to parent. This may be demonstrated by parents seeking fulfillment, which should be achieved through their couple relationship, from their parenting relationship. This places an emotional burden on the children and can evolve into interactions that could be considered poisonous.

In addition to economic marginalization, racism also presents a burden for many African American families. La Taillade, Baucom, and Jacobson (2000) found that African American couples that indicated they had experienced racism and discrimination were more likely to engage in verbally aggressive and violent communication patterns. Displacement of negative emotions associated with race-based stressors, in addition to internalized racism, places burdens on the family system that may lead to unsupportive and negative behaviors within African American couple relationships (Kelly & Floyd, 2001, 2006).

Although this work does not address the interaction between couples' discord and child-rearing or the presence of children, it can be strongly suggested that children who are being raised by parents with verbally aggressive and violent communication patterns will at the least be exposed to these interactions and at the worst be the direct recipients of them. Moreover, the likelihood of internalized racism and the displacement of negative emotions related to race-based stressors finding their way to the parenting relationship is high. The research regarding the negative effects of race-based stressors on the family system is supported by the extensive and comprehensive clinical examples presented by Boyd-Franklin (2003) and Boyd-Franklin and Franklin (1998) of the manner in which anger and frustration related to racism and discrimination can manifest themselves within the African American family system.

One issue extensively explored by Boyd-Franklin (1989) is how internalized racism manifests itself within the family through skin color issues. Due to the sexual exploitation of enslaved African women they often gave birth to children with varying skin tones, facial features, and hair textures. These differences have influenced the lives of African Americans since the slavery era. Enslaved children with Caucasian fathers were often given work within the house rather than the labor of the fields or given other relative privileges. This hierarchy of skin color has evolved over time and remnants of the idea that lighter-skinned African Americans have greater access to resources can be found in varying degrees in the modern era.

Bowen (1976, 1978) identified a process by which families project roles and expectations for individuals based on multigenerational transmissions. Since appearance is a crucial component of these projections, variance in skin color and other features may result in projections that can be described as internal racism. They have the potential to fuel poisonous parenting toward a particular child.

## Case Examples

Couples and families that have been negatively impacted by racism, discrimination, and economic marginalization may be less available for their children or develop coping strategies that distort parenting styles and may evolve into parenting that can be termed as poisonous. This can be illustrated by the cases of Mia, Hugh, and Faith.

### *Mia*

Mia is a 32-year-old woman who has been married for 6 years and was experiencing conflict with her husband because she does not want to have children. She initially described her hesitancy to have children to be related to "not being ready." Further exploration revealed she has never had a close relationship with her mother. Mia characterized her mother as condemning, judgmental, and critical. She stated that their interactions usually led to insulting arguments and left her feeling drained and inadequate. These negative interactions were compounded by the fact that her mother repeatedly pointed out a dislike of her choice of husband. After a connection between Mia's lack of desire to have children and the way her mother parented her was made, the nature of the poison in her parents' style was examined within a systems framework.

Mia was raised by her mother and grandmother in a southern city. Her grandmother was a woman with a fair complexion from a rural community, who at 18 worked as a domestic worker in the home of a rich, White family. Family lore states that she was given the job because the husband found her attractive. Shortly after her employment she became pregnant and went to live in the city with a distant cousin. She got a job in a hotel, gave birth to Mia's mother, Eliza, and doted on her. She viewed Eliza's close resemblance to a White person as a significant asset. She encouraged her to do well in school, and Eliza became a nurse. Shortly after graduation she married a medical student she had been dating. Although he was a physician from a prominent African American family, Mia's grandmother was unhappy with his medium-brown complexion and did not hesitate to express her opinion. She even included Mia in her conversations. Her parents eventually divorced when Mia was 6, and her grandmother moved in. Mia described a childhood where she was constantly being compared to her father and what were perceived to be his negative traits. Although she did exceptionally well in school, nothing she did seemed good enough to be noticed by Eliza or her grandmother. She described being chastised for her appearance and looking "too Black" and then ignored by both women. She left home at 17 to attend college in New England. She remained there for graduate school and married a dark-skinned man. Although she seems to have been parented within the permissive-rejecting framework, race-based stressors appear to have amplified the effects and shaped a poisonous relationship.

Mia remembered being in summer camp at age 8, where she and her fellow campers swam twice a day. She was sent to the swimming pool by her mother with a sweatshirt and sweatpants in the Georgia heat. Her mother gave her strict instructions to keep the sweat suit on unless she was in the water. After the afternoon swim, she put on her sweat suit and went to play on the playground. She became dizzy and nauseous. The camp director insisted she take off the sweat suit and sit in the shade. When her mother arrived to pick her up and saw her outside without being covered, she beat her publically and refused to pick her up again as Mia had embarrassed her. Mia went on to describe similar rejecting situations, which were rooted in her mother's perceptions of being purposefully embarrassed by

Mia and her "Blackness." Mia reported that her mother refused to come to her wedding because she did not want to be embarrassed by her daughter's choice of a dark-skinned groom.

When examining this case, issues of internalized racism that have been intergenerationally transmitted become apparent. Projections based on complexion resulted in a mother and grandmother being hypercritical and neglectful to Mia. The scope and dosage of the rejection was so profound it was impeding Mia's desire to create a family of her own.

The judgmental and belittling behavior experienced by Mia was shaped by internalized racism. This poisonous parenting can also be the result of other race-based stressors, such as economic marginalization, and can be executed within a distorted authoritarian parenting framework. This is illustrated in the case of Hugh.

*Hugh*

Hugh was a 42-year-old divorced male with two sons. He sought treatment to work on the conflicted relationships with his sons, who were repeatedly disobeying rules at school. A review of the family history indicated that Hugh grew up as the eldest in a two-parent household with three boys. Although his father was a gifted mason, Hugh reported that his father was not let into the union due to his race. He was hired as a day laborer on jobs and barely made enough to feed and clothe the family. Hugh had distinct memories of his father working 16 hours a day and having very little to show for it. Hugh and his brothers wore secondhand clothing, never went on outings, such as the movies, and were often hungry. He reported his father to have been highly critical and abusive both physically and verbally. Hugh was made to get a job at 15 and contribute to the household. His father's ridicule and belittling transcended his high school years and continued into the present. Although he had secured work as a mail carrier, Hugh was often called names such as "lazy ass" and "soft" when he showed interest in anything unrelated to physical labor. Hugh stated that his father called him at least twice a week to criticize him for his failed marriage and the way he was raising his sons. Hugh described a recent incident when he called to wish his father a happy birthday and his father could only complain that his grandsons were not on the phone because Hugh was not man enough to keep his family together. Hugh believed the interactions he had with his father were impairing his ability to parent his boys effectively and left him feeling sad and helpless.

Discussion with Hugh's father revealed that he had experienced significant grief and shame about his inability to provide a more financially stable life for his family. He experienced life as being tough and unforgiving and did what he thought was best to prepare his boys for that reality. Similar to administering a vaccination shot, he viewed it as his duty to discourage

Hugh from pursuing anything that might yield disappointment and pain even if he had to inflict both to do so. He stated he had to keep his boys tough so they did not break under the pressure.

Hugh's case reveals how being economically marginalized due to race can distort an authoritarian style and shape a poisonous parenting relationship. The father spoke poignantly about never realizing his potential as a mason and the pain of coming home from the Vietnam War after defending his country and not being allowed into the union. His lack of self-actualization led him to twist an authoritarian parenting style into something he perceived would make his son strong in the face of pain, discouragement, and self-doubt. This inability to self-actualize due to race-based stressors can shape other forms of poisonous parenting. This is revealed in the case of Faith.

### *Faith*

As a 34-year-old mother of one son, Faith was struggling to maintain boundaries with her mother. She grew up the only child of relatively older parents. She described her mother, Joan, as a gifted violinist who was told by a guidance counselor at her inner-city high school that "orchestras did not have places for Negro girls." Joan pursued a teaching degree and taught music throughout Faith's childhood. Faith reported that she did not remember a time when she was not playing an instrument. Her mother enrolled her in piano lessons twice a week when she was 3. When it was discovered that she had some talent in this area, the development of her skills as a pianist took precedence over schooling, social, and family relationships. Her mother insisted they move away from the Virginia city of her birth and her father to go New York. She reported believing the only way to maintain her mother's love was to do well at the piano. If she ever expressed fatigue or an interest in something else her mother expressed more love toward Faith in an effort to prevent what she experienced as abandonment. Faith was accepted at the prestigious Manhattan School of Music, but not her mother's ultimate choice of Julliard, a disappointment her mother still mentions and attributes to a purposeful act by Faith to separate herself from Joan. Faith fell in love with jazz and a jazz musician at the Manhattan School of Music and married.

Due to the desire for a relatively conventional family life, Faith and her husband established moderate performing and recording careers as jazz musicians. Her mother, Joan, constantly pushed both of them toward more celebrity and inserted herself in their lives. She perceived herself as helping them get more established in their careers. Faith described a recent incident involving her mother's intrusiveness. Joan, through connections of her own, learned that Faith had turned down an opportunity to tour for 2 weeks with a world-famous jazz musician because it conflicted with her son's first day of middle school. Without Faith's permission, Joan called Faith's booking agency and asked if it was too late to accept the tour. After being told it was not too late, Joan booked Faith on the tour. Then she phoned Faith and announced she would come to stay with her grandson to ensure a smooth transition to middle school. When Faith attempted to challenge her mother's behavior Joan experienced it as a lack of gratitude for helping her daughter achieve her goals and a rejection of a mother's love. Faith backed down and went on the tour, causing conflict with both her husband and son.

Faith's case illustrates how a parent's inability to self-actualize due to race-based stressors can distort an authoritative parenting style. Although this style has in many instances shown to be healthier than others, it can also be warped and moved into the realm of poisonous (Grusec, 2002). Joan's guidance and support evolved into an intrusive style that inhibited her ability to let Faith create her own guideposts.

## Treatment Implications and Strategies

Treating poison involves three basic strategies. The first involves amputation or sacrificing a piece of the organism to prevent the spread of toxicity. The second strategy focuses on weakening the strength of the toxic agents to minimize the harmful effects on the organism. Creation of an antidote is the third strategy. Before adopting any of these strategies in treatment, the implications of the nature of poisonous parenting within an African American context must be considered. One implication is the strength and resilience of African American families.

### *Strengths Within African American Systems*

Cultural strengths, such as a positive racial and ethnic identity, the support of kinship, and extended family, in addition to religion and spirituality, have been found to support resilience in the African American family and to work as protective factors mitigating the effects of race-based stressors (Boyd-Franklin, 2003; Hines & Boyd-Franklin, 2005; La Taillade, 2006).

Each of these cultural components is embedded in a system. Race and ethnic identity create a functioning system within society. Boyd-Franklin (2003) found that a strong and positive racial identity may serve as a protective factor against racism and discrimination. This protective quality can also be seen in the African American community with respect to religion and spirituality. The church and spiritual associations represent an additional system within society. Generations of African Americans have used religious and spiritual systems to survive enslavement, segregation, discriminatory practices, and racist practices and attitudes (Bowen-Reid & Harrell, 2002; Boyd-Franklin, 2003; Hines & Boyd-Franklin, 2005;

Kelly & Floyd, 2006; La Taillade, 2006; Taylor, Mattis, & Chatters, 1999). Extended family and kinship relationships are also relevant systems for African Americans. Hatchett, Veroff, and Douvan (1995) found that African American women who consistently interact with extended family members are more likely to be in stable marriages.

### *Multisystemic Intergenerational Perspective*

Another component to consider is a multisystemic, intergenerational perspective. When working with African American clients, being aware of their relationship to the various systems in which they function has proven useful in treatment (Boyd-Franklin, 1989). This should also be the case with poisonous parenting. While not all poisonous parenting within the African American community is solely related to race-based stressors, it can be argued that these elements can be found in many cases and should be considered in treatment. The only way to develop a comprehensive understanding and plan for treatment is to conceptualize the presenting problem and treatment plan through a systemic lens. If this is not done the clinician will miss valuable information. This is especially true if extended family and intergenerational systems are excluded. In all three of the cases presented, if the perspectives of multiple generations were not identified, the opportunity for a comprehensive treatment plan would be lost.

Using the case of Hugh as an example, his father was included in the treatment plan. As stated earlier, authoritarian parenting does not involve direct, compassionate communication between parent and child. Hearing his father articulate a rationale for his behavior was a crucial point in Hugh's treatment. He went from perceiving his father as a man who hated him and never thought he was good enough to a broken, frustrated person who did what he thought was best to prepare his son for life. While this could not take away the poisonous effects of years of his father's parenting style, it allowed Hugh to make decisions about his relationships with his father and sons from an enlightened, less vulnerable position.

### *Interaction Between the Poison and the Organism*

When poison enters an organism, it either shuts down to accommodate the toxin or fights back. Clinicians should pay careful attention to how their clients have reacted to poisonous parenting. Clients may not be aware of the maladaptive patterns they employ to protect themselves from the poison, but these patterns often exacerbate the situation. This can be seen in the case Faith. Since her mother, Joan, presented as warm and supportive it was hard for Faith to identify their interactions as poisonous and often made her feel guilty and angry when this was suggested by others. She accommodated her mother's intrusiveness by simply shutting down. Faith's unwillingness to set boundaries just fueled her mother's intrusive behaviors. While Joan had established using guilt to coerce her daughter from a young age, Faith's compliance as an adult allowed Joan to justify her behavior. Helping Faith understand her role in maintaining the poison in the relationship enabled her to move from a shutdown stance to one of fighting back. Clinicians can assist clients in understanding how their attitude and behavior may be sustaining the poison in their relationships with their parents and support them when they take risks to fight back.

*Treatment Strategies*

There are several strategies for treating an organism once poison has entered its system. One approach involves removing the infected part of the organism before the poison destroys the entire living system. Another strategy involves mitigating the strength of the poison to reduce destruction. The last approach addresses developing another agent that will counteract the impact of the poison. All three will be briefly addressed.

*Amputation* As stated earlier poison can be treated by amputation, weakening its effects, or developing an antidote. The first is the most radical and involves the organism sacrificing a piece of itself. Within the context of poisonous parenting clients would cease all interactions with their parent. Therapists should help clients explore the severity and consequences of such an action before it is done. Factors to explore include the level to which the poisonous relationship is impeding the functioning of the client and the willingness of the parents to stop spewing toxins into their interactions with their child.

Such factors were explored in the case of Mia. Although with the clinician's help Mia came to reframe the treatment she received from her mother and grandmother within the context of internalized racism, her mother's unwillingness to explore the issue kept toxins pouring into their interactions. When Mia insisted on addressing the poison, her mother increased the level of toxicity. Its effects eroded her sense of self. The poison had impeded her desire of the possibility of bringing a dark-skinned child into the world fearing he or she would receive the same treatment from Mia's mother's side of the family. As this was likely since one of her mother's complaints when Mia married her husband would be that the child would be embarrassingly dark, Mia decided to sever ties with her mother and grandmother.

*Weakening the Strength of the Poison* With respect to treating adult clients who have experienced poisonous parenting but feel that resolution with their parents is the healthiest course of action, clinicians can help them lessen the effects of the poison. Lessening the effects suggests that the parent is unwilling or unable to cease toxic interactions, but the clinician may help the client experience these interactions differently, which may weaken the toxin.

This is illustrated in the case of Hugh. Once he reframed his father's behavior as emanating from a place of paternal concern for his son, Hugh was no longer burdened by not feeling good enough and felt less hurt by the names his father would call him. Hugh became an observer of his father and initiated contact to get to know him better. As he made himself available to his father the insults and negative statements diminished. No longer fearing parental disapproval, Hugh became more communicative with his own sons and engaged in addressing their behavioral problems.

*Developing an Antidote* Creating an antidote involves actively engaging with the original properties of the poison. When possible, clinicians should speak with or include the poisonous parent's perspective in their client's treatment. Only by dissecting the toxic agents of the poisonous relationship can a cure be developed and implemented. An example of this is the case of Faith and her mother, Joan.

Faith originally sought treatment for feelings of helplessness with respect to disciplining her son, sadness, and marital conflict. To avoid being intrusive she was excessively permissive and gave her son authority over his actions that were not developmentally appropriate. This led to problematic behaviors in school and conflicts with her husband. After several sessions a connection was made between Faith's permissive parenting style and how she had been parented. Examining the role that guilt and coercion played in lessening boundaries helped Faith create a response to her mother's intrusiveness. With the help of the clinician Faith was able to resist the coercive tactics of her mother, set boundaries with her, and confront her when they were breached. The clinician also helped Faith understand that she was establishing a new pattern of interaction with her mother. She was also helped to understand that this change would likely cause an increase in poisonous behavior prior to a decline in such behavior.

## Conclusion

Poisonous parenting within the African American community does not have to be fatal, and its effects can often be mitigated or cured. Clinicians working with African American adult clients who have experienced poisonous parenting should consider the role of race-based stressors in the shaping and manifestation of the poison from a systemic perspective. This will result in comprehensive treatment practices that are relevant to the African American experience.

## References

Baumrind, D. (1989). Rearing competent children. In W. Damon (Ed.), *Child development today and tomorrow* (pp. 349–378). San Francisco, CA: Jossey-Bass.

Baumrind, D. (1991a). The influence of parenting style on adolescent competence and substance use. *Journal of Early Adolescence, 11*, 56–95.

Baumrind, D. (1991b). Parenting styles and adolescent development. In J. Brooks-Gunn, R. Lerner, & A. C. Petersen (Eds.), *Encyclopedia of adolescence* (pp. 746–758). New York: Garland.

Bowen, M. (1976). Theory in the practice of psychotherapy. In P. J. Guerin (Ed.), *Family therapy: Theory and practice* (pp. 42–90). New York: Gardner Press.

Bowen, M. (1978). *Family therapy in clinical practice*. New York: Jason Aronson.

Bowen-Reid, T. L., & Harrell, J. P. (2002). Racist experiences and health outcomes: An examination of spirituality as a buffer. *Journal of Black Psychology, 28*, 18–36.

Boyd-Franklin, N. (1989). *Black families in therapy: A multisystems approach*. New York: Guilford Press.

Boyd-Franklin, N. (2003). *Black families in therapy: Understanding the African American experience*. New York: Guilford Press.

Boyd-Franklin, N., & Franklin, A. J. (1998). African American couples in therapy. In M. McGoldrick (Ed.), *Re-visioning family therapy: Race, culture, and gender in clinical practice* (pp. 268–281). New York: Guilford Press.

Franklin, A. J. (2004). *From brotherhood to manhood: How black men rescue their relationships and dreams from the invisibility syndrome*. Hoboken, NJ: John Wiley & Sons.

Franklin, A. J., Boyd-Franklin, N., & Kelly, S. (2006). Racism and invisibility: Race-related stress, emotional abuse and psychological trauma for people of color. *Journal of Emotional Abuse, 6*, 9–30.

Grusec, J. E. (2002). Parenting socialization and children's acquisition of values. In M.H. Bornstein (Ed.), *Handbook of parenting, 2nd ed., Vol. 5, Practical issues in parenting* (pp. 143–167). Mahwah, NJ: Erlbaum.

Hatchett, S., Veroff, J., & Douvan, E. (1995). Marital instability among black and white newlyweds. In M. B. Tucker & C. Mitchell-Kernan (Eds.), *The decline in marriage among African Americans* (pp. 177–218). New York: Russell Sage Foundation.

Hines, P., & Boyd-Franklin, N. (2005). African American families. In M. McGoldrick, J. Giordano, & N. Garcia-Preto (Eds.), *Ethnicity and family therapy*, 3rd ed. (pp. 87–100). New York: Guilford Press.

Kelly, S. (2003). African-American couples: Their importance to the stability of African-American families and their mental health issues. In J. S. Mio & G. Y. Iwamasa (Eds.), *Culturally diverse mental health: The challenges of research and resistance* (pp. 141–157). New York: Brunner-Routledge.

Kelly, S., & Floyd, F. J. (2001). The effects of negative racial stereotypes and Afrocentricity on Black couple relationships. *Journal of Family Psychology, 15*, 110–123.

Kelly, S., & Floyd, F. J. (2006). Impact of racial perspectives and contextual variables on marital trust and adjustment for African American couples. *Journal of Family Psychology, 20*, 79–87.

La Taillade, J. J. (2006). Considerations for treatment of African American couple relationships. *Journal of Cognitive Psychotherapy: An International Quarterly, 20*, 341–358.

La Taillade, J. J., Baucom, D. H., & Jacobson, N. S. (2000, November). *Correlates of satisfaction and resiliency in African American/White interracial relationships.* Paper presented as part of the symposium (J. J. La Taillade, Chair), The influence of culture and context of the intimate relationships of African Americans, at the annual convention of the Association for Advancement of Behavior Therapy, New Orleans, LA.

Taylor, R. J., Mattis, J., & Chatters, L. M. (1999). Subjective religiosity among African Americans: A synthesis of findings from five national samples. *Journal of Black Psychology, 25*, 524–543.

Tucker, M. B., & Mitchell-Kernan, C. (1995). Trends in African American family formation: A theoretical and statistical overview. In M. B. Tucker & C. Mitchell-Kernan (Eds.), *The decline in marriage among African Americans* (pp. 3–26). New York: Russell Sage.

CHAPTER 10

# Honor Thy Parents? A Religious Perspective on Poisonous Parenting

DONALD J. OLUND

One of the most quoted proverbs on parenting is, "Train up a child in the way he should go, and when he gets old he will not depart from it" (Proverbs 22:6). Parents of a Judeo-Christian orientation cling to this verse with hope that their adult children will embrace the values and beliefs that were instilled when they were young. Commentators and theologians propose various interpretations on the meaning of *train up* in the Hebrew language. One interpretation is based on the etymological root meaning "to touch the palate." The imagery here is of a mother weaning her child by introducing food, perhaps some fig jam to her baby boy. The mother places a small amount of jam on her finger and touches the top of the child's palate so that he can taste the sweetness of the preserve. Repetition of this simple act of exposure with other samples and the process of eating food for the remainder of the child's life is under way. Metaphorically, from a parenting perspective, the implication is that by slowly introducing children to religious beliefs they acquire a taste for spiritual values that will remain with them into adulthood.

Now imagine after a period of time the mother began mixing the jam or other foods with something toxic, perhaps a very small extract from the poisonous herb, gall. The child would ingest something sweet, with a hint of a bitter flavor, followed by reactive symptoms to the poison. While the potion is not lethal, the little boy nonetheless becomes sick upon exposure to the toxicant. Afterward, the child protests that he does not want to eat food because it makes him sick. The mother, reminding her son that she knows what is best for him, insists he eat what is presented or face punishment. Essentially, the mother has boxed the youngster into the proverbial corner of her control. Knowing no way out, the child decides to eat the food, which gains the favor of his mother he desires yet at the expense of his health. To cope, the boy learns to develop a tolerance for stomachaches. Eventually, the child forms an association of something inherently good (food) with an experience that is unpleasant yet unavoidable. Correspondingly, mixed feelings of mistrust and loyalty toward the mother confuse the child.

Fast forward to the time when the boy becomes a man, thus owning the decision of what to eat, and several questions emerge: Will the adult child continue to ingest what makes him sick? Or is his fate already sealed, as the proverb seems to indicate; "when he gets old he will not depart from it"? Furthermore, what becomes of the parent–child relationship?

Juxtaposed with the Proverbs 22:6 scripture is the fifth commandment, "Honor thy father and thy mother that thy days may be long upon the land which the Lord thy God giveth thee" (Exodus 20:12). Included in the Ten Commandments given to Moses when he appeared before the Almighty on Mt. Sinai, the fifth commandment is considered a sacred rule among Judeo-Christian believers. The word *honor* can be interpreted as respect, glorify, or venerate (Gaebelein & Kalland, 1990). The idea here is that children are to honor parents for the role they serve as procreators and caretakers of their lives. The commandment highlights the importance of hierarchy and status given to parents in the Hebrew family system. Failure to keep the command was an act of social disgrace subject to punishment by death or stoning (Exodus 21:15, 17).

Returning to the aforementioned illustration, the adult child is faced with another dilemma. Not only does he have to contend with the demands of his mother to honor her with continued devotion and loyalty, but the young man also has to consider the expectations of the religious community. Furthermore, he may have to take it a step higher and consider the expectation his God has declared in the commandment given. Thus, he finds himself in a predicament of having to give honor at the expense of his own welfare.

The story of the mother and boy seems highly unlikely, except in cases of Münchausen's syndrome by proxy (Lasher & Sheridan, 2004). However, it is intended to illustrate how poisonous parents use religion to control their children. Most parents do not intentionally harm their children. In fact, oftentimes poisonous parents are unaware they are inflicting damage. In their view they are acting in their children's best interests. However, upon closer examination, the negative effect of this parenting style is toxic to their children's development. The poison may come disguised in a variety of potions administered in various levels of potency. For example, poisonous parents may lace the toxicant *perfection* in the messages they send to their children. The expectation for the child is to be perfect in all aspects of life. The message is further reinforced by use of religious overtones, quoting scriptures such as, "Be perfect therefore as your heavenly Father is perfect" (Matthew 5:48). The intent is not primarily for the benefit of the child as it is for the validation of the parent in the eyes of others. Other poisonous potions may include *dependency, shame, blind loyalty, adoration*, and *defectiveness*.

Poisonous parenting in a religious context is complicated because it confuses children on several levels: self-identity, attachment to parents, and God concept. As the previous example illustrates, it can be unclear to children who in fact is delivering the poison injection. The parent? God? Or both? Undoubtedly, this will have serious implications in the development of children throughout developmental stages. For those in mental health and religious-based helping professions, working with individuals affected by poisonous parenting will require a careful, thoughtful approach to healing attachment injuries that may have both a vertical (God) and horizontal (others) dimension. To begin this process it will require some knowledge on what an individual's religion teaches about parenting.

## What Religions Teach About Parenting

To do a comprehensive review on every religion's teaching on parenting is not the aim of this chapter. Therefore, the focus will be on three primary religious groups in America: Christianity (78.4% of population), Judaism (1.7%), and Muslim (0.6%) (U.S. Census Bureau, 2010). A basic overview and the central concepts of religion and parenting are highlighted.

### *Christianity*

Christianity accompanied the pilgrims when they first landed on the soil of the New World (Linder, 1990). Over the course of American history, Christianity rapidly expanded across the country, becoming an influential force in the institution of the family. According to the U.S. Census Bureau (2010), today there are 30 different denominations or groups affiliated with Christianity.

Christians rely on parenting principles from both the Old and New Testament books of the Bible. Scriptural teachings and guiding principles are replete throughout the Bible and are used by parents in child-rearing practices. Legendary Old Testament stories such as Noah's ark, David and Goliath, and Daniel in the lion's den are read to young children to teach them about having faith in God. In the New Testament, the birth and life of Jesus Christ, including his teachings, miracles he performed, his sacrificial death and resurrection, followed by his ascension to heaven are an important part of religious education. The Epistles, letters written by apostles, contain guiding principles and instructions for parents on how to raise children. For example, the Apostle Paul offers the following instruction to fathers: "Fathers, do not exasperate your children, that they may not lose heart" (Colossians 3:21).

### *Judaism*

Parenting practices in Jewish history are recorded in the Torah, a collection of five books written by Moses. Central to Hebrew religious values is the Shema, which means "Hear O Israel." The Shema prayer is a keystone in religious life and child-rearing practices:

> Hear, Israel, the Lord is our God, the Lord is One. And you shall love the Lord your God with all your heart and with all your soul and with all your might. And these words that I command you today shall be in your heart. And you shall teach them diligently to your children, and you shall speak of them when you sit at home, and when you walk along the way, and when you lie down and when your rise up. And you shall bind them as a sign on your hand, and they shall be frontlets between your eyes. And you shall write them on the doorposts of your house and on your gates. (Deuteronomy 6:4–9)

Throughout Jewish history, an intergenerational process of religious instruction was passed along through both written and oral tradition. A principal role of parents is to teach children a monotheistic view of God and to instruct them in the doctrines of the Torah. Today, in Conservative and Reform Jewish sects, instruction remains an important parental responsibility, preparing young boys for bar mitzvah and young girls for bat mitzvah, an entrance into spiritual maturity (Miller & Lovinger, 2000). Family participation in weekly worship services and observances of Jewish holidays such as Passover and Hanukkah at the local synagogue reinforce the importance of instructing children in the ways of God.

### *Islam*

For the past two decades Islam is the fastest-growing religion in America, although it comprises only about 0.6% of the population (U.S. Census Bureau, 2010). Central to Muslim families is the teaching of Islam and the Qur'an, based on the revelation of the Prophet Muhammad born in Mecca in 570 AD (Espisito, 1999). After an encounter with the Archangel Gabriel, Muhammed received what he described as "…the impression that an entire book had been carved in my heart" (Molla, 1989). In the Islam religion the Five Pillars of Islam are foundational to family life: profession of faith, ritual prayer, alms giving, fasting, and pilgrimage (Hedayat-Diba, 2000). The Qur'an stresses that parents exercise patience and forgiveness to their children in their childrearing practices: "And by the Mercy of Allah, you dealt with them gently. And had you been severe and harsh-hearted, they would have broken away from about you; so pass over, and ask forgiveness for them; and consult them in the affairs" (Holy Qur'an, 3:159).

## Effect of Religious-Based Parenting in Affirming Healthy Child Development

The Gospels record an incident when flocks of people were crowding around Jesus to listen to his teachings and witness his miracles. The apostles were pushing away the children who were maneuvering their way in to find a place near the action. His response to the apostles' attempts to deny children access is insightful: "Do not hinder the children from coming to me, for of such is the kingdom of heaven" (Matthew 19:14). Is there an implied message here for parents? Perhaps the message is don't become an obstacle in your children's spiritual development; instead, be the one to lead them to God.

Parental approach, as it relates to instilling spiritual values in children, is critical to the outcome of their religious beliefs as adults. In a recent meta-analytic review of religion in the home during the decades of the eighties and nineties, it was found that parent–child relationships had a significant impact on the outcome of spiritual values on adult children (Mahoney, Pargament, Tarakeshwar, & Swank, 2008). The research indicated that the outcome is largely dependent on the quality of the parent–child relationship. For example, a longitudinal study by Pearce and Axinn (1998), demonstrated how religious-based parenting that encourages the expression of warmth and affection of parents toward children yielded higher incidences of adult children maintaining the spiritual values they were taught.

In religious-based families, parents are more prone to see God as an active contributor in the maturation of their children. Religious ceremonies such as baptisms, bar mitzvahs, baby dedications, communions, and confirmations symbolize the role God plays in shaping and guiding children along predestined paths and the need for parents to yield control as means of exercising their faith. Mahoney et al. (2008) noted that parents often solicit God in a collaborative process to give wisdom and guidance in their parenting endeavors. This triadic approach (God, father, and mother) is more likely to facilitate teamwork in the parental subsystem resulting in more effective parenting skills and healthy child development. Correspondingly spiritually minded parents tend to adopt a benevolent appraisal of their children, handling misbehaviors with appropriate interventions, resulting in a decrease of negative parent–child interactions while increasing cohesion in the family. One of the strengths of faith-based parenting is that the personification of God as Father gives parents a role model to emulate. Divine attributes of unconditional love, acceptance, discipline, mercy, grace, forgiveness, and faithfulness serve as positive traits parents strive to emulate in child-rearing practices. This in turn establishes an affectionate attachment to children and encourages healthy development within protective boundaries. Thus, children experience parents who properly balance love and limits. Moreover, children in these families generally are more responsive to spiritual training, leading to positive spiritual formation throughout life (Barna, 2007). In a summary of meta-analytical research, Mahoney et al. noted that positive family religiousness resulted in fewer externalizing behavior problems, fewer problems with alcohol and substance abuse, lower incidents of antisocial behavior, and higher prosocial traits. In their adult lives they are more likely to consolidate the spiritual values they learned and pass them along to their children. According to Barna, key elements in raising spiritual champions (children strong in their faith) include parents who are proactive in investing time in their children, who seek authenticity in their relationships, who promote character, and who model congruency in matters of faith.

### Use of Religion as a Mechanism of Control in Poisonous Parents

Religion is often viewed as a healthy source providing nourishment to the soul and a spiritual antidote for the problems of life: "Taste and see that the Lord is good. Oh the joys of those who take refuge in him" (Psalm 34:8). However, when administered by a poisonous parent it acts as a toxin, disrupting the developmental processes of children in the family system. A strange paradox occurs when what is intended to give life to the full drains the life out of children whose parents use religion to control them. How does this happen? Are parents misguided by religion? Do the teachings of the Torah, Bible, or Q'uran advocate harsh or neglectful treatment of children? According to Grille (2005), the problem of physical abuse evident in religious practices is not directly correlated with scripture. Rather, the problem is the extremist views individuals adopt:

> Scriptures cannot be blamed for their believers' attitudes. We all interpret according to our personal dispositions, and therefore we each should be held responsible for interpretations. Those who favour violence will find justifications for violence in any text. The rage of the battered and maltreated child lives on in an adult body, hiding itself behind scriptural justifications, insatiably seeking others to punish. (Grille, 2005, p. 114)

It appears that the problem is not with religious teaching on parenting; rather, it is how parents use religious training in their pedagogy. In other words, religion acts as a contaminant when parents use it for purposes not intended. In such cases, religious teachings may be used to control children, to make them overly dependent on parents, and in some cases to justify abusive behavior. This poses serious problems for the maturation of children, including their spiritual formation. Not only do children have to contend with an adult authority figure that uses guilt messages to exert control, but they may also perceive God as a punitive authority figure of whom to fear retribution. So if religious teaching is not the culprit per se, what contributes to the poisonous element in the parent–child interaction? A study in attachment theory provides insight into how this toxic dyad forms.

## The Effects of Early Attachment on Parent–Child Relationships

John Bowlby and Mary Salter Ainsworth were early developers of attachment theory. They proposed that the effect of the parent–child bond in establishing an attachment is a key factor in a child's developmental process. According to Bowlby (1969), caregivers must balance children's need for comfort and security with the need for autonomous exploration of their world. If this is achieved, children are likely to form a healthy internalized view of self. On the contrary, if the parent frequently denies children's requests for protection and autonomy, the children will have a negative view of self (Bretherton, 1992). Bowlby asserted that mature adult autonomy is a by-product of the positive internalizations of the healthy bond with caregivers. Furthermore, he stated that the ability to self-soothe is learned through the comfort one receives in early attachment. Bowlby concluded, "Thus it is seen how children who suffer deprivation grow up to become adults deficient in the capacity to care for their children and how adults deficient in this capacity are commonly those who suffered deprivation in childhood" (Bowlby, 1951, pp. 68–69).

Ainsworth posited that the health of an attachment is directly correlated with the quality of the affectional bond between parent and child. In her research, Ainsworth developed three types of attachment patterns that develop between caregivers and children prior to 18 months old: (1) secure; (2) anxious avoidant; and (3) anxious resistant. A secure attachment is one in which the primary caregiver appropriately responds to the cues of infants, providing their proximity needs for security and comfort. An anxious-avoidant attachment is formed when the caregiver routinely exhibits poor or no response to distressed children, displays annoyance at children's cries, and permits independence as a means to avoid providing care. Adaptively, children rely less on parents and exhibit ignoring or disinterested behaviors in social interactions. Caregivers in this type are often rigid, angry, and rejecting (Ainsworth, Blehar, Waters, & Wall, 1978). In an anxious-resistant attachment, the caregiver lacks consistency in appropriate responses to children's needs. Consequently, children do not achieve a secure base of proximity and exhibit more push–pull behaviors with the parent, seeking contact then resisting it once it's given. Typically in this pattern, the caregiver engages children on their terms and uses children as a means to get their own needs met.

From the vast research in parent–child attachment, certain conclusions can be drawn. First, child developmental needs are largely determined by the affectional bond formed with their primary caregivers. When the parent–child attachment is secure, children progress through the developmental stages with a positive view of themselves and the skills to form healthy social relationships. However, when an insecure attachment forms in the parent–child dyad, a disruption occurs in the developmental process, resulting in negative internalizations of self and impaired social relationships. Second, attachment type determines the health of the parent–child bond. In a secure attachment, children trust caregivers to provide for their proximity needs of protection and comfort. In this environment, children are free to practice autonomy within appropriate limits while receiving nurturance and warmth from a caring parent. Here, parents balance the needs of children and their own without being neglectful or overly intrusive. However, in an insecure attachment, trust is malformed by the confusing messages children receive from their caregivers. When parents behave in a neglectful, harsh, abusive, inconsistent, or overly dependent manner, the security needs of children are compromised, leaving them in a state of vulnerability. Maladaptive patterns form in the parent–child bond exhibited by anxious-resistant, anxious-avoidant, or disorganized or disoriented behaviors. Parent–child relationships may become highly fused or detached. In either case, the needs of children are circumvented by the needs of parents. Mechanisms of control are used to cement the boundaries, abrogating the autonomous development of children. Consequently, children in insecurely attached relationships exhibit poor identity formation and social relatedness. Finally, parent–child attachments appear to have an intergenerational process. In secure attachments, adult children are more likely to develop healthy attachments in marital relations and in parenting. Likewise, when insecure attachments form, adult children are at a higher risk for mental health problems including anxiety-based disorders, mood disorders, and personality disorders.

## Religion, the Poison in Insecure Parent–Child Attachments

As previously noted, the three religions described earlier follow a religious creed based on scriptures that are believed to have a divine origin. For followers of Christianity, Judaism, and Islam, the teachings and principles are intended to serve as a guiding influence in how to live in the world and as a means to express faith in God. Also, it was shown how religious-based parenting has had a positive effect in affirming the healthy development of children. Attention will now be directed toward the use of religion in family systems characterized by insecure parent–child attachments.

If control over children is a fundamental goal in poisonous parenting, religion can prove to be an effective toxicant. The authoritative element in religion reinforces parental hierarchy, instructing children to obey their parents. In a Muslim family, children are instructed by the Qu'ran on how to show respect to parents: "And your Lord has decreed that you not worship except Him, and to parents, good treatment. Whether one or both of them reach old age while with you, say not to them, 'uff' and do not repel them but speak to them a noble word" (Qu'ran 17:23). Likewise, in Judaism children are given the following instruction in the Torah: "You shall each revere his mother and father, and keep my Sabbaths" (Leviticus 19:3). In a Christian household, the Bible teaches children the importance of obeying their parents: "Children, obey your parents in the Lord for this is right" (Ephesians 6:1). There is nothing inherently harmful in the scriptures highlighted here. One of the functions of parenting is to lead children and teach them how to live in the world. Instilling values and establishing rules of conduct are a parent's responsibility. According to Minuchin (1974), hierarchy, structure, and boundaries are key components in healthy family functioning. The problem has nothing to do with religious principles but rather how they are applied in parent–child relationships. In religious households that adopt a literal interpretation of religious teaching, parents typically adopt an autocratic approach in child-rearing practices (Mahoney et al., 2008). A poisonous parent may take the scriptural command previously mentioned to an extreme to force compliance when another approach might be more effective. For example, a Muslim junior high girl joins Facebook because all her friends at school have already joined. When her mother discovers she has a Facebook page, she yells at her daughter and tells her she is sinning against Allah by allowing worldly influences into the home. When her daughter attempts to reason with her about the matter, the mother puts an end to all discussion by quoting the Qu'ran and demanding compliance. The matter could be resolved more effectively by having a dialogue with her daughter about the concerns she has about Facebook and by allowing her daughter to offer a rationale on what purpose it would serve for her. In the end, the mother would make the final decision; however it would be done after giving her daughter an opportunity to express herself. The mother may have discovered that her daughter was using Facebook to connect with other Muslim friends who share her beliefs. In this case, the mother might allow her daughter to have the account with the condition that she supervises her use.

The problem with poisonous parents is that their need for control stifles the growth of their children. Parents who use religion to justify punitive practices may produce children who are more susceptible to maladaptive schemas, including defectiveness, shame, self-doubt, dependency, incompetence, and failure. Furthermore, children raised in this environment are more prone to mood or anxiety disorders (Mahoney et al., 2008). Parents who view their role as a divine mandate may find it difficult to relinquish control of their children during key periods of separation-individuation, including transition into adulthood. Enmeshment in the family system activates relational patterns characterized by dependency or oppositional behaviors in the parent-child dyad. The effect of this style of parenting produces adult children who are either overly religious or cease participation in religious activities.

## A Contrast of Outcomes: How Adult Children View Religious Values

So how do adult children fare when it comes to their view of religious values and participation in religious practices? The outcome is likely determined in the "touching of the palate" approach. In other words, how parents attach to their children will determine how responsive they are to the spiritual influence fed to them. If the parent–child attachment provides protection, nurturance, and autonomous development, children are more likely to trust their parents and therefore to respond positively to religious values. On the contrary, if the parent–child attachment is insecure, trust is compromised, the emerging self is underdeveloped, and children are uncertain the parent always has their welfare in mind. While religion may in general be a good practice, for insecurely attached children it may be used in harmful ways to control behavior.

In families where children were able to form secure attachment with parental figures, research indicates that they are more likely to maintain the religious values in their transition into adulthood (Mahoney et al., 2008). On the contrary, adult children of poisonous parents more often reject the religious values and practices they learned growing up. According to Webb and Otto-Whitmer (2003), social learning theory offers insight on how these decisions are made. It appears that children make associations between what parents teach and how they experience the security of the relationship. If children experience a meaningful relationship with their primary caregivers they are likely to accept the values their parents espouse. Volumes of research support the theory that children who are raised in religious-based families where the parents provided security and nurturance more often view religion as a positive element and continue to follow religious practices (Mahoney et al.).

In the case of adult children who have an aversive reaction to their parent–child relationship, it is probable that they will reject their parents' values, particularly if these were used to control, manipulate, or abuse them. For those raised by poisonous parents the outcome is uncertain, depending on the type of attachment and the adaptive style of the children. For example, adult children who develop a dependent adaptive relational bond with their parents are likely to continue ingesting the poison-laced religious values as a means to gain the favor of the poisonous parent or to avoid the more serious consequence of abandonment. The tendency to form dependent attachments may also surface in religious settings. Adult children may project their dependency needs on God or spiritual leaders who hold authoritative positions. These individuals gain undue attention by evoking the empathic and benevolent reactions of the religious community to rally together to meet their needs. Conversely, avoidant-attached children are more prone to reject the religious values associated with poisonous parenting as a further representation of their emancipation from parental control. The pairing of parents and religion is toxic to children maltreated in their developmental years. Thus, the association makes it highly unlikely they will view religion with endearment. Because of their poisoned views of God as a divine caretaker, avoidant-adaptive adults are likely to adopt a punitive view of symbolic expressions of deity. Research demonstrated how children who were abused by religious-based parents have difficulty forming a personal relationship with God due to punitive associations formed early on in life and reinforced by repeated parental abuse (Webb & Otto-Whitmer, 2003).

## Treatment for Individuals Affected by Religious-Based Poisonous Parenting

Adult children of poisonous parents face several challenges in managing the roles and responsibilities of adulthood. One of the most common fears expressed is, "I don't want to become like my mother." Or, "I don't want to turn into my father." Emancipation provides a means of escape, providing geographical space between adult children and their parents. However, attachment styles are not solely regulated by physical proximity, there is a psychological and emotional element that fuses familial relationships. Consequently, when adult children leave home in an attempt to escape poisonous parents, they often discover the insidious bond taking up residence in their minds. Among the boxes of clothes and belongings transported from their family of origin, the emotional baggage is also unpacked in adult relationships. According to Bowen (1978), a multigenerational transmission process occurs in families regulated by emotional fusion among the members. If parent–child relationships are enmeshed, developmental processes are compromised inhibiting differentiation, individuals' ability to grow autonomously in a family system. The emotionally fused parent–child relationship remains intact into adulthood. So while adult children of poisonous parents may create proximal distance with their parents the unwanted psychological-emotional bond remains. The challenge for adult children is to complete the task of differentiation by learning to think, feel, and act for themselves while also learning how to establish healthy boundaries in adult relationships. This arduous process involves deconstructing negative schemas, clarifying values, finding self-expression, modifying boundaries, and learning how to be true to oneself while respecting others.

For adult children raised by poisonous parents in religious-based homes the process of differentiation raises questions about the role spirituality may or may not have in their newly developed set of values. If religion was used as a toxicant to control or abuse children it is likely to be rejected in adulthood. However, in some cases, religion may become the serum that brings healing to emotionally wounded adult children. Kirkpatrick (1997) described attachment to God in two forms: correspondence and compensatory. The correspondence hypothesis described attachment to God as positively influenced by secure parent–child attachment. The compensatory hypothesis postulates that attachment to God may be sought by adult children to compensate for an insecure parent–child attachment. In this case, God serves as a surrogate attachment figure influencing a healthy transformation of internal working models of self and others. However, research conducted by Miner (2009) indicated that although a compensatory attachment to God proved to promote a positive internal working model the effect of early attachment injuries may continue to cause psychological problems. This raises important considerations for mental health professionals in terms of providing counseling services to clients who are trying to reconcile early attachment injuries and faith in God. The problem for adult children of religious-based poisonous parents is differentiating the harm inflicted by parents who claim religious justification and God, who does not sanction such behavior. Some poisoned adult children project their negative parental images onto God. Consequently, they find it difficult to exhibit trust, seek spiritual intimacy, and internalize the nurturing expression of God's unconditional love, mercy, and grace.

The challenge for counselors is helping clients untangle the relational chords of an insecure attachment to poisonous parents to secure an authentic relationship with God. To accomplish this, mental health professionals must have a working knowledge of the religious beliefs of clients. This would include researching information on the theology and practice of religious beliefs in a family context. Consultation with religious leaders (i.e., priest, minister, rabbi) would also provide valuable information. Sometimes, clients are better served working with mental health professionals who share their religious background. This is important because religious groups, like other cultural or ethnic groups, operate from a set of beliefs, values, and customs that regulate relationships. Furthermore, while adult children may struggle with trust issues, they are likely to be more comfortable talking with a counselor who can relate to their religious background. Finally, working with a counselor who models a secure attachment to God and is able to amend negative schemas associated with the client's view of God can serve as a mediator to repair the attachment wound. Treatment considerations for adult children of religious-based poisonous parents would include repairing attachment injury with God, identifying and replacing negative schema that distort self-perception and disrupt interpersonal relationships, management of anxiety or mood disorders, identity formation, and modifying boundaries with poisonous parents.

### *A Case Study on Religious-Based Poisonous Parenting*

Rachael (35) and her husband, Tom (36), have been married for 14 years. They have two children: a 9-year-old daughter, Alexis, and a 7-year-old son, Tyler. They requested counseling to address problems they are having with extended family members who are causing distress personally and within the marriage. The problems the couple described involved a pattern of interference in their marriage by Rachael's parents, Bill and Tina. Tom stated that his father-in-law constantly undermines his role as a husband and justifies his behavior using the Bible to support his actions. The intrusive behavior includes informing the couple on marital and parenting issues, such as how they should operate their finances. The couple reported that recently things came to a boil when the parents discovered that they planned to move closer to the city. The move would necessitate leaving the neighborhood and the church Rachael attended since she was born. Rachael's parents informed the couple that they were not "in the will of God" and that such a move would result in God's chastening of the couple, placing their children at risk. The couple stated that they attempted to reason with Rachael's parents only to be met with more biblical warnings and a threat to cut them off. To add further pressure, the couple reported that Rachael's siblings called her and voiced their objection to the decision, stating it was disrespectful to their parents for the couple to move to the city. Her siblings informed Rachael that they are united with their parents and will cut off contact if she follows through with her decision. Rachael expressed mixed feelings of anger, guilt, and worry over the situation. She stated that she does not want to be controlled by her father but fears losing the relationship with her siblings and their children. Tom expressed anger toward his father-in-law for manipulating the family to get back control over his daughter. He confessed that he has a hard time sympathizing with his wife for fear it may cause her to act on her guilt and give in to her father. The couple stated that this matter is causing conflict in their marriage and has put a hold on their decision to finalize the move to the city.

A history of the couple's relationship was conducted. The couple reported they met as teenagers in church and dated secretly for a period of time before finally disclosing their relationship to Rachael's parents. Rachael stated that her parents disapproved of the relationship and demanded that the couple break up. When the couple asked for reasons why the parents disapproved, they stated that they would not allow their daughter to date until she was ready for marriage. The parents cited Bible references to support their decision. The couple reported that they complied with the parents' demand and decided to pray for God's will to be done. Over the course of the next couple of years, Rachael and Tom continued contact through church-related activities. They continued to have a fondness for each other and prayed Rachael's parents would change their minds. Whenever the matter was brought up, Bill denied their request. Tina, upon hearing of Bill's decision, would always give her support to him. Rachael stated that when she turned 21 she informed her father that she intended to marry Tom with or without his approval. She reported that he disapproved but consented nonetheless. Tom stated that he attempted to win the approval of his new father-in-law by respecting his role as his wife's father, but his attempts to form a relationship were dismissed. The couple reported that problems began to develop early in the marriage when Bill attempted to assert his authority in the couple's marriage, quoting the Bible as giving him scriptural authority to instruct the couple. When the couple attempted to establish boundaries with Bill he would become angry and triangulate other family members to gain support and impose guilt on the young couple. The couple also indicated that Rachael's parents often provided financial gifts and support at critical times in their marriage that would be used to exert control over the couple.

During the assessment phase, a family history inventory was taken to provide more background information on family relationships. Rachael reported that she is the second-born child in a family of three; she had an older sister, Rebecca, and a younger brother, Isaac. She stated that her parents chose biblical names for the children after they became Christians, shortly after they were married. Rachael reported that the religious instruction was a central feature of family life and that the children were home schooled from kindergarten through high school. When asked why the children were taught at home, Rachael replied, "My parents told us that they did not want their children to be influenced by the sinfulness of the world." Rachael explained that when she became a teenager her parents informed her that she was not allowed to date but that God would choose a godly man for her and he would reveal this person to her father first. When asked to describe her relationship with her father, Rachael indicated it was distant, not like his relationship with Rebecca, who is the apple of his eye. Rachael stated that Rebecca was the perfect Christian girl who did everything according to scripture. Whenever Rachael questioned a house rule, Rebecca was always parroting her father's expectations. Rachael described her relationship with her mother as close at times but mostly distant. "Mom never went against Dad even though you could tell she privately disagreed with him," Rachael stated. She described her family as being the perfect Christian family, except that on the inside she felt like the oddball because she questioned things and did not always agree with her parents' decisions. Whenever she posed a question or voiced opposition, the Bible was used to correct her thinking and gain her compliance. Consequently, Rachael felt loved and accepted only when she lived up to her parents' expectations. She inwardly wondered if it was that way with God too.

Further family background information offered more insight into the parent–child attachment. Rachael reported that her mother Tina came from a large Italian family where the males held a higher status in the family system. In the sibling subsystem, the higher male ranking allowed the brothers to mistreat the sisters. Consequently, Tina was always giving into the demands of the males in the family. Rachael described her father as the apple of his mother's eye.

Bill was the firstborn male in a family of four, with a younger brother and two sisters. Rachael reported that her grandmother ruled the family and that her grandfather was passive. Her father was the center of the family, and everyone catered to him, especially his doting mother. Later when her parents first met, she was told it was love at first sight. "Dad swept Mom off her feet with his charisma and charm," Rachael stated. Because of her upbringing, Tina informed Bill that she would not have sex until they were married. However, after much persuasion Tina reluctantly consented. Later she became pregnant and had a miscarriage before anyone discovered it. This event was upsetting to the couple, and soon after they decided to get married. Within 2 years of their marriage they met a couple that introduced them to Christianity. Rachael reported that her parents became born-again Christians and were actively involved in church. She related that her family life revolved around religious activities, including attending church multiple times a week, daily family devotions, prayer, and annual Bible camp. Home-school education was based on Christian curriculum. Social activities were solely with kids from church or home school to protect the children from worldly influences. Secular entertainment including music, movies, and television were forbidden; only Christian-based media was permitted in the home. As a teenager Rachael started questioning why her parents continued to exercise as much control over her decisions. She wondered why they did not trust her when she never did anything to disrespect them. When Rachael asked her parents to allow her to make some of her own decisions, they scolded her for making such a prideful request and said she had a rebellious spirit. Rachael was left with mixed feelings of guilt and anger. She wondered if she would ever be good enough for her parents. Later, when Tom asked her out on a date she decided to accept his invitation and kept it a secret from her parents. After a couple of dates Tom could tell that Rachael was struggling with her decision to hide their relationship from her parents, and he suggested that they tell her parents together after youth group. Rachael was tearful as she recalled how her father berated her by quoting scriptures and praying for God to "break her rebellious spirit." No matter what Rachael did to try to prove her loyalty and spirituality to her parents, it wasn't enough to gain their approval. So Rachael vowed she would make her own decisions when she became an adult. When she turned 21 Rachael finally made her own decision even though she knew her parents would disapprove.

In initial sessions the counselor reduced the tension between the couple by helping them resolve their conflict, increase cohesion, and clarify their boundaries as a married couple. Tom recognized that his worry that Rachael would choose her parents over him caused him to exert control over her decisions much like her father. He decided to convey his concerns without making demands upon her. In turn, Rachael conveyed to Tom her understanding of how the triangulation with her parents often placed his needs secondary to the demands of the parents. She planned to limit contact with her parents and focus more on the needs of the marriage. The couple determined to make their decision about moving to the city independent of her parents' demands. Furthermore, the couple decided to limit contact with Rachael's parents while they focused on strengthening their marriage.

In successive sessions the couple's religious beliefs were explored to determine how Rachael's parents' use of religion to control relationships had a negative effect in their practice of religion. Rachael described problems with living out her faith and feeling judged by God. She admitted struggling with trusting God to be a source of comfort and strength. Rachael reported feeling alienated by God, abandoned, and depressed. Tom indicated that his faith has been a source of help throughout the ordeal. He expressed concern that Rachael is drifting from her faith and worries that her parents have damaged her relationship with God. Further treatment involved identifying negative schemas that impaired thoughts of self, others, and God. Spiritual themes highlighted in scripture were used to modify cognitive distortions and repair attachment injuries with God. Over time Rachael was able to adopt a view of God independent of her parents' teaching. Biblical themes of unconditional love, inherent value, mercy, and grace helped Rachael to reestablish trust in God while also developing a healthier self-concept. Tom also modified his views about the roles within the marriage. By adopting an egalitarian view of marriage, Tom supported a balance of power in the relationship based on mutual submission, love, and interdependence. This boundary modification in the marital dyad reinforced Rachael's growth process, reduced conflict, and increased cohesion in their relationship. In the course of treatment, Rachael reported that depressive symptoms subsided, her self-esteem improved, and her faith in God was renewed.

In the latter stage of counseling, treatment assisted the couple in clarifying boundaries with Rachael's parents. The couple reported that they decided to move into the city even if it meant Rachael's parents would be angry and cease contact with them. Rachael stated that she was prepared to face the consequences her parents would mete out in response to their decision to move to the city. Rehearsal of cognitive amendments helped reinforce the couple's views as being independent of parents' expectations. In the following session the couple reported that Rachael's parents were furious at their decision to move into the city and followed through with their threat to cut off contact with them. Bill informed them that they would face God's judgment as a means to bring them to repentance. The counselor processed the residual emotional reactions the couple had toward the event and subsequent cutoff from Rachael's family. The couple reported feelings of sadness associated with the loss, indicating it felt like a death occurred in the family. Grief was reframed as a death of a dream they hoped for in their relationships with extended family members.

In a follow-up session with the couple 3 months later, they reported positive adjustment to their move to the city. Contrary to her father's warning, Rachael indicated that the couple and their children were happy living in the city, had made new friends, and joined a neighborhood church. Tom stressed how impressed he was with the change in Rachael. He described her growth as "a rose in full bloom." He noted an increase in self-confidence, improved social relationships, assertiveness in their marriage, and spiritual growth in her relationship with God. Rachael also reported receiving contact from her mother, Tina, about missing the grandchildren. She stated that she informed her mother that she would be welcome for a visit to their home provided there was no discussion about their move to the city. Her mother announced that she was coming by herself without her husband's knowledge because he would otherwise forbid her to come. The couple indicated that they were comfortable having Rachael's mom visit but were uncertain where things would go from there. In the remainder of the session, the couple collaborated to determine a plan on how to manage the relationship should it progress to future meetings.

### Working With the Poisonous Parent

Treatment potential for religious-based poisonous parents is not as promising as it is with their adult children. For starters, poisonous parents often externalize familial problems. In other words, they are more likely to view the problem stemming from their adult children's lack of respect and gratitude toward them than any act of volition on their part. In therapy they may present as victims of their adult children's cruel behavior. If attention is directed toward their behavior they are likely to exhibit resistance and terminate counseling altogether. Furthermore, more extreme religious individuals have negative attitudes toward secular helping professions. For some, counseling is viewed as a substitute for individuals who are spiritually weak and lack true faith in God. Counseling techniques are considered "worldly" or "unspiritual." There is a general mistrust not only of mental health practice but also the professional. This presents challenges for mental health professionals. Unfortunately, it is highly unlikely that the more extreme poisonous parents will ever consider entering counseling.

In the assessment phase in addition to a routine personal history, careful attention should be given to screening for personality disorders and religious-based maladaptive schemas. Narcissistic, borderline, histrionic, and dependency disorders, resulting from early attachment injuries, are often associated with extreme forms of poisonous parenting (Johnson, Cohen, Chen, Kasen, & Brook, 2006). Religious groups, because of their benevolent and compassionate nature, often attract disordered individuals who are looking to fill the emotional void in their lives. Unfortunately, their inability to sustain healthy, reciprocal relationships often causes problems within the religious community.

Spiritual inventories may offer insight into poisonous parents' concept of God. Typically, their scores indicate an extreme view of one sort or another. For example, poisonous parents may have a judgmental view of God, exhibited by their rigidity, dichotomous thinking, and perfectionism. They strive to live to the letter of the law and judge others who don't. Spiritual authority is used to enforce compliance from their children. In contrast, some poisonous parents may hold a conservative view of God but act as if it doesn't apply to them. The contradiction is exhibited by loose morals, diffuse boundaries, and indiscriminate behavior. Here, they may hold one standard for themselves and another for their children. "Do as I say, not as I do" is the unspoken rule. Unfortunately, their incongruent behavior creates confusion in the minds of innocent children.

Treatment should be based on the presenting problem. If it pertains to ruptured relationships with their offspring, treatment goals can help clients address finding common ground with their adult children while respecting differences. Spiritual themes of unconditional love and grace can be used to amend cognitive distortions, giving poisonous parents an alternative way of viewing the problem with their children. In the case of Rachael's family, her father Bill refused to see his daughter's family, entrenched in his position that they disrespected his authority and had fallen out of God's grace. His wife, Tina, on the other hand, chose counseling to explore her unexpressed feelings about the situation. In the course of treatment, Tina was able to resolve the underlying issues affecting her response to the problem. Eventually, she confronted her husband about his abuse of authority in their marriage and family. Tina informed Bill that she would continue to have a relationship with their daughter with or without him. She followed through on her decision and was able to repair her relationship with Rachael and Tom. Having been shown the ultimate disrespect by his wife, Bill emotionally detached from Tina. Months later he began an affair with a single woman in the church. Within a year Tina discovered the affair and filed for divorce. Soon after the divorce, Bill proposed to his girlfriend. When his pastor declined to perform the wedding, Bill angrily left the church in favor of a new church he insisted would not be judgmental. Rachael's siblings were horrified by their father's behavior and refused to see him. Eventually, they reconnected with their sister and also worked to repair their relationships. Within a year of Bill's marriage, they had a baby. When his adult children were less than pleased with his announcement, he invested time exclusively in his new family and rarely contacted his kids.

## Conclusion

Religious-based poisonous parenting can be lethal to the identity and spiritual formation of children. Caregivers who use religion to control children unwittingly inflict psychological harm, distorting their view of God, and impairing a healthy attachment. Spirituality, an inherently good concept, acts as a toxicant in the parent–child relationship and potentially poisons their belief in God. Through guilt by association, religion is indicted along with parents as coconspirators in the abuse of adult children. Consequently, many adult children reject religious values as part of their emancipation from authority figures they view as untrustworthy perpetuators of abuse. However, in some cases, adult children of religious-based poisonous parents find refuge in their faith. Faith in God as a surrogate parent compensates for the insecure attachment to poison parents. In this spiritual relationship, the basic needs for security and nurturance are met, allowing for the repair of early attachment wounds inflicted by caregivers. Mental health professionals or religious leaders can mediate the process of spiritual reformation in adult children of poisonous parents. Providing a nonjudgmental, supportive, and caring environment facilitates the process of emotional and spiritual healing. Attachment injuries are carefully treated with compassion, understanding, and insight. Distorted images of God are modified to provide a more accurate view based on commonly accepted teaching within the religious community. Divine attributes consisting of unconditional love, inherent value, forgiveness, and grace offer a picture of God that provides security and nurturance, the fundamental attachment needs lacking in early development. Models of secure relationships in the religious community can further reinforce the attachment process. In the course of time as trust increases, adult children are likely to develop a secure attachment to God. Another benefit is the positive effect it has on repairing a damaged self-concept and establishing healthy interpersonal relationships. For adult children of religious-based poisonous parents the commandment to honor parents raises serious questions. How do you honor a parent who has inflicted harm and justified their behavior in the name of religion? This poses challenges for mental health providers and religious caregivers in helping adult children who want to adhere to sacred beliefs yet bear the wounds inflicted by their parents. Loving the sinner yet hating the sin is easier said than done. Helping adult children navigate their way through these conflicts and learn how to establish healthy boundaries with poisonous parents is essential in preventing repeated injury. Defining the meaning of honor in the context of a poisonous relationship may help adult children to find the balance between the religious values and avoiding the threat of harm.

## References

Ainsworth, M. D. S., Blehar, M. C., Waters, E., & Wall, S. (1978). *Patterns of attachment: A psychological study of the strange situation and at home*. Hillsdale, NJ: Erlbaum.

Barna, G. (2007). *Revolutionary parenting: What the research shows really works.* Carol Stream, IL: Tyndale House Publishers, Inc.

Bowen, M. (1978). *Family therapy in clinical practice.* New York: Aronson.

Bowlby, J. (1951). *Maternal care and mental health.* Geneva, Switzerland: World Health Organization.

Bowlby, J. (1969). *Attachment and loss, Vol.1: Attachment*. New York: Basic Books.

Bretherton, I. (1992). The origins of attachment theory: John Bowlby and Mary Ainsworth. *Developmental Psychology, 28,* 759–775.

Espisito, J. L. (Ed.). (1999). *The Oxford history of Islam.* New York: Oxford University Press.

Gaebelein, F. E., & Kaiser, W. C. (1990). *The expositors Bible commentary, Vol. 2.* Grand Rapids, MI: The Zondervan Corporation.

Grille, R. (2005). *Parenting for a peaceful world.* New South Wales, Australia: Longueville.

Hedayat-Diba, Z. (2000). *Handbook of psychotherapy and religious diversity* (P. S. Richards & A. E. Bergin, Eds.). Washington, DC: American Psychological Association.

Johnson, J. G., Cohen, P., Chen, H., Kasen, S., & Brook, J. S. (2006). Parenting behaviors associated with risk for offspring personality disorder during adult hood. *Archives of General Psychiatry, 63,* 579–587.

Kirkpatrick, L. A. (1997). An attachment-theory approach to the psychology of religion. In B. Spilka & D. N. McIntosh (Eds.), *The psychology of religion: Theoretical approaches* (pp. 114–133). Boulder, CO: Westview Press.

Lasher, L. J., & Sheridan, M. S. (2004). *Munchausen by proxy: Identification, intervention, and case management.* The Haworth Maltreatment and Trauma Press, an imprint of The Haworth Press, Inc. Binghamton, NY.

Linder, R. D. (1990). Division and unity: The paradox of Christianity in America. In D. G. Reid, R. D. Linder, B. L. Shelley, & H. S. Stout (Eds.), *Dictionary of Christianity in America.* Downers Grove, IL: Intervarsity Press.

Mahoney, A., Pargament, K., Tarakeshwar, N., & Swank, A. (2008). Religion in the home in the 1980s and 1990s: A meta-analytic review and conceptual analysis of links between religion, marriage, and parenting. *Psychology of Religion and Spirituality,* S(1), 63–101.

Mikulincer, M., & Shaver, P. R. (2007). *Attachment in adulthood: Structure, dynamics, and change.* New York: Guilford Press.

Miller, L., & Lovinger, R. J. (2000). *Handbook of psychotherapy and religious diversity* (P. S. Richards & A. E. Bergin, Eds.). Washington, DC: American Psychological Association.

Miner, M. (2009). The impact of child-parent attachment, attachment to God and religious orientation on psychological adjustment. *Journal of Psychology and Theology, 37*(2), 114–124.

Minuchin, S. (1974). *Families & family therapy.* Cambridge, MA: Harvard University Press.

Molla, C. F. (1989). *L'Islam c'est quoi?* Geneva: Labor et Fides.

Pearce, L. D., & Axinn, W. G. (1998). The impact of family religious life on the quality of mother-child relations. *American Sociological Review. 63,* 810–828.

U.S. Census Bureau. (2010). *Table 75: Self-described religious identification of adult population: 1990 to 2008.* http://www.census.gov/compendia/statab/cats/population.html

Webb, M., & Otto-Whitmer, K. J. (2003). Parental religiosity, abuse history and maintenance of beliefs taught in the family. *Mental Health, Religion & Culture, 6*(3), 229–239.

CHAPTER 11

# Saving Oneself

## *Forgiving the Poisonous Parent as an Act of Kindness to Oneself and Future Generations*

TERRY HARGRAVE

It has been over 20 years since the concept of therapeutic forgiveness started appearing in the psychological literature as a serious intervention directed at healing relational problems (Worthington, 2005). Up until that time, forgiveness was strictly thought of as a religious concept (Hargrave, 1994a) that had little applicability to personal well-being or future interpersonal relationships. Since that time, the research has been overwhelming concerning the positive effects of forgiveness:

- Unforgiveness increases stress, anger, and hostility, which has negative effects on individual health (Toussaint, Williams, Musick, & Everson, 2001).
- Forgiveness generates positive emotions and reduces stress (Witvliet, Ludwig, & Vander Laan, 2001).
- Forgiveness has been shown to be effective in promoting repair and reconciliation in interpersonal relationships after interpersonal problems (Baumeister, Stillwell, & Heatherton, 1994; Hargrave & Sells, 1997).

These and many studies over the past two decades consistently show that forgiveness has positive outcomes for individuals who forgive and the relationships with which they are involved (Hargrave, Froeschle, & Castillo, 2009).

Even with these positive findings, however, the issue of forgiveness of a poisonous or damaging parent is difficult and complex. It is difficult and complex precisely because relational transgression, exploitation, humiliation, irresponsibility, neglect, abuse, and hatred are deeply personal and painful issues to the people who have been victimized by such behavior. Forgiveness, then, is always relational because of the story of pain that exists with the victim and difficult because it plays out within a process between at least two imperfect people who are trying to move beyond the painful poison. Forgiveness, most often, takes place a little at a time over a long period of time (Hargrave, 2001).

The goal of this chapter is to help persons who have experienced poisonous or damaging parenting to consider the possibilities of what forgiveness can and cannot do for them and their relationships. The chapter first addresses the root of pain and exactly what pain we are trying to address through the process of forgiveness. Second, it outlines a clear model of how forgiveness can work as a process for individual healing and perhaps relational restoration. Many models of forgiveness have been explored in the literature (i.e., Worthington, 2003; DiBlasio, 1998; Dorff, 1998; Enright & Fitzgibbons, 2000), and these models and more all make significant contributions to helping people forgive. The clinical model explored in this chapter (Hargrave, 1994a) is simply one method that has helped many individuals find their way along this process of forgiveness with integrity, protection, and potential to build future relationships. Finally, the chapter illustrates how the process can work through a case illustration.

## The Roots of Family Pain

Poisonous parenting and how it can be damaging have been discussed in depth in the other chapters of this book, and it is amazing how parents can use different "tricks" that can be so toxic and tragic. But if you take an overall perspective on how these parents can be damaging, you will see a common thread. That common thread is that all of these violations are either caused by a lack of love or a lack of trustworthiness or both at the same time. These two elements—love and trustworthiness—are the two pillars on which family relationships stand (Hargrave & Pfitzer, 2003).

Violations of love have much to do with the identity that we develop about ourselves (Hargrave, 2000). If you think about it, all that we know about ourselves—whether we are lovable, precious, unique, and worthy of sacrifice—was dependent on how our caregivers treated us in our earliest formations. This has been described as attachment in previous chapters, but it is worth noting here that we learn something significant about ourselves in the process of being attached or not to our parents. We learn our sense of self (Hargrave & Pfitzer, 2003). If we were cared for in such a way where our parents sacrificed for us, cherished us for who we were, and desired to be with us, then we likely grew up with the sense of self that had a healthy identity. On the other hand, if we had poisonous parents who were stingy in their sacrifice and giving, were condemning or unaccepting, and used us at their convenience, then we grew up with a sense of self that was weak from feeling unloved and uncherished.

But the lack of love is only one of the issues when it comes to pain people carry from poisonous parenting. The other issue is that of trustworthiness. Basically, trustworthiness teaches us that relationships are safe (Hargrave & Pfitzer, 2003). What makes relationships safe? First, the relationship has to be predictable. In other words, the person that cared for you behaved in predictable and consistent ways so you could determine how you were going to act. Second, the relationship has to be one of openness. When we are in relationships that are secretive, we consistently try to interpret or guess what our intuition tells us is incomplete. This element of openness allows us to act freely because we can be confident of the situations and obligations that exist and are required of us. If caregivers are not open, then we are always unclear about the nature of the emotions that go on around us (Hargrave, 2000). For instance, if parents are consistently depressed or upset but do not tell their children what they are upset about, the children will sense the emotion but get no read on how to behave since they will not communicate. As a result, the children will either be overfocused on the parents or will internalize the problem as something they have to solve. The effect is anything but safe for the children, and they learn not to trust.

Predictability and openness are clearly important in forming safety for a child, but the most dynamic element in forming trustworthy parent–child relationships is found in what is balanced or just. Boszormenyi-Nagy and Krasner (1986) discuss from a contextual family therapy point of view the importance of trustworthiness and justice in relationships. If we look at relationships at their most basic level, then we see that they consist of actions that one takes to give to the other and, as a result of that giving, an entitlement to receive the giving from the other in the relationship. This balance of give and take in relationship is essential in maintaining fair giving between relational partners (Boszormenyi-Nagy & Krasner). If this balance is not present and one partner gives and receives nothing, that partner will eventually feel the injustice of the relationship and will stop giving (Hargrave & Anderson, 1992). In other words, the lack of balance or justice deteriorates trustworthiness and makes giving to one another difficult. Relational partners begin to look at one another and demand or expect the other to give first before they reciprocate. They may begin to threaten or try to manipulate one another to force or cajole the other to give. Finally, they withdraw from one another and terminate the relationship because they feel that they receive nothing from the partner (Hargrave

& Pfitzer, 2003). Justice is such a relational resource because it promotes trustworthiness, which in turn promotes giving in relationship (Hargrave & Pfitzer).

This concept of balance is usually easily seen when we are talking about partners in relationships that are equal in give and take with friends, siblings, and spouses. These are called *horizontal relationships* (Boszormenyi-Nagy & Krasner, 1986), and the giving and taking basically balances out between the partners. *Vertical relationships* (Boszormenyi-Nagy & Krasner) exist between successive generations such as parents and children. Balance and justice here are a little different from that of a horizontal relationship where, for instance, spouses would basically be expected to take care of and give to one another equally. In vertical relationships, parents are responsible for giving to and nurturing the children without expecting to receive something in return. It is not just that children are not as capable as parents of giving that makes this fair but also that one day children will grow up and be in the position to be the caregiver and nurturer of children from the next generation. It is a balance that goes through the generations of a family instead of being between partners. In vertical relationships, parents give to children so when those children grow up they can give freely to the next generation of children. In this way, justice and trustworthiness are built through intergenerational giving (Hargrave & Pfitzer, 2003).

The problem, of course, is the poisonous or damaging parent. Instead of freely giving love and nurture to children without expecting anything in return, poisonous parents expect children to love and nurture them. Children are extremely compliant and will even try to fulfill this unjust request, but they will find themselves unable to compensate for the love and trustworthiness poisonous parents are requesting not only because they lack the maturity but also because they are not the parents of the parent who is able to compensate for the nurture and love the parent lacks (Hargrave & Pfitzer, 2003). As a result, poisonous parents will likely become even more passive, withdrawing, manipulative, aggressive, or even abusive. These actions are called *destructive entitlement* (Boszormenyi-Nagy & Ulrich, 1981).

Why would poisonous parents take such action against innocent children? It is most likely because when they were children themselves, they were robbed of this just and balanced love and nurture. Contextual therapists believe that this sense of justice is innate (Boszormenyi-Nagy & Krasner, 1986). In other words, children know that they should be the recipient of their parents' love and nurture without the requirement to take care of their parents in return. When children are required to love and nurture their parents and get very little in return, they do not forget the injustice but instead seek the love and nurture from innocent parties.

Children are entitled to love and nurture, but since poisonous parents do not give it to their children, the children then feel justified in getting it from someone else even if the means are destructive through manipulation, withdrawal, or threats. The likely innocent parties involved when this destructive entitlement plays out are these adult children's spouses and children. When children of poisonous parents are grown, they will become poisonous parents because they are destructively seeking the love, nurture, and trustworthiness from their own children to make up for what was not given in their childhood. This destructive entitlement is insidious in family relationships and is the root of much family pain (Hargrave, 1994b).

These are the roots of family and emotional pain that comes from poisonous parenting. Adult children of poisonous parents will either feel that they were not loved by their parents or that they were in a situation that was not trustworthy or safe. In almost all of these instances, these adult children will have been raised to feel like it was their job to make things right for their poisonous parents or, at the minimum, not bother their parents with any need at all. This is the reason the work of forgiveness is so necessary: If the victims of poisonous parenting do nothing, they will carry the same legacy of destructive entitlement in them. They will seek love, nurture, and safety from inappropriate and innocent relationships. They will feel entitled to be passive, withdrawing, manipulative, aggressive, and abusive with their spouses and children in some of the same ways as their poisonous parents (Hargrave, 1994a). Without the work of forgiveness, the victims will likely become the victimizers, and their children will eventually become another poisonous parent.

## A Model of Forgiveness as a Process

Much has been discussed in the literature on forgiveness concerning the idea of letting go of past injustices or even hurt or anger associated with the injustices (Hargrave et al., 2009). As good as this sounds, it may not reach into the heart of what forgiveness is all about. In this particular model, I would argue that forgiveness is not so much about letting go as it is putting back. In other words, forgiveness is about restoring as much love and trustworthiness to relationships is as feasible and possible (Hargrave, 2001).

Figure 11.1 shows the model used in this chapter to illustrate forgiveness. This model conceptualizes the work of forgiveness as having two broad categories: *salvage* and *restoration*. These are two important distinctions. In the work of salvage, victims of poisonous parenting are not seeking necessarily to restore or reestablish the relationship with the parent. Instead, they are seeking to prevent the parent from continuing to hurt them, ways to prevent their own destructive tendencies, and ways to understand and

| The Work of Forgiveness | | | |
|---|---|---|---|
| **Salvage** | | **Restoration** | |
| Insight | Understanding | Giving Opportunity for Compensation | Overt Forgiving |

**Figure 11.1** Hargrave's model of forgiveness.

address the tremendous emotional pain that poisonous parenting causes (Hargrave, 2001). Salvage, therefore, is about victims learning how to restore love and trustworthiness for themselves and the current or future relationships in which they participate.

The category of restoration has quite a different relational implication. Restoration implies that victims are trying to restore love and trustworthiness in the relationship with the poisonous parent. In this category, victims may try to restore this love and trustworthiness by slowly reengaging victimizing parents to see if they are not as destructive and more loving and trustworthy, or victims may engage in the act of overt forgiving, which is intended to confront the old relationship and together decide how to proceed in a new and more fulfilling relationship. The work of forgiveness may or may not entail a future relationship with the poisonous parent. Forgiveness is about victims becoming more loving and trustworthy in all relationships. As such, forgiveness is much more about a process instead of a one-time act that results in different behavior (Hargrave, 1994a).

Under these two broad categories of *salvage* and *restoration* are the stations of forgiveness. It is important to point out that these four stations are not *stages* in which victims will proceed from insight to eventual overt forgiving. Instead, the stations represent the different ways that victims go about the work of forgiveness. For instance, one victim may find that she forgives through insight and that is all the work that is needed or can be accomplished with a poisonous parent. Another victim may find that the station of understanding is helpful and eventually leads to his engagement with the poisonous parent through giving the opportunity for compensation. In other words, there is not prescribed path for this work of forgiveness, and it further emphasizes that the work is a process and not a one-time act (Hargrave, 2001).

### *Insight*

Under the category of salvage, there are two stations of progressing in the work of forgiveness. The first station is called *insight*. Insight enables victims of poisonous parenting to explore the mechanisms and interactions by which they were harmed and victimized by the parent. Simply stated, poisonous parents did their damage in a way that can be understood through the sequence of interactions. If poisonous parents were more concerned about their own needs instead of the needs of their children, then they likely ladled accusations or guilt at their children. If poisonous parents were emotionally or verbally abusive, then they took on actions or behaviors that communicated this destruction. It is impossible for children to protect themselves from this type of parenting because of the lack of understanding and the inability to take care of themselves. But as adolescents or adults, they can become aware of this behavior and the sequences that their parents use to become manipulative or abusive. When they understand the sequence of their poisonous parents' behavior, they then can be much more active in stopping the behavior or the abuse. For instance, they can say to a manipulative parent, "That issue does not belong to me but belongs to you for resolution." Persons who were victims of emotional abuse can get in the car or leave (Hargrave, 2001).

One may look at the actions in the station of insight and wonder why it is part of the work of forgiveness. First, it is the work of forgiveness in that no love or trustworthiness can be restored to any relationship if violations are continuing to occur. If victims do not learn that they can protect themselves or, more importantly, do not choose to protect themselves, then they will react and be burdened with the painful violations that get in the way of other healthy relationships. If I do not believe that I am worthwhile and important and able to stand up for myself, then even if I am not around my poisonous parent I will have a tendency to behave in ways that reflect my self-doubt and lack of safety. I will likely act in destructive ways that are passive, manipulative, or aggressive. In short, victims must learn that they can stop the damage of the poisonous parent whether they choose to be in a continuing relationship with that parent (Hargrave, 1994a).

### *Understanding*

Second, the station of insight is forgiveness because it allows victims to clearly see their own destructive interactions. When victims understand the sequences and mechanisms by which they were hurt by a poisonous parent, they are able to understand and see the mechanisms that they use to hurt others. If victims are able to stop the poisonous parent from causing more damage to themselves, then they are also able to stop themselves from perpetrating damage to other innocent relationships (Hargrave, 2001). In these two ways, victims of the poisonous parent not only salvage themselves from the continuing effects of the violation of love and trustworthiness but also restore love and trust to other relationships with which they are involved.

The second station in the category of salvage is called *understanding*. Understanding enables victims of poisonous parenting to make human identification with the victimizing parent. As discussed before, poisonous parents are usually destructive not because they are inherently evil but rather because they were the victims of poisonous parenting themselves. When victims realize that their victimizer had these limitations with regard to love or trustworthiness, development, or past abuse, it gives the opportunity to realize that the victimizer is not evil. This is a significant issue in the work of forgiveness. Often, when persons are victimized by another, the pain from the victimization leads them to only feel contempt, disgust, or hate for the wrongdoer. In turn, this contempt, disgust, or hate fuels the very kind of action or behavior that becomes destructive and damaging in other relationships. In addition, many times persons who have been victimized by another believe that they deserved the mistreatment and abuse. They feel that being treated in unloving or untrustworthy ways were deserved because they were not lovable or did not deserve to be safe and nurtured. Without this station of understanding, victims of poisonous parenting are often left with the emotions of hate for the victimizer, hate for themselves, or both (Hargrave, 1994b).

Almost all poisonous parents are people just like the victims they exploited. They are not evil but are rather victims themselves. Victims did not deserve their abuse but are lovable and well deserving of safety. When victims understand, they relate to their own humanity as well as the humanity of the victimizer. They acknowledge that if they grew up and were victims of the poisonous parent's past, development, and history, they might not have done any better than the poisonous parent. This kind of understanding does not remove responsibility from poisonous parents or their victimizing behaviors. It does not excuse it or let parents "off the hook." Instead, it holds parents responsible as parents and for the damage they perpetuated (Hargrave, 1994a). It also allows victims to realize that their poisonous parents are not some evil monster to be hated or abused. Instead, they were simply human beings who had issues they handled in irresponsible ways. The victims did not deserve this victimization but instead are lovable and deserving of protection. Understanding removes the need to hate the victimizer and the resulting pain of victims thinking they deserved abuse (Hargrave, 2001). When this type of understanding takes place, victims do not feel the bite of the painful emotions associated with this hate and lack of worth (Hargrave, 1994a). The result is that victims are freer to live in loving and trustworthy relationships without old and past emotional pain.

### *Giving Opportunity for Compensation*

When one crosses over into the category of *restoration*, the work of forgiveness usually goes in the direction of correction and transformation of the victimizer from destructive patterns toward loving and trustworthy action (Hargrave et al., 2009). The intent, in other words, is to rehabilitate the damaged relationship with poisonous parents by interacting with them directly. It should be noted here that this work of forgiveness comes at risk. While the work of salvage does not demand that victims have anything to do with their victimizer, this category of forgiveness demands interaction. Anytime there is this kind of interaction and learning, there is risk of the victimizer being unloving and untrustworthy once again. Therefore, it is wise for victims to be cautious and thoughtful about the work of forgiveness in this category to ensure that there is reason to believe that the relationship actually can become loving and trustworthy (Hargrave, 2001).

The third station in the work of forgiveness and the first in the category of restoration is *giving the opportunity for compensation*. In this station, victims allow their previously poisonous parents small interactions to test out if they are more loving and trustworthy. For instance, victims may go to a family gathering with their parents to see if the parents can be free of making caustic or damaging remarks. In another example, victims may speak with their poisonous parents on the phone to find out if there is more loving concern for them instead of their poisonous parent. In both of these examples, if the poisonous parents had not changed, the victims could reasonably extricate themselves with minimal trauma and with the knowledge that the victimizing parents had not changed enough to trust (Hargrave, 1994a).

However, if the parents were respectful and appropriately concerned, it might be reasonable for victims to engage in a little more of a complex interaction that would risk more love and trustworthiness. For example, victims might invite parents to a family gathering at their house or might have a meal with their former poisonous parent. If their parents proved loving and trustworthy, the victims would continue to relate in more and more complex ways to see if the relationship could recover a sense of love and trustworthiness to the point of losing dysfunction. In this way, love and trustworthiness would be restored to the relationship a little at a time over a long period of time (Hargrave, 2001).

There are, of course, issues with this station in the work of forgiveness. First, it is rare that poisonous parents will do everything well and that they will be perfectly loving and trustworthy. Change is slow, and victims who want to pursue this area of forgiveness must have some patience as their poisonous parents learn how to become more loving and trustworthy. They are not and cannot be perfect but can and should make progress in being different if this station of forgiveness is to be effective (Hargrave, 2001). Second, the issue of the violation and the roots of poisonous parents' behavior may or may not ever be discussed. In this station in the work of forgiveness, the concentration is not on understanding, talking things out, or even discussing correction. The focus is on changed behavior. If the former poisonous parents have learned how to avoid being toxic, victim and victimizer may not ever have the discussion about the previous violation. Forgiveness, in this station, is achieved because love and trustworthiness have been reestablished, and the memory of the violation fades in light of the current behavior (Hargrave, 1994a). Finally, giving the opportunity for compensation does not ever fully give victims what they missed out on from their poisonous parents. Love and trustworthiness can be present, and in a substantial way this can be some compensation for victims to enable them to have a healthy relationship with their parents. But they do have to reckon with the reality that nothing their parents can do in the present will correct or erase past pain or distress (Hargrave, 2001).

### *Overt Forgiving*

The last station in the work of forgiveness, *overt forgiving*, is many times what most people think of when they think of forgiveness. In this station, victim and victimizer come together to talk overtly about the relational transgression with the intent of correcting the relationship to become loving and trustworthy in the future (Hargrave, 2001). Although there are many ways to go about this process, it can be extremely volatile and may produce a destructive interaction. For this reason, it is often reasonable to take this step with an involved third party or therapist to keep the process and intent on track (Hargrave, 1994a).

In overt forgiveness, the victim and poisonous parent first look to come to some *agreement* about the crux of the violation. This agreement basically confirms the facts and behaviors that resulted in lack of love or lack of trustworthiness on the part of the poisonous parent. Obviously, this may take time as people have very different recollections of relationships and occurrences and may be particularly defended around certain issues. Second, the victim looks for the poisonous parent to *acknowledge* responsibility for the damaging or destructive behavior. This acknowledgment is key because it has much to do with who holds the responsibility of the lack of love or trustworthiness. In many ways, victims must hold the victimizer responsible for their violation to make sense of emotional pain. When poisonous parents acknowledge responsibility for their damaging behavior, victims are no longer required to carry the responsibility (Hargrave, 1994a). Although this acknowledgment is the key process in overt forgiveness, *apology* seals the promise or intent of victimizers that they will seek to live differently with regard to the relationship (Hargrave, 2001).

Can a conversation really have the effect of restoring a relationship? Yes and no. It has been amazing to see two people who were previously enemies walk away from overt forgiving filled with new hope and love for one another. At the same time, the process of forgiveness continues as they learn how to work out the details of living in interactions with one another in loving and trustworthy ways. Even in this station where there is a one-time action, forgiveness and restoration usually play out in a process of learning from the other stations (Hargrave, 2001).

*Love, Justice, and Power*

No matter the station of forgiveness chosen, it is helpful to keep in mind that what victims are seeking to do in the work of forgiveness is to balance love, justice, and power. Tillich (1954) makes the theological point that these three aspects of reality are actually mutually dependent to achieve healthy relationships. Individuals who have power without love and justice run the risk of being abusive and dictatorial in seeking only what makes them satisfied. If individuals have justice without power or love, they will likely be concerned only with vengeance for perceived wrongs. If they have love without justice or power, they will likely be weak and passive to the point of having no power to move relationships forward in a healthy way. Only when the three are balanced do you have meaningful caring acts that are loving and fair that are based in true agency and action (Tillich).

This concept has much to teach us when we consider the work of forgiveness. The real process of forgiveness includes the ability to protect oneself, to have justified and trustworthy balance and give and take, and to have love that infuses others and self with worth and companionship. When there is a violation, as there is with poisonous parenting, it requires victims to start piecing back together a life that has this balance of love, justice, and power. Violations of love and trustworthiness have the effect of people misusing or overcompensating in the use of power. The more power is used to manipulate and abuse, the more untrustworthy and unloving relationships become (Tillich, 1954).

Potential forgivers may start with the process of emphasizing power with the station of insight where victims learn to protect themselves and their relationships, but the eventual intent of the exercise of power now becomes to start moving toward a balance of love and trustworthiness. In other words, even though this insight might be overemphasized in reforming from the damage caused by the poisonous parent, the hope would be that victims would be able in other relationships to start moving toward more love and justice. In the station of understanding, victims may emphasize the power of love as they make human identification with their victimizer and understand the poisonous parent's past pain. Finally, victims who decide to restore the relationship through giving the opportunity for compensation or overt forgiving are actually trying to correct the balance of giving in the relationship to achieve justice. The point is that the model of forgiveness presented here accounts for a methodology that moves victims toward an integration and balance of love, justice, and power (Hargrave, 2001). Any model of forgiveness must some way or another account for the balance necessary in these three issues or it runs the risk of exploiting the former victimizer, innocent parties, or the victim themselves.

### Case Example: Jean and Her Poisonous Parent

Jean was a 32-year-old graduate student who was working on a graduate degree in business. Although bright, successful, and ambitious, Jean was consistently displeased in her progress in relationships with men and was frustrated in the way she related to her mother and father. Her parents were divorced when Jean was 12 and her brother was 10. Her father remarried 2 years later, and her mother remained single. She and her brother grew up in the home of her mother. Although there were significant issues between Jean and her father, her primary frustration was with the way her mother "made me feel like I had to take care of her."

It was evident in talking with Jean that she felt trapped in the relationship with her mother through the mother's manipulation. "I remember from as long as I can remember that I was always my mother's confidant." She went on to explain that her mother shared all of her relational frustrations with Jean's father with her and would ask for Jean to emotionally comfort her when upset. "She would crawl into my bed when I was 7 or 8 and talk and cry for hours about how Dad was mistreating her. She would ask me to rub her back and stroke her hair—tell her how much I loved her. Of course, I would try to comfort her but I hated those times. No place—not even my bed—was safe."

After Jean's mother and father divorced, Jean ran into the requirement of taking care of her mother and brother instead of being free to pursue her adolescent activities. "After the divorce, I really became the father of the family. I would want to go out with my friends, but my mother would say something so sad and pitiful that I felt guilty for doing anything." When asked to give an example of what the mother would say, Jean stated in a weak voice, "I try so hard and you just don't seem to realize how tired I am. If you can't see your way to just help out a little, I don't know how we are going to make it as a family."

When asked about the current relationship, Jean stated that her mother calls her up to five times a day with many of the same needy requests. "Can you just spare some time to come and see me? I am so lonely. I never left you alone when you were younger." It became clear that Jean was victimized by being manipulated into being a parent for her mother from a very early age. This dependent behavior of the mother not only was poisonous for Jean's emotional health; it also frustrated and angered her. Her reaction was to become very independent and highly suspicious of any intimate relationships for fear that it would trap her in dependency.

#### *Moving Toward Insight*

We started the process of forgiveness by detailing some of the sequences that would lead her mother to engage her in such manipulative ways. Jean identified that any time her mother felt an uncomfortable or lonely emotion she would move to make some statement to Jean that essentially made Jean responsible for making her feel better. Jean reported that she would often feel resentful and burdened by the responsibility but would accept the fact that her mother was not capable of taking care of herself and therefore, Jean had to care for her. As Jean would care for her mother she would become more resentful and angry and pull back from the relationship. When the mother would respond with more dependence, Jean would often "blow up" in anger and say or do things that would hurt the mother's feelings. This in turn would lead Jean to feel terribly guilty and so she would eventually move toward the relationship, giving in to the mother's emotional dependency. "This is the same cycle that goes on now with Mom and probably a similar cycle that I go through when I start feeling closer to men."

Jean worked on the station of insight to find a new way she could interrupt the damaging sequence between her and her mother. The first step was to make the mother responsible for her own emotional well-being. Jean stated, "Last week when my mother started whining, I reminded myself that she was responsible for her own emotional health. Instead of distancing myself from her when she was sounding needy, I told her that she needed some professional help and that I could not provide that for her. When she came back at me and said that I always was the one to make her feel better, I told her that she had been sad since I could remember and that I had come to the conclusion that I could not make her better. She would just have to find another way to make herself feel better. I then made myself go home." Although Jean stated that the pull of guilt was significant, she kept reminding herself that if she gave into caring for her mother that she would then become part of the problem. As a result, she left her mother alone. "She called the next day and basically started the same process again. I stood fast and gave her the same answers and got off the phone."

What Jean noticed immediately was how much the action she took reduced her anger and guilt. "I felt so much freer not being constrained by all that anger. The guilt was harder, but I kept reminding myself that I really was not responsible for my mother's emotional health and that was better." She reported having more energy and feeling much better in knowing just how to stay out of her mother's sequences of dependence. Although Jean did have instances where her mother did get her into a similar sequence, within a month she was spending only about a fourth of the time she was previously spending with her mother and reporting that she was also not feeling so frightened by intimacy in her other relationships.

This is classic to boundary making and sequence interruption in the process of dealing with a poisonous parent. It was not that Jean was not able to see the sequence before, but she was so trapped in the sequence that she could not make sense of something to do that would be different nor give herself the message that she was not responsible for her mother's emotional health. With more insight and the damaging interaction greatly curbed, Jean was ready to take on an additional station of forgiveness through understanding.

*Moving Toward Understanding*

Since Jean was experiencing much less emotional dependence and manipulation from her mother through the insight of effective boundaries, she had a great decrease in the amount of anger that she felt toward her mother. "I feel better because I feel free and I am not as angry, but I really do still have the guilt that I should be doing something different and that I am a bad daughter." This indicated that Jean had reached the limit of what insight could do for her and that she had additional pain that needed to be addressed through the station of understanding. We did this by discussing her mother's background and development.

Jean said, "My mother really came from an environment where everything was done for her. She was an only child and her father and mother doted on her consistently. Even today, my grandparents still treat her like she is 16." When questioned about what she thought this environment was like for her mother, Jean thought for a long time and answered, "I think that it is a two-edged sword. Sure, it is nice that you have someone taking care of you, but I don't think my mother ever learned that she was capable herself. She never learned that she could make it on her own and that she had something to contribute." We discussed this aspect of her mother's past and made clear that even though she was not abused in a traditional sense, she was likely left feeling incompetent and dependent. Jean said, "Hmm, I never really thought about it in that way but that now makes perfect sense to me. I always thought that she had it easy, but it is now a little clearer to me that she was really robbed of her competence. She may have robbed me of my freedom to be a child, but she was robbed of her right to be competent as a growing adult." Through these and more discussions over the next 6 weeks, Jean realized that she actually felt a real sense of sadness for her mother because her mother had many competencies like intelligence and a sense of humor that were never appreciated. "It is like those things never had a chance or encouragement to come out of her." But mostly, Jean realized that her mother being emotionally dependent upon her had mostly to do with her mother's feeling of incompetence and fear. Jean understood where this came from in her mother, and therefore she realized that it had nothing to do with her being a good or bad daughter to her mother. The manipulation and dependence came from her mother's past pain. This had a remarkable effect in lifting a good part of Jean's guilt.

"Whenever that guilt comes knocking, I simply remind myself that my mother puts that on me because of the incompetence that was put on her. That clarifies it for me, and I don't have to take that guilt on."

As a result of the work of forgiveness through the stations of insight and understanding, Jean reported after 2 1/2 months that she was continuing to spend much less time with her mother, feeling freer to be more intimate in her relationships and not having the nagging guilt. In essence, the work of forgiveness in these two stations had enabled her to stop her painful interactions and become emotionally available to other relationships. For many, this would be remarkable work and be sufficient in dealing with poisonous parenting. But Jean wanted to explore the possibility of reforming a loving and trustworthy relationship with her mother.

*Moving Toward Giving the Opportunity for Compensation*

The work of salvage in forgiveness, when it is effective, is beneficial for what it does for individuals in terms of emotional well-being and their future relationships in terms of love and trustworthiness. But salvage often opens up new possibilities of relationship with the victimizer (Hargrave, 2001). In Jean's case, the skills and boundaries that she had learned through the process of insight allowed her to be in her mother's presence without getting trapped in the same old cycles that produced pain and distress in her. In addition, the understanding of her mother's past and the identification she made with her mother's emotions relieved a great amount of guilt and anger as she realized that her mother had issues of pain of her own.

After 4 months, Jean returned with the desire to work through some additional issues related to forgiveness with the purpose of "finding a place in my life for my mother." She explained that even though her mother was damaging in the past, she suspected that her mother had grown some as the result of their changed interactions and her mother's growing lack of dependence on her. After careful discussion about the possibilities of forgiveness, Jean thought that giving the opportunity for compensation might give her mother a chance to show that she was more loving and trustworthy but at the same time would offer some protection to her by not getting too involved with her mother. "I do want to see if I can find a place in my life for my mother, but I'm not willing to go back to the old dependent relationship."

Through discussing possibilities and Jean's current status, Jean revealed that she was now finding it much easier to be involved in relationships. She said, "There is this one guy in particular that I have been spending time with that I see some possibilities that we might go further in the relationship. I notice, though, that sometimes we get locked into a similar battle to the one I had with my mother. I want him to pursue me and I start saying things that put guilt on him. I want that to stop." One way of opening up

Jean's relationship with her mother to see if she could handle a new type of relationship was to see if her mother could offer a listening ear and eventually become more of a confidant. It was decided that Jean could go through a sequence of interactions with her mother to see if her mother could (1) listen to some of Jean's issues with men; (2) express appropriate and motherly concern for Jean instead of what the possible relationship with a man might do to the mother–daughter relationship; and (3) express some of her own regret about being too dependent in relationships. To provide some sense of safety for Jean and ease a way of disengaging if the relationship with the mother became too overwhelming, it was decided that a reasonable pace would be to make two phone calls a week over the next 5 weeks.

After the first week, Jean came back expressing some tentativeness. "My mother was surprised that I called since my contact with her had been minimal. It was like she knew that she couldn't behave the old way, but neither of us knew exactly how to behave. I expressed some vague purpose for the call but really didn't tell her that I wanted her to listen to me." After some work and role play, Jean was encouraged to give her mother another call and express overtly what she wanted her mother to do during the conversation. The next week, Jean returned very encouraged. "I started the conversation telling her that I didn't know if she could do this for me, but I needed someone to just listen to me as I processed some of my feelings with this guy. She didn't do it perfectly and would slide sometimes into giving me advice, but I would say to her that I just wanted her to listen. You know, that is basically what she did. I really saw some possibilities. I limited the conversation to 20 minutes as we discussed, and I felt for the first time that I had a mother who listened to my issue instead of listening for the implications of what it would mean for her. She really has learned something from our change in interactions."

This is clearly reflective of the goal of giving the opportunity for compensation. Without talking about the bigger issues in the relationship, Jean was able to have a loving and trustworthy conversation with her mother. In the subsequent weeks, she progressed in having more conversations with her mother. A turning point came during the fourth week of calls to her mother. Jean said, "I could tell that we were doing much better at connecting, so I decided to go to the next step and see if she could express some care and understanding for me as a daughter. I asked her if, after listening to me the past few weeks, she had any idea of what I was feeling. After several minutes, she said she thought I would feel a combination of hopeful and fearful in relation to this guy. She nailed it exactly. I felt tears well up inside of me, and I couldn't talk. After some silence she said that she understood those feelings and that she wanted me to know that she would be with me through the process of sorting those things out. She didn't protect herself or feel sorry for herself; she just supported me."

Although Jean's mother never did get to the point where she expressed regret over her own dependent interactions, Jean and her mother eventually began seeing one another. Jean was careful to tell her mother exactly what she wanted from her mother during these interactions, and it helped in the process of restoring their relationship when the mother complied. As in most cases of giving the opportunity for compensation, there were times of retrograde in the relationship when Jean had to employ tougher boundaries in terms of insight and moderate her own pain by understanding. However, the relationship recovered a healthier sense of balance, and Jean was able to find a place of comfortable relating to a once poisonous parent.

## Conclusion

Any work of forgiveness is worthy work because it is about the process of restoring love and trustworthiness (Hargrave, 2001). As such, it has the possibility of helping individuals, their future relationships, and even the poisonous parent who was responsible for the pain. As the previous case illustrates, it is not an easy process and has many imperfections because the players are unpredictable and may or may not be capable of change. In addition, most work in the area of forgiveness takes time to unfold. But the process and work of forgiveness through salvage and restoration offers hope of love and trustworthiness. Since these are the essential elements of relationship, there is little doubt that forgiveness in the model outlined herein can move any victim of poisonous parenting forward in recovering and relating better.

## References

Baumeister, R. F., Stillwell, A. M., & Heatherton, T. F. (1994). How stories make sense of personal experiences: Motives that shape autobiographical narratives. *Personality and Social Psychology Bulletin, 20,* 676–690.

Boszormenyi-Nagy, I., & Krasner, B. (1986). *Between give and take: A clinical guide to contextual therapy.* New York: Brunner/Mazel.

Boszormenyi-Nagy, I., & Ulrich, D. N. (1981). Contextual family therapy. In A. S. Gurman & D. P. Kniskern (Eds.), *Handbook of family therapy* (pp. 159–186). New York: Brunner/Mazel.

DiBlasio, F. A. (1998). The use of a decision-based forgiveness intervention within intergenerational family therapy. *Journal of Family Therapy, 20,* 77–94.

Dorff, E. N. (1998). The elements of forgiveness: A Jewish approach. In E. L. Worthington, Jr. (Ed.), *Dimensions of forgiveness: Psychological research and theological perspectives* (pp. 29–55). Philadelphia, PA: Templeton Foundation Press.

Enright, R. D., & Fitzgibbons, R. P. (2000). *Helping clients forgive: An empirical guide for resolving anger and restoring hope.* Washington, DC: American Psychological Association.

Hargrave, T. D. (1994a). *Families and forgiveness: Healing wounds in the intergenerational family.* New York: Brunner/Mazel.

Hargrave, T. D. (1994b). Families and forgiveness: A theoretical and therapeutic framework. *Family Journal, 2,* 339–348.

Hargrave, T. D. (2000). *The essential humility of marriage: Honoring the third identity in couple therapy.* Phoenix, AZ: Zeig, Tucker and Theisen.

Hargrave, T. D. (2001). *Forgiving the devil: Coming to terms with damaged relationships.* Phoenix, AZ: Zeig, Tucker and Theisen.

Hargrave, T. D., & Anderson, W. T. (1992). *Finishing well: Aging and reparation in the intergenerational family.* New York: Brunner/Mazel.

Hargrave, T. D., Froeschle, J., & Castillo, Y. (2009). Forgiveness and spirituality: Elements of healing in relationships. In F. Walsh (Ed.), *Spiritual resources in family therapy*, 2nd ed. (pp. 301–322). New York: Guilford.

Hargrave, T. D., & Pfitzer, F. (2003). *The new contextual therapy: Guiding the power of give and take.* New York: Routledge.

Hargrave, T. D., & Sells, J. N. (1997). The development of a forgiveness scale. *Journal of Marital and Family Therapy, 23,* 41–62.

Tillich, P. (1954). *Love, power and justice.* New York: Oxford University Press.

Toussaint, L. L., Williams, D. R., Musick, M. A., & Everson, S. A. (2001). Forgiveness and health: Age differences in a U. S. probability sample. *Journal of Adult Development, 8,* 249–257.

Witvliet, C. O., Ludwig, T. E., & Vander Laan, K. L. (2001). Granting forgiveness or harboring grudges: Implications for emotion, physiology, and health. *Psychological Science, 12,* 117–123.

Worthington, E. L., Jr. (2003). *Forgiving and reconciling: Bridges to wholeness and hope.* Downers Grove, IL: InterVarsity Press.

Worthington, E. L., Jr. (2005). Initial questions about the art and science of forgiving. In E. L. Worthington, Jr. (Ed.), *Handbook of forgiveness* (pp. 1–13). New York: Routledge.

CHAPTER 12

# Helping Clients Become Compassionate Parents, Partners, and Friends

SHANNON B. DERMER and SHEA M. DUNHAM

It is impossible not to have shadows of one's own childhood emerge with the birth of a child. Usually new parents want to recreate for their children the best parts of their own childhood and avoid the worst parts. Parents might say, "I will spend more time with my kids than my dad did," or "I won't spank my kids." Yet parents often find themselves doing the very things they disliked or hated when they were children. When adult children become parents they may find, much to their surprise, themselves empathizing with their parents as they try to contend with the same struggles that made life difficult for their parents. After all, parenting does not occur in a vacuum. Parents are influenced by financial pressures, social support, the parenting values of their partner, religion, education, and the prevailing knowledge about parenting at the time children are being raised. Children are usually not aware of these pressures; all they know is that they want the full attention and love of their parents.

No parent is perfect, but there is a qualitative difference between the mistakes most parents make and poisonous parenting. It is impossible for caretakers to be physically and emotionally available every moment of every day. Sometimes good parents ignore their children's needs or put their own wishes and desires for their children above what children need or want. While all parents make mistakes, poisonous parents systematically ignore, criticize, or overshadow the needs of the child. These patterns exist across developmental stages, although they may be heightened or soothed at particular stages. Poisonous parents may express their toxicity in different ways, but they have the commonality of creating insecure relationships and playing out insecure strategies through extreme relational styles—anger, smothering, or avoidance.

Firestone (1990) believed there are three reasons parents act in unloving ways: (1) Children remind them of painful experiences from the past; (2) children become the lightning rod for critical, negative thoughts and feelings that parents have toward themselves; and (3) negative messages from childhood were internalized and affect how they parent. He described parents' motivations as both benevolent and malevolent. He believed that most parents love their children even when they are "indifferent, neglectful, or even abusive" (p. 4) and that parents often give contradictory messages of wanting their children to be self-reliant and happy but act in ways that demand conformity and submission. They mistake anxious attachment for genuine love and regard. Unfortunately, love can be the most lethal weapon in the parental arsenal.

Despite the fact that poisonous parents may state that they love their children and are doing what is in their best interest, love is more than a feeling. A compassionate, loving parent displays observable, loving responses: smiling, a friendly look, warm humor, physical affection, sensitivity to children's wants and needs, and companionship (Firestone, 1990). No matter what their stated intentions and feelings are, poisonous parents tend to display behaviors that contradict generally accepted definitions of love (Firestone).

In this chapter, the authors provide general guidelines for working effectively with poisonous parents. Specific interventions for specific issues have been reviewed elsewhere in this book. The guidelines in this chapter are guiding principles for working with clients who need assistance identifying, exploring, and labeling emotion in themselves and others. Clinicians need to pay special attention to the therapeutic alliance when clients have insecure attachment strategies. They tend to be difficult clients to work with because they have attachment injuries and may have anxious, avoidant, or fearful-avoidant styles. Clients with insecure relationship strategies are more prone to feeling rejected and criticized, which makes it more difficult to create a secure therapeutic alliance (Mikulincer & Shaver, 2007). When working with both the parent and the adult child it is important for both to feel validated and heard. It is a difficult, but not impossible, task to validate each person's experience without invalidating the experience of the other person (Johnson, 2004).

### The Role of Clinician

Clinicians can play a key role in helping poisonous parents and their adult children identify and understand their destructive cycle. The goal is to heal attachment injuries and increase the emotional availability of poisonous parents. In addition, therapy explores: values about the expression of affect (meta-emotion), attributional processes, and automatic responses to internal/external emotional cues (Gottman, 1999; Hughes, 2007; Moran, Forbes, Evans, Tarabulsy, & Madigan, 2008). Clinicians also interact with the family system in ways that will enhance attachment and security (Hughes). When therapists act as and are perceived as a secure attachment figure, clients are more likely to have positive outcomes (Cozolino, 2006; Johnson, 2004; Mikulincer & Shaver, 2007). With poisonous parents, interventions that focus on developing mindfulness, interpersonal skills, emotional regulation strategies, empathy, emotional responsiveness, and reflective functioning are necessary. Interventions focusing on helping people become more attuned to their own needs and the needs of others are important for those with insecure attachments, whereas with parents who are already emotionally intelligent behavioral interventions tend to be more beneficial (Moran et al.). Clients with insecure attachments need a clinician who can provide safety, warmth, and unconditional positive regard and can help clients manage their distress when investigating and discussing hurtful memories, behaviors, thoughts, and feelings (Mikulincer & Shaver). The pain of exploring these issues activates the attachment system and need for support and security.

Several general guidelines will help therapists work with poisonous parents or their adult children. First, clinicians need to know and understand how strong and healthy attachments are created so they can assist parents in learning how to develop a more secure bond (Goldsmith, 2010). This process begins with normalizing attachment needs as healthy and adaptive (Johnson, 2004; Karakurt & Keiley, 2009). Second, as previously mentioned, for clients to explore their relationships effectively, creating a safe relationship by establishing a solid therapeutic alliance is requisite. This involves a conscious effort to validate each person's experience without invalidating or marginalizing the core elements of the experience of the other person. This may be particularly difficult because "clients tend to project attachment-related worries and defenses onto their therapist" (Mikulincer & Shaver, 2007, p. 412). Because of their attachment histories, poisonous parents and their adult children are prone to feeling criticized, rejected, and misunderstood. The key is for the therapist to maintain an attuned and empathetic stance even in the face of clients' overwhelming distress and insecure attachment strategies (Mikulincer & Shaver). Desirable therapist characteristics include being egalitarian, authentic, and transparent to create a safe haven in session. Consistently maintaining an atmosphere where safety and repair are a priority creates trust, openness, and the ability for clients to look at their inner resources that are uncovered through the therapy process. The clinician focuses on the parents' safety and assists the parent in maintaining safety for the adult child. Poisonous parents, due to their own attachment insecurities, may easily shift into distancing or attacking. When this occurs, the clinician must immediately slow things down in session, validate parents' efforts or hurts, and explore what made them reactive or is keeping parents stuck in negative interactional cycles. Third, focusing on in-the-moment emotions and using experiential interventions to label and make meaning of those emotions helps correct conflictual interactional cycles. Clinicians may have to "speak for" clients at times because family members may not be fully aware of thoughts, feelings, and intentions (Hughes, 2007; Johnson, 2004).

The more clients struggle with being aware of and taking responsibility for emotions and behaviors, the more the clinician may have to actively reflect feelings and reframe attributions in terms of attachment needs. This assists clients in becoming aware of, naming, and expressing feelings and experiences that are confusing, frightening, or shameful (Hughes, 2007). Furthermore, clinicians help clients stay in the here and now by taking an active role in sessions and engaging in a meaning-making process (i.e., understanding cognitions, emotions, and behaviors in terms of attachment needs). The goals are to assist the parent and adult child to become more aware of emotions, label them while they are being felt, accept feelings, and be able to communicate what it is like to experience an emotion. It is not that clients merely get "insight" into things that they did not know before; rather, they experience, bodily, the emotion they are talking about (Greenberg & Watson, 2006). Once the clients are aware of their emotions, the therapist facilitates clients in learning how to soothe and regulate emotion and use adaptive emotions to transform maladaptive emotions (Johnson, 2004; Greenberg & Watson). It is a balance between experiential and conceptual exercises, with experiential taking precedence.

In addition to specific clinician characteristics and behaviors in session, taking an extensive attachment history supports the meaning-making process. Meeting with parents and adult children in separate sessions creates the opportunity to strengthen the therapeutic alliance and empathy with each party. Also, clients may feel freer to honestly answer some painful questions in individual sessions. During the attachment interview clinicians ask questions about major caregivers, friends, and romantic relationships from the past and the present. In gathering attachment history, it is particularly important to focus on (1) what people learned about comfort and connection in relationships, (2) past traumas and how people adapted, and (3) how people may have found healing in relationships (Johnson,

2004). Based on past and current experiences, internal working models develop over time to determine feelings of self-worth and expectations regarding if and how others will meet one's needs. Determining specifics about clients' internal working models and attachment styles helps therapists match interventions to their particular coping mechanisms that get activated under distress (Stiell, Naaman, & Lee, 2007).

Finally, because people involved in poisonous relationships tend to be reactive, using an overall style that reduces reactivity and supports general emotional engagement is useful. Reactivity is an extreme form of emotional expression or the avoidance of emotional expression. The goal is to express primary emotion (an instinctual, unedited expression of emotion) rather than secondary emotion (a learned emotional response used to protect one from being vulnerable). Emotion is an important form of communication that regulates one's own behaviors and the behaviors of others (Greenberg, Rice, & Elliott, 1993). Johnson (2004, p. 109) uses the acronym RISSSC—repeat, images, simple, slow, soft, and client's words to remind therapists to maintain behaviors and a stance that will create safety and enhance clients' ability to express primary emotions and help people, especially those in poisonous relationships, improve their emotional availability.

R, Repeat: it is important to repeat key words and phrases a number of times.
I, Images: Images capture and hold emotion in a way that abstract words cannot.
S, Simple: It is essential to keep words and phrases simple and concise.
S, Slow: Emotional experience unfolds in a session; a slow pace enables this process.
S, Soft: A soft voice soothes and encourages deeper experiencing and risk taking.
C, Client's words: The clinician notes and adopts the client's words and phrases in a collaborative and validating way.

Overall, the priority is to be authentic, engaged, and affected by the clients and their narratives. The therapist–client relationship should be a model for a secure parent–child relationship, wherein the therapist provides security and a safe haven while encouraging exploratory behavior and connections with others (Cozolino, 2006; Hughes, 2007). The therapist is acting like a caring parent in many ways, but he or she is not "reparenting" the client. The clinician is using the principles of creating a secure relationship to guide attitudes, actions, and goals. "The therapist constantly monitors the state of the therapeutic alliance and the current therapeutic tasks to judge the best balance of active stimulation with responsive attunement. The relationship always takes precedence over the pursuit of a task" (Greenberg & Watson, 2006, p. 95). Guiding principles include creating an empathetic relationship, being present, being responsive, guiding moment-to-moment experiences and interactions, and a collaborative relationship wherein both client and therapist sometimes lead and sometimes follow (coexploration) (Elliott, Watson, Goldman, & Greenberg, 2004). "Therapist interventions are offered in a nonimposing, tentative manner as conjectures, perspectives, 'experiments,' or offers, rather than as expert pronouncements, lectures, or statements of truth" (Greenberg & Watson, p. 94).

## Conclusion

People with insecure attachment strategies tend to be difficult clients with which to work. In addition to insecure styles, poisonous parents also have the pressures and expectations associated with the title of "parent" and another human being who literally and, later, figuratively depends on the parent for survival. The deficiencies in caregiving along with the high expectations create a pressure cooker that is oftentimes on the verge of exploding. Parents, children, adult children, partners, friends, and future generations are the casualties when these relationships detonate over and over again. Nevertheless, no matter how painful the relationships can be, children and adult children still yearn to connect with attachment figures in times of distress.

Although clients seek therapy to quell life distress, the process of therapy raises levels of distress, especially in those with insecure attachment styles. A strong therapeutic alliance, which resembles a secure attachment, is the hallmark of effective therapy with all clients and is at the forefront of ongoing goals with poisonous parents and their adult children. For those with poisonous styles, interventions that focus on identifying, normalizing, expressing, and making meaning of emotions are most important. Although behavioral interventions are effective with many client populations, for those who struggle with emotional security, emotion-processing approaches are more effective. Experiential, person-centered, and emotionally focused models are probably the most useful with poisonous parents, but other models can be used successfully to understand and intervene in destructive family relationships. No matter what the approach, the goal should be to help adults to develop into people who can effectively request warmth, security, and support and into people who can effectively give warmth, security, and support to others. When, for various reasons, relationships cannot be restored the goal should be understanding and forgiveness. In the end, it is about helping clients find empathy for themselves and others.

## References

Cozolino, L. (2006). *The neuroscience of human relationships: Attachment and the developing social brain*. New York: W. W. Norton.

Elliott, R., Watson, J. C., Goldman, R. N., & Greenberg, L. S. (2004). *Learning emotion-focused therapy: The process-experiential approach to chanage*. Washington, DC: American Psychological Association.

Firestone, R. W. (1990). *Compassionate child-rearing: An in-depth approach to optimal parenting*. New York: Glendon Association.

Gottman, J. M. (1999). *The marriage clinic: A scientifically based marital therapy*. New York: W. W. Norton.

Greenberg, L. S., & Watson, J. C. (2006). Emotion-focused therapy for depression. Washington, DC: American Psychological Association.

Greenberg, L. S., Rice, L. N., & Elliott, R. (1993). *Facilitating emotional change: The moment-by-moment process*. New York: Guilford Press.

Hughes, D. (2007). *Attachment-focused family therapy*. New York: W. W. Norton

Johnson, S. M. (2004). *The practice of emotionally focused couple therapy: Creating connection*. New York: Brunner-Routledge

Johnson, S., Makinen, J., & Millikin, J. (2001). Attachment injuries in couple relationships: A new perspective on impasses in couples therapy. *Journal of Marital and Family Therapy, 27*(2), 145-155. doi:10.1111/j.1752-0606.2001.tb01152.x.

Karakurt, G., & Keiley, M. (2009). Integration of a cultural lens with emotionally focused therapy. *Journal of Couple & Relationship Therapy, 8*, 4–14.

Mikulincer, M., & Shaver, P. R. (2007). *Attachment in adulthood: Structure, dynamics, and change*. New York: Guilford Press.

Moran, G., Forbes, L., Evans, E., Tarabulsy, G., & Madigan, S. (2008). Both maternal sensitivity and atypical maternal behavior independently predict attachment security and disorganization in adolescent mother-infant relationships. *Infant Behavior and Development, 3*(2), 321–325.

Stiell, K., Naaman, S. C., & Lee, A. (2007). Couples and chronic illness: An attachment perspective and emotionally focused therapy interventions. *Journal of Systemic Therapies, 26*(4), 59–74.

# Index

## B



## C



## D



## E



## F



## G



## H

## V



## W